KISS THE RED STAIRS

KISS THE RED STAIRS

The Holocaust, Once Removed :
A Memoir

MARSHA LEDERMAN

McCLELLAND & STEWART

This paperback edition published 2023
M&S hardcover edition published 2022

McClelland & Stewart and colophon are registered trademarks of
Penguin Random House Canada Limited.

LIBRARY AND ARCHIVES CANADA CATALOGUING IN PUBLICATION
Title: Kiss the red stairs : the Holocaust, once removed / Marsha Lederman.
Names: Lederman, Marsha (Western arts correspondent), author.
Identifiers: Canadiana 20220415161 | ISBN 9780771049385 (softcover)
Subjects: LCSH: Lederman, Marsha (Western arts correspondent) | LCSH: Children of
    Holocaust survivors—Canada—Biography. | LCSH: Children of Holocaust
    survivors—Psychology. | LCSH: Holocaust, Jewish (1939-1945)—Psychological aspects.
    | LCSH: Holocaust survivors—Family relationships. | LCSH: Holocaust, Jewish
    (1939-1945)—Influence. | LCSH: Divorce—Psychological aspects. | LCSH: Psychic
    trauma. | LCGFT: Autobiographies.
Classification: LCC D804.3 .L43 2023 | DDC 940.53/18092—dc23

Quotes from "Man's Search for Meaning" by Viktor E. Frankl, copyright ©1959, 1962, 1984,
1992, 2006 by Viktor E. Frankl. Reprinted by permission of Beacon Press, Boston.

Quotes from *After Such Knowledge* by Eva Hoffman, copyright © 2004. Reprinted by
permission of PublicAffairs, an imprint of Hachette Book Group, Inc.

Quotes from Oscar Groening used with permission of Der Spiegel, "The Bookkeeper
from Auschwitz" by Matthias Geyer May 9, 2005 used with permission.

Quotes from Oscar Groening used from the BBC documentary series Auschwitz: The
Nazis and the 'Final Solution' episode 6, 2005, used with permission.

Quotes from Vivian Rakoff used with permission of University of Toronto Archives.
Vivian M. Rakoff fonds. B2015-0011/002(16)

Book design by Talia Abramson
Typeset in Adobe Caslon by M&S, Toronto

Printed in the United States of America

McClelland & Stewart,
a division of Penguin Random House Canada Limited,
a Penguin Random House Company

www.penguinrandomhouse.ca

1st Printing

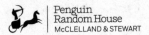
Penguin
Random House
McCLELLAND & STEWART

For Jacob

Contents

A person is literally a cemetery where multitudes of living corpses are buried.

ISAAC BASHEVIS SINGER, *Shosha* (1978)

KISS THE RED STAIRS

March 2020

THE WORLD IS QUIET beyond the dusty slats of the living room blinds. There are two playgrounds across the street: one wooden, at the school; the other, at the park, a fading rainbow of primary colours on metal. Both are roped off with caution tape. The school has closed its doors, for what will be months. The gates to the tennis courts will soon be padlocked, but not yet. The twice-daily bootcamp, with the instructor who sings Italian standards and eighties pop hits and displays obvious love for her would-be-fitter wards, is gone from the gravelly schoolyard, silenced by a global pandemic. This is the view from our window.

"I just want to go outside," my son says. "I just want to play with my friends."

Like any eleven-year-old, Jacob wanted to run around and do what it is not-quite-teenage boys do. Scoot down hills. Play hide-and-seek. Call on his buddies. Buy candy from the convenience store. Maybe get into some mild, harmless trouble.

When your child wants something that he has every right to have and you cannot give it to him, it is a special kind of agony. I know that, throughout the pandemic lockdown, other mothers in my neighbour-hood, across the country, around the world, were feeling the same ache that comes with denying a child this fundamental right: to run around outside, free. To see their friends. To go to school.

Then, a sudden shift. With my crackling knees folded into our sagging brown couch, my back turned to the room, my eyes aimed out through the window at the almost-spring day, I was no longer in Vancouver. My body was, of course—nobody was going anywhere. But part of me was now somewhere else. In Poland: Radom, Lodz. I was the child who would grow up to be my mother, or not grow up to be an uncle, wanting to go outside and play. I was in the place I had actually planned to be on this very day—only it wasn't today's Poland I was imagining.

In 2020 Canada, I could say to my son: yes, this is terrible. But *nobody* can go out and play. It's hard for everyone. This is what we have to do to stay safe.

What if, through that window, he was able to see other children at the playground? What if he was denied the ability to play on the swings and go to school—or walk on the main street, or sit on a park bench—while others continued to blithely live their lives? What if he looked outside and instead of the empty park and schoolyard, he was tormented with the sight of blond, blue-eyed kids squealing with delight, scaling the monkey bars, tunnelling down the slides, hiding behind the park's large trees for fun, not survival? Kids whose lives would also soon be changed, but not the way my Polish-Jewish would-be uncles' lives were: suffocating drawn-out deaths in a gas chamber, after the years of humiliation, torture, starvation, thirst. Forced, in one case, to dig a giant pit in the forest where people he knew, stripped naked, would soon be shot.

Those boys, the uncles who never got to grow old, who would never get to know each other, were eleven—or maybe thirteen—and twenty when they were murdered by the Nazis.

This is where it goes for me. Where it always goes. Auschwitz, Treblinka, the ghetto, the forest, the farm. What if all the other kids could play but my child could not, because he is Jewish?

One moment my son was my mother, and then he was her little brother. I looked at this disappointed boy peering out the window, and I was imagining him rounded up in a chaotic scream of desperate people, separated from me, pushed on a train, stripped of his clothes, his little eleven-year-old dignity, and in a few hours, his life.

Outside, the caution tape wrapping the swings blew in the March wind.

After all the work I had done, after the divorce that nearly defeated me, after the therapy and the reading and the countless attempts to learn to "be present," here I still was, instantly transported to my horrific past. Not really mine. *The* horrific past. The past that I haven't lived, but that I think lives in me.

The worst thing, the worst fear, is that it could continue to live beyond me, in this growing boy next to me.

There is more work to do.

PART ONE

Generations

ONE

My Trauma

November 2017

THE STARS WERE PAINTING the sky a twinkling kind of magic and everyone around me was oohing and ahhing, squinting through powerful telescopes at galaxies billions of light years away. There were shooting stars and distant planets and rings around Saturn that we were appreciating while buffered from the immediate atmosphere in multiple layers of clothing. We warmed ourselves with the steam rising from our New Zealand hot chocolate, and with the intergalactic view. It was a once-in-a-lifetime dreamlike night, the mysteries of the universe there for us to drink in, and imagine.

And I was thinking about Auschwitz.

Did they see these same stars? Did they look to them for comfort? Did they wonder if their missing loved ones were looking at the same sky, or were up there, with the stars?

This did not make sense in any way—my darkness under the bright New Zealand night sky. Even logically it was nonsense: this is not the sky they would have seen in Poland—wrong hemisphere—and the light pollution from those Nazi searchlights would surely have been murder for any dark-sky viewing. Also, stargazing? I'm not sure how much time—or inclination—the prisoners would have had to kick back and ponder the universe.

I should mention: it had been a really, really bad time—for the world, but also for me.

And in this bad time for the world and for me, I was once again deported to the worst place. Even here, in this beautiful place.

I was looking at the stars near the base of Aoraki Mount Cook, New Zealand's tallest peak, and I was thinking about a death camp. I was there because I work for a newspaper with editors kind enough to recognize that my life was falling apart, who decided to throw me a subtle bone, sending me to this remote country to write a couple of travel articles outside my usual arts beat.

And by my life falling apart, I mean my marriage.

At the same time that I was trying to get used to life on my own in my half-empty home, it felt like the world outside it was also falling apart. There were Nazis marching across my computer screen, and not in black and white. They were angry and sweaty and they were there *now* on the same landmass as me—well, they were when I was back home in North America. They could drive to where I live! They were in full colour, carrying tiki torches and iPhones and being uploaded to YouTube. *Jews will not replace us*, they were yelling.

There were Nazis on my Twitter feed—neo-Nazis if you want to be particular about it—and my nightmares were back. Well, they had never left, but the nightmares were vivid, sticking with me through the day, right there, within reach, as I made the coffee in my Vancouver kitchen and got my son dressed and I boarded the train to work.

Then, through the day, I suffered brief memories of the dreamed terrors: it's Kristallnacht on my street and my house is next, or I'm hiding in the closet hearing the muffled German shouts of soldiers approaching. My mother is alive! And warning me that they're coming for my son. These flashes came at the oddest of moments. Crossing the street to grab lunch, wiping down the cutting board in my kitchen as I hastily prepared a working-mom dinner for a hangry kid.

I cried sometimes listening to the news. The nightmare—the real one—was back. I was despised, again.

I was walking around, fearful and slow with the weight of mass graves filled with strangers' bones. The what-ifs of my entire life had turned into *what now?* I ached for my parents. Also, I was a little bit glad they were dead, saved from having to see this.

And yet through the hatred, the violence, the terrifying possibilities, I wished this was the thing that was really pushing on my chest—the dominant source of my despair. If only the tiki terrorists could have obliterated all my other shit. But even they were not that powerful. I had more pressing issues to obsess about.

My husband had finally, after a year of an in-home freeze-out, said he was going to take off "for a couple of months to get some space," and then decided, without bothering to mention it to me, to make the arrangement permanent. A detail I figured out when our seven-year-old reported a fun trip to IKEA during which they'd purchased a bed for him to sleep in at his dad's place. And ice cream.

I had been pretending to be myself but the me I had been did not exist anymore. She had been destroyed. That happy person with a future to look forward to was gone, along with that future I had allowed myself, against my better judgment and skeptical nature, to believe in: a future of retirement road trips à deux, milestone celebration dinners, a paid-off mortgage.

It wasn't that I couldn't imagine what was gone from my future— I was well aware that there were no anniversary dinners ahead—it was just easier not to. It felt so tempting to disappear, like the life that I'd had. The anguish was so heavy, sometimes I felt like I couldn't move. And I didn't. I was stuck. Glued to the grief.

It seemed almost paltry. *It's only a divorce*, I tried to tell myself. It happens all the time. People move on. A broken heart is not insurmountable, nor is the financial catastrophe that comes with it. You'll figure it out. Think about what your parents went through.

Since I was old enough to know what my parents had gone through, this is where any personal sadness has inevitably led. It becomes impossible to complain about anything to people who lost their entire families in a frenzied haze, who were marched to ghettos, deported to labour camps, carted off to Auschwitz. Any problem I could have had, did have, could not begin to compare. The scales of grief were imbalanced: my parents' side hovering down near the ground, my side way up high, light and airy.

And so, the problem would be dismissed, silently, by me. It did not feel right to appeal to my mother about anything that might have been plaguing me. How dare I unload on her about a disappointing biology test result, a friend's broken promise, even my own broken heart? These problems were luxuries, I knew.

And yet, this is what I was craving as my life was falling apart. To sit with my mother at her kitchen table and cry into a cup of milky tea with her fleshy arms around me, her blue tattoo close to my breaking heart. To have my father, big and strong—a survivor!—drive his boat of a car over to my house, grunt a few awkward sympathetic words, and go about his business hanging curtains or fixing my kitchen cabinet, the one whose door had fallen off the hinges. The stuff my husband used to do.

In my grown-up heartbreak, I became like a little kid calling for my mummy and daddy, the terms I still use when I think about them. But my parents were nowhere they could hear me. I was going to have to do this alone.

...

At one point during this quiet turbulence, one of my therapists (there were a few) asked if we could talk about the Holocaust.

The Holocaust? No, no; that was irrelevant. I was here to figure out what was happening in my home, now.

I had mentioned at some point that my parents were Holocaust survivors—maybe on the intake form, maybe during that first rambling, teary session. But that was not the point of these visits. The point was the figurative, then literal, disappearance of my once-loving husband.

So no, I did not want to talk about the Holocaust.

But now here I was, staring at this magnificent New Zealand sky, and thinking about the worst things.

And here it was, the worst thing—and not in grainy black and white. There was evidence of global anti-Semitism brewing on my computer, on my phone, on my TV, in the national newspaper I write for. It had become the subject of many of my conversations.

Was that therapist onto something? Was it at all possible that the Holocaust maybe did have a tiny bit to do with the way I was dealing with my marital breakdown? With my refusal to let go, despite the terrible evidence? With my futile quest to hang on, even if that attachment was threatening to destroy me?

Or, worse, did my background mess me up so badly that I had actually caused my divorce?

Was I so screwed up by my family history that I was a broken person who sends people fleeing from me? I like to joke that I'm neurotic, but in an entertaining way. The joke didn't seem so funny anymore. My anxiety, suspicion, my tendency to think the worst, my legendary talent to catastrophize—did this have something to do with the trauma my parents experienced? Had Hitler ruined my marriage?

It was hard to think about anything other than my separation. I was in a constant obsessive state; worried, terrified. So scared. What would become of my child, our home, my sanity, such as it was? I hid it pretty well in the world, but a few close people knew otherwise.

When I got back from New Zealand, I was in my kitchen, confiding to a friend about my grief—the divorce, not the Holocaust. She sat on one of the counter stools my husband and I had picked up together from a warehouse in the suburbs, back when we were furnishing this house, starting this life, and she told me: your ancestors are singing for you, crying out to you, they are supporting you, they are sending you strength.

Normally I would have found this suggestion a little too out there for me, a little too woo-woo, a little too convenient. Even silly, even bordering on insulting.

My ancestors, the ones whose lives had ended in the most inhumane way, who had been gassed to death in purpose-built execution chambers, were sending me strength from the beyond? Because of my little heartbreak?

But I surprised myself by loving this idea. I wanted to believe her. I wanted the comfort of this type of spiritual care. I clung to this beautiful possibility.

But I couldn't feel my ancestors in me. I just wanted my mom.

The thought stayed with me, though. That my ancestors were in my bones, still. That they helped create me. That they *were* me.

...

The Internet knew my marriage was in trouble before I told anyone else. "How to hold on to your husband" became a frequent search. And, eventually, "You can survive divorce."

But thinking about what the therapist had said, and starting to hear bits and pieces of news reports about studies examining intergenerational trauma, I began to cast my Google net wider.

I entered variations of "Holocaust and intergenerational trauma" into the search bar. For a break from all the sad-sack marital breakdown stories, I told myself. And there they were: studies that suggested children of survivors were not just messed up from our understandably imperfect upbringing, but that we were actually altered, epigenetically—whatever that meant.

Really? My mother hauled boulders while starving in Auschwitz and this had genetic consequences on me, born more than twenty years later? It seemed a little far-fetched.

The study of science has triggered my deepest insecurities ever since grade eleven physics challenged my perceptions of myself as an across-the-board (minus phys. ed) straight-A student. But I forced myself out of my academic comfort zone. I'm a reporter, I told myself. I do this kind of work all the time: investigate. I was desperate for answers and sleeping maybe three hours a night. I had a lot of time on my hands to research possibilities.

While I was much more inclined to think that the Holocaust had nothing to do with my failed marriage or my inability to shed my grief over it, it was something to look into. Or maybe more to the point, something to hang on to. I was grasping at what few explanatory straws I could find, clutching at any thin, brittle branch in my path as I slipped backward toward that boiling lava pit of divorce.

Why was it that this horrific event, something that did not even happen to me, insisted on following me everywhere, even to that twinkly bucket-list night on the other side of the world?

And as I contemplated navigating the kind of existence I never thought would be mine—abandoned! divorced! single motherhood!—I did start to wonder: did the Holocaust have anything to do with what had happened, or how I was dealing with it? And what else had Hitler done to me?

TWO

Childhood

I MADE MY FIRST friend at five. I am not counting the boy across the street who befriended and bullied me at fairly equal intervals (a child of survivors himself) or the boy who lived next door and tried to charge me twenty-five cents to play basketball with him on his driveway until his father caught wind of the scheme and put a swift end to it.

No, my first real friend was a girl I met in the school gym on kindergarten registration day. Pearl was light and positive and fun—everything I wasn't. Even then. She lived a few doors away, and as kindergarten progressed, I increasingly embedded myself at her house, which was alive in a way mine was not. Her basement was warm, carpeted. There was a toy box. A closet full of board games. A big brother who wrestled with her. A mother with a driver's licence. A gas barbecue in the backyard. A whole bunch of things I didn't have.

Grandparents.

Pearl's maternal grandparents were around a lot; her Zaidie—her grandfather—pinched my cheek as a greeting, and her grandmother—they called her Mamu—was a warm, sharp, lovely presence.

I liked these people, a lot—the oldest people I had ever known. I saw how nice it was to have them around. They cooed over Pearl and her siblings. They gave them hugs and presents. Cash! They brought an almost tangible warmth to the home. They made family meals extra-crowded and lively. I compared these mealtimes to the silent, efficient food-shovelling operations at my own kitchen table and it wasn't much of a contest.

After one of these visits, I came home from Pearl's house with a question for my mother. I inquired as to the whereabouts of my own grandparents.

When I think back, and I know memory is imperfect—especially mine—I see this as the first click of the lock on the invisible Pandora's box that enveloped our house. Its contents oozed into every room of our tidy bungalow, even before the lid was opened. This turn of the key would unleash all sorts of challenges to my psyche, a barrage that followed me from our Holocaust survivor–dominated Toronto sub-division, around the world as I travelled and found new places to plant myself, and to my little duplex where I now live in East Vancouver.

It was an innocent question, but it elicited an answer that was maybe a little too frank. It pretty much put an end to my five-year-old innocence.

That was not my mother's intention, of course; I affix no blame. How was she to know what to say? There were no social workers to help people like my parents then—or at least none they would have known of, or taken advantage of. There were no support groups or parenting workshops, no self-help books or Google results to offer advice or aid the traumatized.

Sitting at our kitchen table, a brown-and-white Formica number that was probably out of date then but that would be at home in the hippest loft apartments today, I stated a fact and posed a question: *Pearl has grandparents. Why don't I?*

My mother's answer was stunningly matter-of-fact—and honest; I'll give her that. There was no beating around this particular burning bush.

Your grandparents died in concentration camps, she informed me. *The Germans hated the Jews and sent them to take a shower, but gas came out instead and they were murdered.*

I had heard my parents talk about "camp" fairly frequently. This happened "in the camps," or "in camp" we did this. I did not know what exactly this camp was, but I instinctively understood that it was different from the day camp I had attended for one week that summer, or from the overnight camp north of Toronto, called Mothers and Babes, where I had travelled with my mom. It had been set up to give mothers a break, but I clung to mine and refused to join any of the kids' activities; Gitla Lederman—although by now people in Canada were calling her Jean—received no break.

So, this was the camp they so often spoke about. A camp with showers. Where water was replaced with gas. Run by Germans. Who hated Jews!

I was a precocious kid, and I somehow understood at this moment to keep my questions to myself. There were a lot of them, though. To begin with: So not everybody was Jewish?

As a small child, before the world opens up to you, you just presume that everyone has the same kind of life and experience as yours. Okay, so not everyone is Jewish. And the Germans (who are . . . ?) hated the Jews. Why? Did we do something wrong? And, oh my God—do they still hate us?

And even if those Germans did have some sort of reason to hate us, the Jews, were those showers an appropriate response to this hatred? We must have done something very bad.

Most concerning to my five-year-old self was the very existence of those showers. Were these showers still around? Was there any chance that I might encounter one, once I graduated from taking baths? Did the gas just come out of the showerhead rather than water? And if so, what did that feel like? Did it burn? How did that kill you exactly?

And how could I tell if someone was German? I would need to be on the lookout.

Over the years, I have thought a lot about this conversation. At some point I recognized it was a really bad answer to offer to a five-year-old. And I felt some judgment about this. How dare my mother provide such a graphic, potentially scarring response? It wasn't until it was too late to ask her about it, when I had my own child asking all sorts of questions I couldn't answer off the top of my head, that I began to consider what this moment must have been like for her.

Your kid walks in the door from a friend's house and asks a question that you haven't exactly been dreading—because I really don't think she had anticipated it, not yet, anyway—but a question that would trigger an avalanche. The grief that would come tumbling from the dark place where she kept it hidden—hidden so that she could go about her day doing menial, crucial tasks like making chicken soup from scratch and ironing for a family of five.

These missing hypothetical grandparents I was wondering about were very real to her. They were her parents, loved fiercely and missed with an intensity I probably still can't understand. What is it like to be a teenager and come home one day to a house emptied not just of its contents but of its people? Your people? And to have no idea where your family has gone? And to never see your mummy and daddy again?

And then, what is it like when you get shoved into a cattle car and find yourself at Auschwitz, lugging giant rocks in an empty pursuit, in the shadow of smokestacks pumping out death, and realize that this is probably what happened to your parents? And your little brother? And your grandparents, aunts, uncles, cousins, friends? How can I even begin to imagine what that moment of comprehension was like, even if I wanted to? Was the content of that sick-smelling smoke revealed to her by a fellow inmate? Or did she figure it out herself? And if so, did it dawn on her slowly—a gradual, horrific, unreal kind of realization? Or did it arrive as a lightning bolt of sickening truth?

It would be decades before I knew the answer to this, and I didn't hear it during a conversation with my mother; it was too late for that.

When I look back on that moment that I have since established as a turning point in my little emotional life, I realize that this encounter in our kitchen must have been terrible for my mother. After she provided me with that answer, did she escape to her bedroom, close the door and lie down on the bed? Did she lock herself in her little pink ensuite bathroom and weep? Or did she turn to the kitchen sink, wash a few dishes and get on with her day, keeping it together as she knew she must, because no alternative was offered? I'm guessing that one.

Did she tell my father about the conversation when he came home at the end of another long night at his job? Confide in him? *Marsha knows!* Or ask: *Do you think I said the right thing?* Most likely, I think she would have chased it from her mind, or kept it to herself so as to avoid upsetting her husband too. Or maybe by the time he steered his Pontiac into the driveway, she was dead asleep, anesthetized by the endless household chores and the unexpected grief of the day.

...

The Holocaust—we didn't call it that then; it was simply "the war"— came at me in bits and pieces that read more like adventure stories than the actual flesh-and-blood, life-and-death nightmare that it was. Hiding places, false names, serendipitous encounters, a lot of hunger satisfied in unusual ways.

The stories were generally not told to me, parent to child, but mainly overheard. My parents had a large social circle consisting almost entirely of other survivors. They recounted war stories as they played rummy on Tuesday nights and poker on Saturdays, breaking for elaborate meals—and later, when those late-night meals became problematic for cholesterol counts and jammed-up arteries, abundant snacks served in crystal bowls. From these conversations, I would glean fragments of what had happened to them before I was born, back home ("home") in Poland and later, Germany. I don't think I gave it much thought, but rather absorbed these stories through some sort of domestic osmosis.

It came up again and again, probably daily, and yet I did not have a clear picture of this war they kept talking about, these camps. Other than those showers, which I dared not ask about again, the unspeakable details remained, for the most part, just that: unspoken.

Until I was seven.

That year, my parents signed me up for Hebrew school at a local synagogue, not the one we personally attended, which was Orthodox and did not offer this kind of casual, part-time religious education. These were after-school lessons, for a couple of hours on Tuesdays and Thursdays and then a three-hour session on Sunday mornings. This seems preposterous now. What kid would stand for all that post-school-day classroom time and God talk? What, we have to learn *another* alphabet? And *pray*—something most of us didn't even do with our own families? But in the age before democratic child-rearing, before talking back was tolerated and children were empowered to make their own choices, this is what we endured. In my neighbourhood, Hebrew school was the thing to do. Many of the kids from my public school were packed into those desks along with me, seven hours a week.

The instruction was somewhat uninspiring—and our behaviour, pretty unruly. None of us, not even goody-two-shoes teacher's-pet me, cared very much for this experience—although I did try to excel at whatever testing the school bothered to conduct.

I still harboured respect for those poor souls who were charged with trying to teach us Hebrew words and a few Bible stories. (They also, one year, tried to talk us out of going trick-or-treating—Halloween, they implored, was not a Jewish holiday! This directive, although most definitely ignored, did produce a small twinge of guilt as I went door-to-door gathering candy and pennies for UNICEF.)

It was probably Yom HaShoah—Holocaust Remembrance Day, which occurs in the spring—when the entire Hebrew school was herded down to the basement of the synagogue: a large, soulless room that hosted Jewish holiday-themed parties and, on this afternoon, a film screening. Seats were set up and a projector loomed near the back.

I recall absolutely no preparation for what we were about to see—neither gentle explanations nor child-friendly trigger warnings so we could brace ourselves for the horrors to come.

What I do remember is sitting in the dark—it was so dark—one row behind Pearl, and watching what I now understand was some sort of documentary about the Holocaust. One scene in particular struck my little second-grade soul, leaving a dent that I'm beginning to think never quite got punched back out. In footage that has since become sickeningly familiar—but was then the most shocking revelation—a front-end loader pushed what looked like hundreds of naked, skinny bodies into a giant pit. Watching scenes of corpses being bulldozed into mass graves is horrifying by any standard, but when you're seven, it's off the charts. And when you happen to know that your grandparents were killed in those concentration camps, you look at those naked bodies and you think: *One of those women could be my grandmother.*

Years later—my God, more than forty-five years later—I called Pearl to ask her about this. Did she remember seeing this movie? Yes—she in fact vividly remembered it. "It felt so grotesque that I couldn't even imagine that it was real," Pearl said. "I think the truth is, it removed me from the Holocaust; it dehumanized my experience."

After the film, we all shuffled upstairs and went on with our lessons. Maybe we learned about the things we weren't supposed to do on Shabbat (travel in a car, turn on the lights, write anything down), or maybe we learned another letter of the Hebrew alphabet. I don't recall. Perhaps we even discussed the film, but I feel like I would have remembered that.

What on earth was the school thinking, right? Showing a bunch of kids those horrific images without preparing them in any way?

I feel pretty certain that this was a damaging introduction to the truth of what happened to my grandparents, just like my mother's gas showers answer was a traumatizing response to my innocent question about why I didn't have a grandfather to pinch my cheek or slip me a few bucks. My mother's not-family-friendly response subtly taught me another lesson, a really rotten one—the grave consequences of which did not occur to me until it was far too late: be careful with these kinds of questions. They are dangerous. Keep them to yourself. Never work up the courage to ask the right questions and find out what exactly happened to your parents, from your parents.

And then, long after your loving parents are gone, when your loving husband kind of just disappears into himself, you might also be afraid to ask the hard questions—even if you are desperate to figure out what on earth is going on. Because the answers could be death.

I don't remember being picked up that day from Hebrew school, but I usually got a ride home with my dad, who would proudly steer his LeMans through the massive synagogue parking lot to collect me. I am certain that I said not a word about the afternoon's cinematic experience to him, nor to my mother. She would have served us some sort of traditional Jewish dinner—not always to my taste—and on this day it must have been extra hard to swallow.

Did I sit there and refuse to eat? Or did I choke the meal down somehow, in the silence of our kitchen? I am fairly certain of the answer. Food did not go to waste in our house. The extravagance of scraping uneaten bits into the sink or garbage can was prohibited. Due to my parents' former starvation, a fact of life to which they would often allude minus most of the details, food was a luxury, always appreciated—even the most basic offering: a piece of rye bread with butter, a bowl of warm oatmeal. And so, if we pulled a piece of bread out of the bag and there was mould on it, we did not toss the bag or even the slice; my father would cut around it and we would eat it anyway. This was the rule with food: it was to be eaten, no matter what. A giant piece of liver on your plate that your mother insists on serving, at least once a week, despite your protestations? Blanket it with ketchup and choke it down. An overripe banana? A bruised apple? Raisins, which are the grossest snack food ever invented? Tough. Eat.

I did manage to draw the line at a few items: *galleh*—jellied calf's feet, a delicacy ("delicacy") my mother made every now and then; fried cow's brains (which my mother tried to convince us would make us smarter); and, once I figured out what it was, *kishka* (stuffed cow's intestine). Somehow I managed to convince my mother that these items were simply off the table. I wonder if it was compassion or a tiny bit of selfishness that led her to agree: if I didn't take a serving, there would be more for the grown-ups.

In our basement we had a large recreation room, and at the back of that room, a door that led to what we called the cold storage room. Shelves and shelves were lined with canned goods and other edible non-perishables. Piles of the stuff were often replenished by my supermarket-flyer-reading, bargain-hunting father, who spent his days off work cruising from one store to another, purchasing the best deals. There were also rows of jars of homemade pickles and other preserves. Our basement shelves were bulging with food, something that didn't strike me as odd until I started having friends over, who marvelled at the stockpile. Should war strike again, we were ready.

...

In Canada today, immigrants are celebrated—at least in the crowds I run with. Things weren't quite that way in the 1970s. My parents felt a strong sense of being viewed with derision. They joined in, in fact, referring to themselves self-deprecatingly as *greeners* (this must be pronounced with a thick Yiddish accent), knowing they were second-class citizens (but citizens!) and lucky to be here along with the Canadian-born parents of my friends. Even if their brick-heavy emotional baggage was stored deep inside, my parents' accents gave them away immediately—*greeners*. And their imperfect English was a constant source of self-doubt. It was I who was dispatched to write notes to the teacher, explaining that I had been ill. It was I who spell-checked the sentences my mother would draft onto a piece of plain notepaper, which she would then, after receiving my corrections, carefully transcribe into greeting cards wishing brides and grooms a hearty Mazel Tov.

You'd think at that post-war time, other people would have looked at my parents, heard them speak and thought—my God, what they must have gone through, those poor souls. But no, that was not the response to which my parents became accustomed.

Nor did they have a pedestal of wealth to protect them from the disparagement—real or imagined—they felt they received from born-in-Canada Canadians.

While so many of their fellow immigrants struck it rich, my parents were firmly middle class, leaning toward the lower end of the spectrum. My father did not drive a Cadillac like many of his friends did, and he never would. There were stories of unfortunate business decisions: a turned-down opportunity to buy farmland in what was then the middle of nowhere but that later became a giant subdivision just north of the official Toronto border; we would have been millionaires! A decision to sell houses my parents owned in downtown neighbourhoods that would become extremely desirable not too long afterward, in favour of buying a cookie-cutter house up north in suburbia. A decision to sell a retail property in the 1980s right downtown, at Queen and Sherbourne, which would today be worth many millions of dollars.

My surprise arrival on the scene probably did not help matters financially—and also emphasized how different my family was in comparison with the other kids I knew. I was a late-in-life baby, their third—an accident, my father used to chuckle in acknowledgment to anyone who inquired. This made me feel, as you might imagine, not exactly spectacular. Looking back on it now, I wonder if the unspoken boast in that chuckle was that my father was still virile and getting action, even at his advanced age. (At some point, upon learning the facts of life, I calculated that I was born nine months, minus three days, after he would have celebrated his forty-sixth birthday.)

I bring up my parents' bedroom activities not because I want to gross myself out, but because they speak to the weirdness of my upbringing. Back in my day, there weren't many kids born to forty-one-year-old mothers, as I was. And while I grew up in a neighbourhood that was teeming with Holocaust survivors, their children were mostly older. My peers had parents, for the most part, who had been born in

Canada. They did not have accents. They dressed in modern clothing.

My parents were different, and as I became aware of this, I became ashamed of them.

I'm not sure exactly when I awakened to these differences—but I viewed them as inadequacies. I remember working with my mother one year on her wardrobe before the annual elementary school open house, when parents would visit the school and meet the teachers. My mother had one designer (mass-produced or a knock-off, surely) sweater—a rust-coloured Pierre Cardin number with a little zipper at the neck—and I suggested ("suggested") she wear it. I wanted so badly for her to fit in, so I could fit in.

I am mortified when I think about this. What a terrible way to behave, to treat my mother. What a terrible way to be.

But I wonder now if I was aware of not just their differences—the accents, their advanced age—but also their vulnerability. They had been victims of something catastrophic, even if I didn't exactly understand it. Perhaps I wasn't only aware of this vulnerability, but afraid—even disdainful—of it. Maybe there's something primal in that: we are supposed to be protected by our parents. And if our parents had been victims of something very, very bad—would they be able to protect us? Or, along with checking the grammar and spelling on their notes to my teacher and bar mitzvah boys all over North America, would I be called upon to fulfill that duty, to protect them?

Part of the joy of childhood is feeling safe, secure, even immortal. I wonder now if those feelings eluded me, given the danger that had befallen my parents and their siblings when they were just kids, just Jewish kids, like me. The Pierre Cardin sweater would not have protected anyone from this, but it would have provided some sense of normalcy for me, I guess. A wool-blend armour in rust.

There was one story from my elementary school life that my mother delighted in telling. I heard it countless times. I will preface it by explaining that, the odd Hebrew school class aside, I was a very diligent student.

There was some sort of meeting between the principal and some of the parents. And by parents, I mean mothers. One of the moms (definitely not mine) inquired about acceleration—the practice of allowing high-achieving children to skip a grade or do two grades at once. My sister Doris, ten years older than me, had accelerated by completing grades three and four together; my sister Rachel, seventeen years older than me, had skipped grade five altogether. Both had been excellent students. This sort of thing, however, was no longer done.

"But if we did still do this," the principal explained to the group of mothers, "the first student to skip a grade would be Marsha Lederman." I can still hear my mother telling the story, in her thick Yiddish accent. The other mothers were aghast; at least, that's how my mother perceived it. The child of this *greener* would be the first to accelerate?! Over their brilliant kids, with actual Canadian parents? How could that be?

I don't think my mother ever felt so proud.

It's a stupid story, but whatever joy it gave my mother then gives me comfort now.

...

My sisters left home early. I was not yet five when Rachel married Jack; I was the flower girl in a green gown and a beehive hairdo.

I was eight when Doris spent a summer in Israel and met her future husband, Sam. This was destiny: Doris was spending a day off from her kibbutz work visiting our great aunt, Raisel. Raisel had survived Auschwitz with my mother; we called her Doda Rushka. Sam, who was Swedish, was in Israel as an exchange student at a hospital in Haifa. On a day off, he travelled to Tel Aviv to visit his great uncle Tzvee, also a survivor—and Raisel's husband. After a day together, there were sparks. Many letters were exchanged between Toronto and Stockholm; Sam—whose parents were also Holocaust survivors—visited Canada for the 1976 Olympics (but I think he had something more than viewing amateur sport in mind); and they met up in Canada or Sweden about every six months. Doris moved to Sweden, where Sam was a medical resident, when I was twelve.

And then the house got really quiet. Then it was just me and my parents. It felt like a home in which nothing really happened, beyond the basics: meals, chores, bedtime. It felt a little dead.

But to wish for fun in my family seemed frivolous, given what my parents had been through.

My father often retreated to the basement, where he would sit at the wall-to-wall built-in desk in the cold rec room on a little hard chair and read about World War II. A few steps away was the door to that enormous cold storage room, its shelves filled with canned goods accumulated over years, bought on sale, waiting for the next war.

I don't believe that as a child I asked my mother very much, if anything, about her wartime experiences. Not what kind of work she did, what kind of bed she slept in, did she make any friends "in camp"? I guess I learned my lesson with the gas shower answer. But I do remember working up the courage to ask her one thing: had she ever seen Hitler? Like, in person?

It's a curious question and I wonder now where it came from. I think I was fascinated by the idea that one man could be that terrible and have so much power that he could order other people to carry out those atrocities on such a grand scale. Or perhaps I was trying to make connections—connect what had happened to my mom to this image of the madman I kept seeing in grainy films, whose name had become shorthand for evil. Maybe there was, for me, an element of celebrity in it. Would her having seen Hitler in the flesh somehow legitimize her status as a survivor of this terrible war? Or was my motivation more about schoolyard notoriety: was this something I thought I could brag to my friends about?

I really don't know why I would ask such a question. But I remember her answer like it was yesterday.

"Are you kidding me?" she said. "If I had seen him in person, I wouldn't be here to tell you about it."

THREE

Jacob Meier Lederman

I WISH I KNEW more about this story. I wish I knew the chronology, the details; I wish I had a folder stuffed full of facts.

But what disappeared when my father did—his sudden death on a trip to Europe in 1984 felt like a disappearance to teenaged me, anyway—is inaccessible now. It all took place, that's a fact, even if nobody knows the exact facts. If a 1940s-era Polish Jew is persecuted in a forest, does anybody here . . . really know what happened?

The unknown facts begin with his birth. Jacob (also spelled Jakub and Jakob) Maier (also spelled Meier and Majer) Lederman was born, so we were told, on October 15, 1919, in Chojny, what is now a suburb of Lodz—a large industrial city in Poland. Lodz had an enormous Jewish population before the Second World War: about 233,000 people; more than one third of the city's residents, making it the second-largest Jewish community in the country, after Warsaw.

Jacob's birth was auspicious: a son born on Erev Yom Kippur, the evening that marks the beginning of Judaism's most important holiday. (Jewish holidays begin the evening prior; think Christmas Eve, minus the Christ part.) Yom Kippur is a sundown-to-sundown holy day of fasting and non-stop prayer, during which Jews atone for their sins of the past year, asking God—and, leading up to the day, any people they have wronged—for forgiveness.

It sounds super-religious—and it is—but it's the one holiday on the Jewish calendar that even many secular non-believers observe in some way—or are aware of, at the very least. Kol Nidre, the evening service that begins the holiday, is generally a standing-room-only affair at synagogues around the world. And if even the most non-observant Jew goes home afterward and proceeds to pour themselves a glass of water or grab a bedtime snack, my money is on them feeling at least a twinge of guilt about it. This stuff is ingrained in us from early on.

But in 1919 Poland, when Jews were Jews in a way many of us are no longer and you had a son—your first!—born on Erev Yom Kippur, trust me: this was an occasion, an omen—a very good one, the hugest of deals. This person was special, he was going to be something, do something very important with his life.

That he did. There was no Nobel Prize awarded to my father or great fortune accumulated or even a university degree to his name. But Jacob lived. He lived—the only person in his immediate family to survive the Holocaust. When you consider that some three million Jewish Poles—about 90 per cent of Poland's Jewish population—were obliterated over those six years, the fact of my father's survival is very special indeed.

My family celebrated my father's birthday on October 15, which was the date on his passport. But years after his death, my sister discovered that Erev Yom Kippur and October 15 did not line up in 1919. The holiday in fact began on October 3—a Friday night (the beginning of the Sabbath), which would have made it even more special. So my father was probably born on October 3, 1919. Or, alternatively, that Erev Yom Kippur business was somehow mixed up with being born on the last night of Sukkot, which was October 15 that year—still auspicious, but far less so as Jewish holidays go.

I feel fairly certain that my father's secular calendar birthdate must have been misunderstood or misrecorded. I just don't think his family would have gotten that very significant religious date so wrong. So that's the story I go with: my father was born on Erev Yom Kippur. Even so, I commemorate his birthday (insofar as any commemoration takes place anymore) on October 15. I know both can't be correct. But when there is nobody left to ask, you find ways to honour the bit of history you inherited before all primary sources vanished.

Jacob—they called him Yankel or Yankele (roughly Jack); I know: so many names, so many spellings—was born to Sara (also spelled Sura; née Sierpinski or Sierpinska) and Moshe (also spelled Moszek) Aron Lederman. The family operated a general food store and café on a busy street in Chojny, which was outside the main Jewish area of Lodz but was still home to a Jewish community.

Moshe Aron and Sara had a daughter, Devorah (or Deborah) Raizel (also spelled Rajzel), who was born the year before my father, on April 25, 1918, I believe. When my father was two, his brother was born. They named him Isaac (I'm spelling it that way for ease and because that is how I have always thought of him; I have also seen it spelled the Hebrew way, Yitzhak, and Izchak). Isaac was born on November 25, 1921, according to a document my father filled out long after the war. His birthdate was something I had never known until my sister Rachel unearthed a photocopy of that piece of paper with my father's handwriting, nearly one hundred years after the fact.

My father's paternal grandparents, Nacha and Mordecai (also spelled Mordechai and Mordchai) Lederman, were still alive when my father was born. I know very little about them, and very little about my father's parents, my grandparents.

My grandfather Moshe Aron came from a large family—he had nine or ten siblings; my grandmother Sara also came from a family of ten, we believe, including her identical twin sister, Esther.

My grandmother Sara's parents were Samuel Josek and Zysla Gutmer, 26 and 28 years old when she was born on December 6, 1889 at 6 a.m. in the village of Aleksandrow. Her twin sister Esther (also Ester and Estera) was born an hour later, according to records.

My father's family's business on busy Rzgowska Street was a combination café and deli food store that sold some groceries. I do not
know the name of the store—did little stores like that even have
names? As a committed lifelong shopping devotee, not being able to
picture this store or even know what it was called bothers me in a
way it should not. To think that there was a retail establishment in my
family and that I do not know what it was called. But of course, much,
much bigger fish, etc.

My father's first cousin—also a survivor, her name was Roza, but
we also called her Ruzia (also spelled a variety of ways, including Rusia
and Rujia)—referred to the business as a "Kafehouse." I found this in
a letter Roza wrote to my sister Doris after our father died. I loved this
term so much when I read it. Kafehouse. So European. So not tragic.

There was a big barrel of fruit near the entrance, mostly apples, a
friend of my father's recalled more than half a century later. They sold
halva, nuts, cheese, sausage—not kosher. The shop, with an earthen floor,
was next door to the small apartment building where the Ledermans
lived in a rented unit. Both my father and his sister, Devorah—a quiet,
gentle type is how I have heard her described—helped out at the store.
They were a hard-working family and it was a thriving little business,
affording them a nice apartment and little luxuries like a bicycle—my
father's, which he shared with his siblings.

Devorah was blond with fair skin. Her youngest brother, Isaac, was
tall, blond, good-looking and very funny—a jokester, full of life. Moshe
had a blond beard, and Sara was also blond. *A doomed family of blonds*,
I thought, when I heard these descriptions years after my father died,
also too young. But not as young as they had been.

"My memories about your grandparents," Roza wrote in her letter
to Doris from Israel, where she found refuge after the war, "were:
delicate, speaking short but very interesting, they hosted guests very
lovingly." (English was probably Roza's fifth (!) language, and her
handwriting was a little difficult to read, so my interpretation might
be a little off.)

"Your father was a beautiful and nice boy; his behaving was very sympathetic."

Doris had written to Roza, asking about our father's family—what they looked like, what they *were* like. Roza remembered very little. "I was there not more than three times and I remember that during my visit there, all of us had a very good time, they were very nice and polite people." The hospitality, she stressed, was excellent—good food, an immaculate home; they pulled out all the stops for their guests.

They spoke mostly Polish in the household, but Yiddish too. My father also learned German. That, down the road, would help him survive. At school, he was training to be in the textile business as a sewing machine operator. This might have also become a lifeline.

As an adult, my father was an eloquent writer and a voracious reader. I like to think of him as having been a high-achieving child and excellent student. But the truth is, I really don't know. His marks, his academic feats, even the name of the school he attended—these are unknown to me.

I do know that my father loved animals. The family had cats in the store—maybe for practical reasons, to deal with mice—and he adored them. He also cared for stray cats, who would come around a lot—maybe because he fed them.

My father was good at art, very proficient at drawing. Athletics, on the other hand, were not his strong suit (this latter deficiency I inherited).

A story I heard: The neighbourhood kids played soccer at a field near the store, and my father was made goaltender. He was a terrible goalie, no great surprise, earning him a nickname: "Yankel the Himmel Kicker," meaning "Yankel who looks at the sky." (This works exceedingly well for a soccer nickname, because in Yiddish, at least the version my parents spoke, "kick" means "look.") As I understand it, a lot of the opposing team's balls made it past the goal posts as my distracted father looked up, dreaming of who knows what.

I learned this story not from my father, but, years after he died, from a childhood friend of his younger brother Isaac. Stanley Fried had survived the war and lived in New York, where my sister Rachel and I travelled in November 2000 to meet him. Stanley told us that the Lederman family store was a hangout for the kids, who would challenge each other to halva-eating contests, cramming huge amounts of it into their mouths, sometimes to the point of getting sick. The group of them, trying to avoid my grandmother's watchful eye, would use long sticks to steal apples out of that barrel at the front of the store— for fun, not necessity. Necessity would come later.

Learning these details sixteen years after my father died—almost as many years as I had him in my life—was illuminating and excruciating. I remember my father's love for halva. Did he think about those contests with long-dead friends when he ate this exotic confection as an adult in faraway Toronto? When we sat on our front porch, eating sliced-up apples, was he quiet because he was thinking about that barrel, and his murdered family?

It is shocking to me that I know nothing else of my father's childhood. What were his hobbies? Career plans? What was his bar mitzvah like? Did he share a bedroom with Isaac? Who was his best friend? Did he have a favourite book? Did he even have access to books? I know so little I could kick myself, shake my fists at the sky. I'm so angry at the world for allowing the destruction of my father's youth, of his family—of all those families. I'm so angry at myself for not asking him more about it.

But war stories—those we heard plenty of. Well, maybe not plenty. But stories from the war dominated conversations about my father's past—almost as if when the Jews were erased from Poland, so were their pre-war lives. At least, that was the experience at my house. And I was too young to understand that. Once I did, it was too late to fill in all those blanks.

...

The Germans invaded Poland on September 1, 1939. Lodz, in the centre of the country, was captured one week later, put under German rule and renamed Litzmannstadt.

Decrees against the Jews that would have stripped the Ledermans of their livelihood and their liberty quickly followed. New laws would have closed their shop; forced them to at first wear Star of David armbands, then, later on, yellow stars; and subjected them to a curfew. The synagogue they attended—did they attend?—may have been one of the four major synagogues that were burned down that November. My father's career plans would have been finished, with Jews forbidden to trade in textiles and leather. (His last name, Lederman, suggests the leather trade went way back in his family; it has manifested itself in me through an unhealthy passion for footwear and handbags.)

The Lodz Ghetto was established in February 1940; by April, it was sealed with wooden fences and barbed wire—nobody could leave. It was four square kilometres, but crowded, as transports arrived from other places in Poland as well as Germany, Austria, Luxembourg and elsewhere. In June 1940, the ghetto held more than 160,000 Jews. Thousands more arrived in 1942, including about 5,000 Roma. The ghetto grew while supplies dwindled to virtually nothing. Conditions were, as we can all imagine, indescribably awful. Starvation, filth, disease, crazy desperation. "Deplorable" would be far too mild a word. Then came the deportations—off to a place much, much worse. And then, nothing.

At some point, Sara, Moshe Aron, Devorah, my father Jacob, and Isaac left Lodz, relocating to Piotrkow Trybunalski, about forty kilometres away. It's unclear why. They might have been forcefully resettled there by the Germans, as Jews from Lodz and elsewhere were in some cases—maybe because they did not live in a Jewish area, where the Lodz Ghetto was established. Or they may have gone there because Sara was originally from Aleksandrow, close to Piotrkow, and she may have still had family nearby. Maybe they chose to go there because they thought it would be safer, or a somewhat easier imprisonment.

It was, of course, neither safe nor easy.

The Germans entered Piotrkow Trybunalski on September 5, 1939, and began killing Jews immediately, setting fire the next day to the Jewish Quarter.

"The borders of the ghetto were marked by signposts bearing the word Ghetto (in gothic script) above a white skull and cross bones on a blue background," I read in a volume of endless horrors, the *Encyclopedia of Camps and Ghettos, 1933–1945*. When I got to that passage, I pictured my father, a young man of twenty or so, seeing those scary signs. But then, would he have seen them? Or were they meant for those on the outside, the non-Jews—a warning to stay away?

The ghetto in Piotrkow was much smaller than the one in Lodz, and while it was the first ghetto in Nazi-occupied Europe, it was not enclosed by a fence, and it was not sealed off until April 1942, so residents would sometimes be able to leave. Maybe my father did see those scary signs, after all.

There was a relatively thriving economic scene—underground food production and other industry. There was also, however, starvation, filth and disease. Refugees who came from other cities—like the Ledermans—were low on the hierarchy, apparently, and did not generally fare well.

I do not know what my father and his family did for food. I do not know what they talked about. Where they lived. Eventually, they might have been put to work. But in that rotting world, as they were living at the very least five to a room—the whole family—there must have been moments of joy. This is what I tell myself. I have to, because the weight of their certain miseries is a torment.

In the fall of 1942, the ghetto was liquidated. My father was spared; he was not with the family. He might not have been there at all.

Sara, Moshe Aron, Devorah and Isaac would have been among the Jews in the Piotrkow Trybunalski ghetto who had to walk more than two kilometres en masse to the railway station, where they awaited the arrival of a train to take them . . . somewhere. They were loaded onto a cattle car. The train arrived at Treblinka, where the only option was extermination. The women would have been separated from the men; all would have been forced to undress and to run naked down a fenced-in path known as the tube or the funnel to the gas chamber. They would have been forced inside, the entrance sealed, the gas dropped. They would have choked to death in that room, naked.

There is a page of testimony at Yad Vashem, the Holocaust museum and archive in Jerusalem, that my father must have filled out on a trip to Israel; probably the first time he visited, in 1976. The form offers a skinny box in which to record the circumstances of death. He filled one out for each member of his immediate family. "Treblinka, October 20th, 1942—gassed" my father wrote on each form, in all caps.

...

My father had a job in the ghetto. I do not know how he managed to obtain this life-saving work. I assume he was selected because of his strength, or his smarts. Maybe for his excellent German. Or was it his experience working with textiles that landed him this golden ticket? I know little about the actual job he was doing. Cleaning things up, is what I've always imagined. But maybe he was sewing. Or building. Or destroying.

That encyclopedia, though, describes horrific chores forced on the Jews of the Piotrkow ghetto: digging canals and trenches, removing tons of earth, the slaves working up to their knees in water all day. Or removing large amounts of earth from a pit while foremen with sticks would beat them. That same entry also recounts a terrible scene: some of those workers—they were employed ("employed") in a glass factory—witnessed the trains departing for Treblinka, heard the cries of their desperate family and friends, saw their hands groping at the window gratings.

The story that I do know is of my father's final day on the job, of his escape. I am unsure if this happened before the deportations or afterward, but we think it was before.

Some vile Kommandant told his workers to line up. He announced that every tenth (or was it every fifth?) man would be selected for execution that day. One, two, three, four, five, six, seven, eight, nine, ten.

One, two, three four, five, six, seven, eight, nine, ten. One, two, three, four, five, six, seven, eight, nine, my father.

This story, the defining story of my father's life—and the reason I am here to tell it—was recounted to me second-hand; I did not hear it from him directly, but from my mother long after he died.

My father begged one of the Nazis overseeing this seemingly rogue operation for his life. He did not appeal to the guard's humanity; he was too smart for that. Humanity? Please. Jacob offered concrete rewards. He had a watch with him somehow; a good one—gold. He offered it to the soldier—who of course would have been able to take it off Jacob's dead wrist immediately after shooting him, or order another Jew to do so and hand it over. The watch, though, was just a tease. My father had more to offer. He told that Nazi executioner that he had a cache of jewellery hidden back at home. Jacob would dig it up and bring it to that monster in exchange for his life. This negotiation was all happening in the pre-execution frenzy.

The Nazi said he would think about it. He ordered my father to hide. He sent him to a tiny room—a basement bathroom is how I have pictured it, but I doubt that is accurate—and there my father crouched and waited, shaking, hearing the shots murdering his every tenth friend (or was it every fifth?) knowing that one of those bullets had been destined for his head. And still could be, depending on how things went.

My father was able to keep track of time; he still had that watch. And he was there for hours. *Hours.* He could not see what was going on beyond the closed door that kept him hidden. But you can imagine what he was imagining.

At last the door opened. The guard, probably trying to keep this deal secret from his colleagues, had waited until there was no one else around. He took my father's watch, and told him to go get those jewels and bring them back in the morning. Then he would be able to continue to work, continue to live.

Weak with the trauma and confinement of the day, my father bolted as best he could. He ran to the jewels. Because there actually were jewels; that much was true. They were hidden at the home ("home") in the ghetto where the family had been staying; at least that's where I think they were. But they were not destined for that Nazi whose greed overcame his desire to be a good soldier that day. My father was too smart to take that chance. What would stop that pig from shooting him as soon as he had the valuables?

It occurs to me now that this soldier might have been very young— maybe nineteen years old. A kid.

If this happened before the deportations, as we believe it did, then when my father went back to his place in the ghetto, his parents and little brother and big sister would have been there. He would have told them the story; my sister Doris thinks at that point they told him to run away, to save his own life. Maybe the valuables were handed to him directly by his mother, Sara, or his father, Moshe Aron. Did they pack them in a little bundle, place them in a tiny bag? My father would have taken those valuables, and then he would have had to say goodbye.

My father took his bribe and his breaking heart and took off into the night. He had heard about a Polish official who would issue fake documents for a price. He knew where that official lived. In the darkness, he made his way out of the ghetto to that man's home and gathered the courage to knock on the door. I suppose when your life is on the line, the courage somehow presents itself.

To leave the ghetto alone was a treacherous proposition. The dangers for a Jew at that time, especially outside the ghetto, were immense. Anyone could turn him in—not just a soldier, but someone out for a stroll who spotted him. A child, even, who had been fed evil rhetoric about the Jews, or who simply noticed a strange, skinny man on the street. Some zealous citizen could have killed him on the spot, become a hero for taking matters into their own hands and doing away with a Jew on the loose. There might have been a reward.

There would have been no record of Jacob's death, of his life.

It was with that knowledge that my father left the ghetto for this Polish official's home.

A woman answered. My father explained his reason for being there. She told him her husband was out, but that he could come in and wait. She, amazingly, let him into the house. Perhaps they talked then, which would help the next part of this story make sense.

When her husband returned home, he was not happy to find this man, this Jew, inside. *Who is this?* he snarled (as I imagine it). *What is he doing here?* My father made his case, and his proposal. *Please can you help me? I have these things to offer you.*

I don't know what was in that package—his parents' wedding rings? A Star of David in gold? Silver candlesticks? Jewels taken from other ghetto inmates?

It didn't matter. The official was not interested in helping. Maybe he was thinking about what the punishment would be if he was found out—death. Maybe he was feeling some heat from the brass, some suspicion. Maybe he just didn't feel like doing it that day. Maybe he didn't need—or couldn't stomach the sight of—more stolen valuables.

No, he said. *No.*

My father's shot, gone. What did Jacob feel in that moment? Did he start to die, a little bit? Did whatever hope for life he had maintained begin to dissolve into defeat? Or, ever resourceful, did he quickly begin plotting alternate strategies?

And then the Polish official's wife spoke up. This woman, this saint, took pity upon my father. *A gentle soul*, she said. *Look at his eyes*, she said. *His beautiful eyes.* (My father did have remarkable eyes—a piercing shade of blue. Clear and bright. You might say Aryan.) There was something in his eyes—maybe it wasn't the colour, but the sorrow—that made this woman pressure her husband to help my father. Or perhaps it was the conversation she may have had with my father while waiting for her husband to come home. Or the way my father waited, patiently and anxiously, as if his life depended on it. Which, of course, it did.

Maybe that man loved his wife very much. Maybe he too saw something in my father's eyes. Or maybe he just didn't want the aggravation of a domestic impasse.

He went to get the papers together.

And his wife, this woman whose name I will never know and to whom I owe my life, prepared something for my father to eat. His first meal all day. And his first decent meal in who knows how long. It was Jacob Meier Lederman's last meal.

After that day, he became Tadeusz Rudnicki, Polish Catholic. Tadek.

...

It is the great irony of my father's life that he survived the war by taking a train into Germany. When he was asked for his papers—my God, what must have been going through his head—Jacob presented the fake documents that identified him as Tadeusz.

Tadek now, he ultimately disembarked near Lippstadt, about 220 kilometres north of Frankfurt. I can't know the route he took, but based on the map, the train likely would have gone through Lodz, and Berlin.

He ended up in the area of Holsen, in the state of Westphalia.

Holsen was a scattered settlement with excellent agricultural conditions near the Lippe river. Fertile farms, growing good food in spite of the hell all around them.

My father landed work at a farm in the area, where he would also live. He laboured in exchange for meals and a place to sleep and, apparently, a very small amount of cash. It was a life-saving arrangement. For him, at that time, these were unimaginable luxuries: Food. A bed, in his own room above the area where grain or hay would be unloaded.

In the ghetto, how many people would have had to crowd into a room that size to sleep, live and eat? Eat, that is, when they could find food.

For the farm family, my father would have presented a bit of a wartime miracle. Male help would have been scarce; able-bodied men were all off fighting for the Reich. Did they suspect he was Jewish? If they did, they did not ask.

Tadek was bony and starving, but even so, one of the first meals he was served at his new home was hard to choke down. It was a local delicacy, *Schwarzsauer*—soup made from the blood of pigs. As hungry as he was, digging into that goop was a challenge. Yet, to avoid any suspicion, he had to pretend that he was loving it. That was one of the few stories from this time in his life that I heard, growing up.

I had always pictured this place as a sheep farm (although it wasn't, I learned many years later), simply because I had always thought my father had a strong aversion to lamb. And believe me, other than blood soup, my father would eat just about anything—those cow's brains, the jellied calf's feet, a cow's lung in his soup, bring it on. But a nice lamb chop? No thanks.

But about even this I did not have the right information—or had somehow absorbed the wrong impression. According to both of my sisters, it was our mother who couldn't stand lamb, and it had to do with something that happened after the war. Funny how sisters who grow up in the same circumstances remember things so differently. Funny how the simplest thing—a distaste for a certain kind of food— can become such a mystery.

Then years after my mother had told me the story about my father and the watch—a story both Doris and Rachel had also heard— Rachel's husband Jack told me a different story, one he said my father had told him directly. That his escape had nothing to do with the count-to-ten execution exercise, was not the result of a bribe with a gold watch. That what happened was one night, when the prisoners were marching somewhere—back to their beds, perhaps, after a long day of work in the ghetto—my father took advantage of the darkness and quietly escaped by rolling down a hill.

...

The farmer, his wife and their children were a church-going family, Catholic; and my father, posing as a Polish Catholic himself, was ter- rified about this weekly activity. Would church be his undoing, the thing that exposed him as a fraud? He knew nothing about the religion or the service; he did not know how to conduct himself. On that first Sunday, he remained at the back of the church and observed. This is when people stand, this is when they kneel. This is *how* they kneel. The following Sunday—and for nearly three years of Sundays after that—he put what he had observed into practice.

My father had obtained a little Polish Bible; my mother told us that he would clutch that black book and pray silently to God—Jewish, Catholic, who cared—to keep his real identity secret. The fervent, wordless prayer, from that young man who sat in a pew in the back of the church, must have presented to the other congregants as piety personified—a man of faith, devoted to God and Christ.

I don't know if my father was praying to survive the war; I don't know if he thought in those terms. Did he think the war would end and so too would the persecution of the Jews? In that vacuum of information and facts, did the Jews believe that if Germany was defeated, they would be okay? Or did they just think this was how it was going to be forever?

My dad's only plan at the time must have been to just keep concealing who he really was. For as long as it took.

Concealing who he really was presented particular concerns for my father, a Jewish male. These days you see a circumcised penis and you think, whatever. But back then, it would have raised an immediate alert: Jew. Circumcision was not standard procedure in Europe at that time—but it was for Jewish boys.

So going to the bathroom would have been by necessity an ultra-private event for my father—a man working on an early 1940s German farm, out in the fields for what I can only assume were long days. Somehow, he managed. But I imagine a full bladder could have been terrifying, if anyone was around.

Sex, of course, would have been out of the question. My father was then in his early twenties—and so probably pretty interested in such activities once he had the whole survival thing worked out. That said, I have since heard some talk of a girlfriend from those days—non-Jewish.

I can only assume that things never got to the pants-off stage. It's an unconventional form of birth control, concealing your circumcised penis so as not to be found out and sent to the gas chambers.

There was a story my father told repeatedly—or maybe he told it once and, unlike the others, it stayed with me. He had to spend two days—or was it a month?—hiding in a pile of hay while a woman he knew brought him bread. My sisters recall the story somewhat differently—that while hiding he ate green, unripe apples and got sick as a result. I knew this clandestine event occurred during the war, and I knew that it was because he was hiding from the Nazis, but I did not know the context for this exciting caper. I figured it was on the farm—the haystack—and I figured, of course, that the Nazis were searching for Jews.

In fact, I have since learned from my sisters that the Nazis were not hunting for Jews—the area was Judenfrei, as far as the Germans were concerned. They were looking for new recruits. It was toward the end of the war, Germany was desperate for manpower and the army was going from town to town looking for able-bodied men of any stripe. At some point, they came to the Holsen area. So my father hid. It wasn't just that he didn't want to fight for Germany (of course he didn't), but he knew being recruited would have amounted to an instant death sentence. He would have been found out and executed—that penis again.

So, the haystack.

But after a couple of days—which seems to make more sense than the month I had once imagined—it became untenable. Something drove him out of hiding—diarrhea from the unripe apples? It must have been something pretty substantial—and the acting job of his life took on a new twist. In order to avoid recruitment into the German army, my father pretended to be severely developmentally delayed.

The Germans bought it. They laughed at him, poked fun at him, and dismissed him as incapable. I'm not sure why they didn't kill him. Maybe they couldn't be bothered.

Eventually, they left town and my father could return to his other life-saving performance as Tadeusz Rudnicki, Catholic Pole.

Years later, when I caught wind of a possible girlfriend on that farm, I immediately pictured the bread-supplying haystack woman. If so, if that was his girlfriend and she was in on the scheme, what story had he told her to justify his need to hide in the hay? Did he just say that he didn't want to fight in the army—probably a death sentence in itself?

Or did she know the truth; did she know, in fact, that he was Jewish? Had she seen that circumcised penis? Boy, I hope so.

I'm not sure if this girlfriend I know almost nothing about was a member of that farming family, someone from a local village, or perhaps another wartime orphan who had found employment and a surrogate family on that farm or one nearby.

I am also unsure of the family's attitudes toward Jews. Did they hate them, as they had been taught? Did they speak ill of them in the home or in the fields? Maybe as a mindless insult, at the dinner table, as they were being served? *Hey, more potatoes, please. Don't be such a stingy Jew!*

My father told my sisters a story about heading out on an errand with the farmer toward the end of the war. They were riding in the horse-drawn cart when they passed a Jewish cemetery. My father, probably petrified, somehow worked up the courage to inquire, as nonchalantly as he could, about the whereabouts of the local Jews. The farmer offered no details, just a terrifying answer: they were all gone. There were no more Jews. Conversation over.

When the war ended and my father felt safe revealing his identity, the family was in utter shock—at least that's what I was led to believe, growing up. They couldn't fathom that this man, really a part of the family by now, was a Jew. The Jews had been demonized perhaps since they could remember—the kids anyway—and there were supposed to be none left. Yet here they had been living with one all along? It couldn't be.

The story I was told was that they embraced him nonetheless, felt no anger or upset.

It is to my utter disgrace and shame that I let my father and then my mother die without finding out who this family was, what their name was, what happened to the farm, or where their descendants live now. I used to see my father pack up large boxes full of gifts—coffee and other non-perishables, clothing, some trinkets—and send them off to Germany. They were going to that family, the people he lived with for years, who had unwittingly saved his life. He also, according to my sister, sent packages to that girlfriend.

I wonder what my father thought of this family. With all the loss and grief he must have been silently bursting with back in his twenties, imagine what it would have meant to have a mother feed him a meal (even if it was pig's blood soup) or, I don't know, give him a hug. How my father didn't collapse into tears at even the slightest kindness is a mystery to me, like most of what happened to him during the war and before.

I am certain that a great deal from his experience on the German farm stayed with my father all of his life. Certainly, his love of gardening; he had a green thumb and tended to gooseberry, raspberry and red currant bushes in our Toronto backyard, as well as a couple of peach trees, and he later planted cherry trees. Another thing that stuck for sure was his name. Everyone, including my mother, called him Tadek. Once in Canada, Ted for short.

...

My sisters, ten and seventeen years older than I am, remember the day two photographs arrived at our suburban Toronto home in an envelope addressed to my father. One was a class photo taken at some point in the 1930s—rows and rows of children standing on the steps of a school. I don't know if a single one of those Jewish girls survived the war. My father's sister, Devorah, was one of them.

The other was a picture of two slightly older girls, probably teenagers, one with stark black hair and piercing eyes, the other with shoulder-length light brown hair. They stood in a lush backyard or a park, their arms around each other, clearly very close, giving off a serious air, as people tended to in photographs from that era. The girl with the shoulder-length hair—maybe it was blond, or had darkened a bit with age, as mine had—was also Devorah.

She looked exactly like my own big sister, Rachel. My aunt. My father's big sister—for whom my other big sister, Doris, was named. She was a real person with sad eyes and a pretty necklace. Did she babysit my dad when he was a little boy? Did they fight? Pull pranks on their parents? Giggle together? Compete for their mother's attention?

I wonder what my father saw when he looked into my sister Rachel's face. Was he reminded of his sister? How often? I know that he loved Rachel very much, seemed to have a particular fondness for her. Was it because of his sister's face that lived on in her? Maybe it was because she came first, born on German soil, the ultimate defiance to those who had drenched it with Jewish blood just a few years earlier.

I do not know the name of the girl with the dark hair or what happened to her, although it's pretty safe to say her fate probably mirrored my aunt's. I picture that nameless girl, that silky dark hair shorn off, her brave, fuck-you eyes giving the Nazis who saw to her death a look that would haunt them for the rest of their lives.

I don't know if she has any family who lived to mourn her. So, I try to do it for them. I mourn this nameless friend of my father's sister.

When Rachel took the old black-and-white picture to some sort of photography miracle worker and had the image reproduced, the girl with the dark hair digitally removed so we could all have a photo of our aunt to display in our homes, I installed it above my fireplace in Vancouver. Still, the image of Devorah never felt right without her best friend's arm around her. It felt like a crime. This unnamed woman, eradicated, again.

I do not believe in fate or meant-to-be; I certainly don't believe that there's someone up there in heaven looking out for us (nor do I believe in heaven). But wow, every now and then you have to wonder about coincidences and sheer dumb luck. Like how those photos of Devorah made it to my parents.

After the war in Toronto, before I was born, my parents knew a woman they called Miss Milada; I don't know her full name. She was a friend who would every now and then treat my sisters and my mother to a meal at a Hungarian restaurant, a luxury, as in those days my parents would never have sprung for dinner out.

Miss Milada worked for a wealthy man; she was a cook at his home. When she died, my father was notified; Miss Milada had left some things in her will for my mother.

My parents went to her boarding house to retrieve what their friend had left for them. But there was nothing left—just some odds and ends; nothing worth keeping. The landlady, they suspected, had already gone through Miss Milada's things.

Some time later, my father went to a function hosted by the Lodzer Society (survivors from Lodz, like many other cities in Europe, formed or joined societies in North America with their fellow former *landsmen*—to both help each other out, and get together and socialize). Would you believe, Miss Milada's landlady was there. She and my father got to talking, recognizing each other from their earlier encounter. My father mentioned that he was from Lodz, and maybe told her a bit about his family. Some sort of lightbulb went off in her head. She said she knew of someone in the U.S. who knew his family—and had a photograph of his sister. I don't know how she put two and two together, but she did. And she said she would get the photograph to him.

My parents, loyal friends to Miss Milada but cheated out of her will, received a posthumous inheritance because of her anyway, more precious than anything that would have come out of her jewellery box. Two photographs: the schoolchildren and the girlfriends.

My father was jubilant the night the pictures arrived at our house. Then later, inconsolable. I recall hearing that he took those two photos into the master bedroom at the back of the house and did not come out again until the morning. I picture him in the blue bedroom, sitting on the little varnished wood stool that stood next to his side of the bed—the only chair in the room, where he would sit to watch television—looking at the photos and weeping.

When I imagine this scenario, I am always distracted by this stool. Why was that the only seat, beyond the bed, in that room? Why would my father choose to sit on a hard, backless stool to watch *All in the Family* or the nightly news or the odd Bob Hope special? Why not splurge on something comfy?

I suppose one could apply some psychology—or just plain logic—to this weirdness, and hypothesize that having his own stool next to the bed he shared with his wife in the house that he owned was indeed a great luxury, after the horrors he had suffered. That it was solid, sturdy. That it was his. That he wasn't tempting fate with any sort of extravagance like a comfortable, upholstered chair.

But why not allow yourself the indulgence of a cushioned seat, or at least some sort of back to rest against? Hadn't your aching body done enough work for a lifetime? Did you not deserve to lean back and enjoy Archie Bunker's armchair racism from the comfort of a real chair?

Of course, I never asked.

...

The day before I turned eighteen—official adulthood, old enough to vote—I drove my parents to the airport. I steered my dad's bulky blue Pontiac LeMans into a quiet area where I was able to pull over, drop them off and say good-bye. They were going to Sweden for the first time, to visit my sister Doris, who had been living there for years by this point. The long-delayed visit was due to big news: she was about to have her first child. My parents would arrive a few days before the due date, see the sights, be there for the birth and the traditional festivities—the *bris* (if it was a boy) or ceremonial baby-naming (if it was a girl)—stick around to help for a bit, and fly home in mid-August.

Nobody was happier about this plan than I was: I was getting the house to myself for the summer.

My parents departed on July 11, 1984. In Stockholm, they visited the Vasa Museum, with its hulking seventeenth-century Viking ship, salvaged from the ocean bed after 333 years underwater. They saw the Royal Palace, visited the Skansen open-air museum, strolled through some city parks. Stockholm, a beautiful city, appealed especially to my father's European sensibilities.

One evening, a few days into their trip, my father began feeling unwell. There was some sort of pressure over his chest. My brother-in-law Sam, who is a physician, called an ambulance and followed it in his car to the hospital where he worked. It was around midnight. My father was sent to cardiac intensive care.

The next morning, Sam called the house and told my sister and mother to come to the hospital—that this was serious. My father was alarmed to see Doris, who was very pregnant. *What are you doing here?* he asked. She made up a story, told him she had an appointment herself. She didn't want to scare him.

That day, July 16, 1984, four days after my eighteenth birthday, for which I received from my parents a triple-strand freshwater pearl brace-let—very fashionable at the time—my father, Jacob Meier Lederman, died of a massive heart attack in Stockholm, Sweden. He was sixty-four. He did not live to see his fourth grandchild, Melissa, born twelve days later.

Once all the red tape had been untangled and worked out, my mother had to fly back to Canada alone. Her husband's corpse was somewhere in the cargo hold below, sealed in a lead casket.

We picked her up at the airport, my oldest sister Rachel, my brother-in-law Jack and I, and while we waited at the gate, I watched all the joyful reunions around me. Happy hugs and bouquets of flowers, tears of joy. How I wished we were one of those families. Our family was never the happy one.

At my father's funeral, a rabbi who had never met him delivered the eulogy; our synagogue's rabbi was away on vacation. The eulogy was short on details. No mention of my father's intelligence, his wicked sense of humour, his infectious laugh that I can still hear in my head today. The beautiful way he wrote—even a letter to me while I was away at summer camp was carefully composed, with florid detail. His voracious reading. How he made the best fried salami sandwiches. How, when he sneezed, the whole house shook. There was no tribute to his green thumb—to the bushes in the backyard, which delivered fruit year after year, thanks to his attention. Or the two cherry trees he had planted the year before, the last full year of his life. Or the German farm he had once lived on, in disguise.

All of my anger, and there was a lot of it, zeroed in on this eulogy and the rabbi who delivered it. How had this alleged man of faith not taken an hour out of his life to come around and ask us some questions about my dad? Or incorporated some of what he had learned about my father from whatever research he had done into this eulogy? Anything. One thing. It seems absurd as I write this now, even cruel.

But I understand something else now too: the real target of my anger. Who is the person who should have been asking questions but did not?

What was your job in the ghetto? Why were you in Piotrkow Trybunalski and not the Lodz Ghetto? Was it a haystack—and for two days? Or a whole month? Who brought you that bread—or was it apples? Tell me every detail about that story where you bribed the guard with your watch and then escaped and got false papers and went to Germany and lived on a farm pretending to be a Polish Catholic man named Tadek. Every. Single. Detail.

Who is the person who let her father die four days after her eighteenth birthday without asking any of these things?

I did not get to know my father very well and he did not get to know me very well. We did not connect in his lifetime and that has left a hole in mine. Because it turns out we had—we have—so much in common: the reading, the writing, the sense of humour. The darkness.

Was he protecting himself from getting too close to his youngest daughter, from throwing himself into what could have been a beautiful relationship, because of the losses he had already suffered? Because he could not take one more heartbreak?

Something that occurred to me as I was writing about him in this book: he had his father in his life longer than I had mine.

FOUR

Gitla Lederman

THE STORY I HEARD my mother tell most often about her child-hood concerned a new pair of shoes, a teary disappointment and an ominous foreshadowing that I did not clue into until much, much later.

Twice a year, my mother took me shopping for a new outfit: once in the fall for the High Holidays—Rosh Hashanah, the Jewish New Year, and eight days later, Yom Kippur. And once in the spring for Passover. And every year, on every mall visit, I heard the same story.

As a child, my mother—real name Gitla, most people called her Gucia, Guta or Gittel—received a new pair of shoes. That Passover, my mother was the proud owner of a brand-new pair of Mary Janes. I understood this to be a very big deal. New clothing was not some-thing that happened on a regular basis in my mother's 1930s Poland world; she would no doubt have lived her young life in a wardrobe of hand-me-downs from her older sister, Ella. My mother was over the moon about these new shoes.

She was wearing them when one of her many uncles, this one a particular favourite, arrived at her home for the Passover Seder. The uncle complimented the shoes, and he followed the observation with an expression my mother led me to believe was common in

Yiddish—or maybe it was Polish (I have yet to find anyone else who is familiar with this idiom in either language): *May you wear them until they fall apart.*

This was devastating to my mother. What sort of uncle would wish upon her the destruction of her beautiful shoes? She burst into tears.

What her uncle meant, of course, was: may you live so long and be so healthy that you outlast the shoes. The Polish or Yiddish—or his personal—version of "wear them in good health." It was just an expression.

But then.

...

My mother's father, Moshe Rafael Lindzen (also sometimes spelled Linsen—yes, prepare for more multiple spellings of every name), was an observant Orthodox Jew who taught boys at religious schools in Radom, where they lived. He and his wife, Rachel, owned a textile business, operating, we think, out of a stall at the market.

Moshe was also spelled Moses, Mojses, Mosze and Moszek in documents that tell me he was born in September 1893 in nearby Jedlinsk, north of Radom. Moshe Rafael was an only child—somewhat unusual then, and we recently found a clue as to why. Information we received from Jewish Records Indexing in Poland included a column for Comments or Extra Information, taken from his birth certificate. It indicated that his mother was the daughter of Jankiel, a merchant from Jedlinsk. And then: "Father unknown."

When I first read this—father unknown!—I found it a little bit thrilling. My initial, visceral response was a weird kind of joy. His mother, Maria Brajndla or Brandla (Breindl, they called her), had an illegitimate child at the age of thirty-five. I pictured a passionate love affair, clandestine romance, soul-nourishing fun.

But upon reflection, the possibilities turned darker, as they generally do when I reflect upon pretty much anything. Although in this case, I have a hunch it was warranted. I had to consider a different backstory to "father unknown": that perhaps Breindl had been raped. Somehow this seems a more likely scenario than having a secret romance in a late-nineteenth-century shtetl. Of course, it is one of the many things I will never know.

Breindl recovered. She later married a wealthy man, described as kind and intelligent, and this makes me very happy. They lived in Kielce. She was well dressed and elegant, sporting large hats and long earrings, items purchased during her travels to Germany, Vienna and Czechoslovakia. She visited spas in Carlsbad and Marienbad. A good life.

My mother's mother, my grandmother, was Rachel Chaia (also Chaja), maiden name Zweigenberg, spelled in many different variations (Cwajgenberg, Zveigenberg, etc). Ruchla, as she was called, was born into a religious and wealthy family from Gniewoszow, east of Radom, one of six siblings (we think). When she was sixteen, she was told she would be married.

It was an arranged marriage: the couple—Moshe Rafael was seventeen—met on their wedding day, during the ceremony. But the shock that stayed with Rachel, more than meeting her about-to-be husband as she was about to be married to him, was seeing her long, beautiful black hair shaved off, as was the custom for Orthodox Jewish women upon marriage. She promised her daughters, my mother and her sister Ella, that she would never allow that to happen to them. She was adamant about this. It was a story I heard from my mother many times. Maybe even more times than the one about the shoes.

It must have been easier for Rachel to talk to her children about the grief of losing her hair than telling them she was freaked out about meeting their father in that strange, cruel way. They would have been expected to have sex a few hours after first setting eyes on each other.

I think my grandparents liked each other, or grew to, and they stitched together a sweet life in Radom. A smallish city about two hours' drive today from Warsaw, Radom was heavily Jewish; Jews accounted for about one third of its population—about thirty thousand people. (Estimates vary somewhat, but this is the figure Yad

Vashem uses.) They lived in an apartment building, on the top—what we could call the third—floor, the children all sleeping in the big main room while the parents slept in the only bedroom.

"We were a very happy bunch at home," my mother said in her interview for the Shoah Foundation, Steven Spielberg's post-*Schindler's List* project to get as many survivors' stories recorded on video as possible.

I was by myself in a museum in a strange city when I was able to watch that tape for the first time since she died—many years after her death. And there she was, alive again: in her condo in the north part of Toronto, dressed up for the occasion. Alive again. Among all the feelings that swirled, a prevailing one was a profound sense of irritation, both as her daughter and as a journalist. The woman who conducted the interview did not elicit many details. "That's all what I can tell you," my mother would say, and the interviewer did not pursue the matter.

I felt the interview focused too much on the religious aspect of everything—had they observed the Sabbath in the ghetto? In Auschwitz?

Oh my gosh, who cares? They were in a death camp, for God's sake.

But I know that at the core of this irritation is my anger with myself for not getting those details down during the many years I had with my mother. According to my sister Doris, the interviewers were discouraged from being aggressive in their questioning. (Although I would argue that tenacity does not necessarily equate to aggression.) In any case, when I watched that video almost fourteen years after my mother died, I had to stop it at that point. Her description, "a very happy bunch," slayed me.

As Orthodox Jews, my mother's family would have observed the Sabbath and gone to synagogue every Friday night and Saturday—the males at least. Moshe Rafael was religious and scholarly, very learned in the Torah and Talmud. But he also possessed a catholic curiosity and tasked his older daughter, Ella, with bringing home books from the public library for him.

Moshe Rafael did the buying and selling of the textiles, while Rachel ran the store or the market stall, whatever it was. At home, she did all the domestic work—cooked, cleaned, in addition to running the retail operation. Annoying, but I'm sure not unusual.

In the evenings, while Rachel was manually washing dishes from the meal she had spent hours preparing without any modern conveniences, Moshe would play his violin, which I like to think would have made Rachel's chores more pleasant. He often got together with a neighbour, a non-Jew who also played violin, and they would make music together.

This neighbour would later offer to shelter my mother's little brother, Rachmiel, to save him from a horrific fate.

Rachmiel was the youngest, a blond-haired, blue-eyed boy who could have passed for a Gentile, and often did.

The eldest, Yakov—Jacob—generally called Yankel (middle name Yosef or Joseph), born in 1917, was a bit of a rebel—he didn't like the Orthodox ways and dreamed of living a more secular Jewish life in Palestine. And Yankel went for it, that different life, leaving Radom with the aid of a Zionist organization in the mid-1930s, likely in 1936.

(I learned years later that there was another Lindzen boy, born between Yankel and Ella, who died at a young age, perhaps two years old. I don't know his name. I didn't even know he existed until long after my mother died. The things we never talked about.)

We think Yankel made it to Palestine, based on postcards he sent home, but it is unclear what happened to him. Did he fight in the underground? Did he die under an assumed name? Did he become a spy? A Mossad operative? Or something more run-of-the-mill, less political? A firefighter? Was it a noble death—was he saving someone from harm? Or was he hit by a car trying to cross the street while on some pedestrian errand, picking up bread or milk, and labelled a John Doe with no family? My family hired researchers over the years. We never found out what happened to him.

The second-oldest was Esther—although I don't recall anyone ever calling her that; she was always Ella to us. Her occupation was corset-maker, according to a document we found years later. She was born

July 3, either 1918 or 1920. Next was my mother, Gitla, born January 10, 1925. She was athletic, so she told me, an aptitude that, let me repeat, did not survive to the next generation, my sisters and I can assure you. Little Rachmiel (I have also seen it spelled Rachmeel) was born in 1929 or 1931. It's possible he would have begun his studies for the bar mitzvah he would never get to have when it all turned dark.

...

Long before the war, anti-Semitism in my mother's Polish city was an expected and accepted part of life. Nothing to write home about—an inevitable, common irritation. Like mosquitos in the summertime, ants at a picnic. At least that's how my mother remembered it. I guess being called "miserable Jews" by shitty kids in the schoolyard or even getting beaten up the odd time pales in comparison to your parents being marched off to the gas chamber and you never, ever getting to see them again.

Still, from the perspective of afterward, I'm surprised that my mother didn't see this behaviour as any kind of warning. Would the bullies who called her "dirty Jew" stand up for her when their own lives were being threatened by the invaders? Or would they join in? We know the answer.

A particularly harrowing time was Easter, when, as she described it to me, Catholic congregants would get riled up during Good Friday services as their trusted priests railed in venomous sermons about how the Jews had killed Christ. Afterward, boys would run from the church looking for Jews to pelt stones at, or worse. My mother learned to lie low on Easter weekends.

Easter is the one Christian holiday that moves around on the secular calendar, overlapping with the Jewish holiday of Passover. The Last Supper is often interpreted to have been a Passover Seder. This was the time of year when the old lie of the blood libel would circulate—the made-up slander that matzo, which Jews eat at Passover, contained a sinister ingredient: the blood of Gentile children whom they had murdered.

My mother's experience of anti-Semitism before the war is not surprising, given what was going on for the Jews in parts of Europe at the time. And it was mild compared to what others suffered.

Long before the Second World War, pogroms—group massacres targeting Jews and their homes and businesses, which were looted—were common in Poland, and elsewhere. The prevalence of these attacks may, ironically, have saved many from the fate experienced by the victims of the Holocaust. Scared off by the violent anti-Semitism, many Jews emigrated from home for strange lands abroad—finding refuge in places like Palestine or North America.

The Jews were derided for being either dirty communists—loyal to the Bolsheviks rather than Poland—or for being dirty capitalists, in control of all the money, as in the world banking system. This other major lie was contained in the hoax publication *The Protocols of the Elders of Zion*. "Hoax" is maybe not the right word; this was no prank but a deliberate construct to promote anti-Semitism. The book—which was serialized in a Russian newspaper—was a work of fiction disguised as a non-fiction text, blaming the Jews for a litany of horrible things. It included minutes from a meeting where Jews were said to be strategizing to take over the world. It was preposterous. But it caught on. A Polish-language edition of the *Protocols* appeared in 1920.

And people believed it—or found it convenient to believe it, as justification for their anti-Semitic beliefs and actions.

This was the atmosphere in which my mother grew up, even before the Germans arrived in her city. This was what the Nazis marched into.

At one point, likely after Hitler rose to power in Germany but long before he invaded Poland, Moshe Rafael and Rachel had the wisdom to get the hell out of dodge, and obtained visas for Palestine. They would emigrate to the Holy Land, a reprieve from the constant threat of anti-Semitism. A lifeline they could not yet understand the significance of.

It is evident that they did not understand its significance. Because in the end, they decided not to go to Palestine, but to stay home in Poland.

We think they might have heard that life in Palestine was difficult, and so different from what they were used to. Staying was a decision they agonized over—and, of course, came to regret deeply. I can't imagine the amount of self-blame they must have felt. Was one of them more reluctant than the other? Did it cause a rift in their marriage when they realized that they had made a fatal mistake? That the one who persuaded the other to stay put had sealed their fate with his or her reluctance? Or did they share the guilt, and look at their three youngest children, their two daughters and their little boy, and feel a sickening culpability for what was to come next?

Moshe Rafael and Rachel had photos taken, we believe, for those visas. Someone dug them up in an archive many decades after the war; I must have been in my thirties by then. And there, suddenly, they were: my mysterious grandparents. They were so serious-looking. No, they actually looked very unhappy, maybe a little scared, staring at the camera, already anticipating the worst. Still, I was able to see, finally, what my grandparents looked like.

...

My mother's family did not live in a Jewish area; Gitla had to walk an hour each day to get to her school. Nearing the end of August 1939, she was excited: she would be starting at a new school in September.

When Germany invaded Poland on September 1, 1939, the news came blasting out of the radio. Gitla's chief disappointment was related to her education: school would not be starting. Her parents had other worries.

Gitla didn't know this yet, and maybe thank goodness for that, but that was the end of her formal education. At least until she took English lessons at night school decades later in Toronto, a city she had probably never even heard of at that point.

"Nobody could know what's ahead of us," my mother said about this time in a live interview I conducted with her on a radio show I hosted in 1998 (this interview was too brief, too public, too weird, with me having to cut her off so we could go to commercial breaks as she was talking about Auschwitz or the last time she saw her parents).

Moshe Rafael could no longer teach; Jewish schools were forced to shut down, although he continued to tutor privately. The textile store—or was it a market stall?—was closed; no Jewish-owned businesses allowed. My mother received some private lessons. She sewed and helped around the house to pass the time.

Moshe had to stay inside, hidden. It was dangerous for men, especially Orthodox men, to venture outside; they could be forced into labour—or worse. Men would be beaten, tortured, humiliated. One SS pastime ("pastime") in the Radom Ghetto that I have read about involved cutting the beards off Jewish men, often on just one side of their face, and making them pose for photos in grotesque positions. There were instances, that I read about in a wartime history book on Radom, of setting the victim's beard on fire with matches while the Orthodox man's hands would be tied behind his back. In another book, I read of Jewish men in the ghettos having their beards plucked out of their faces, one whisker at a time.

In April 1941, the Lindzens were forced to leave their comfortable home. There were two ghettos in Radom; the Lindzens were sent to the smaller one. Three families lived in two rooms. "We all were packed in like herrings," my mother told me. My mother's maternal grandmother, I believe, and one aunt were with them, along with another couple and their four children. I don't know any of their names. I wish I could mine one detail about that other family, something to keep them alive in the tiniest of ways, after they were no doubt murdered like almost everyone else. The names of the children, their ages, what the father did for a living, anything. All of that information is lost.

I learned from an unpublished memoir my mother's Radom friend Hela Morder wrote that that winter was brutally cold. The ghetto—Hela was in the larger one—was covered in snow and ice. "It was difficult to tell who was young and who was old," Hela wrote. "The combination of the cold and starvation had turned us all into uniform beings, bent and twisted and skeleton-like in our misery."

My mother's family was able to take some of their belongings with them; they would trade these later for food. Here Rachmiel's non-Jewish looks were put to practical use: he would leave the ghetto to trade these items for food they no longer had access to.

"Did you ever think about escaping?" the interviewer asked my mother in that Shoah Foundation video.

"From the ghetto? There was nowhere to escape," my mother said.

"What did your parents tell you about what was going to happen?" the woman asked.

"They didn't know. Nobody knew. That they were going to kill us."

...

There is another Passover story my mother told me, this one from wartime, from the ghetto, shortly after they were forcibly relocated there. The family managed to have some semblance of a Seder. A key part of this ritual meal comes after everyone has eaten, when one of the children opens the door for Eliyahu—the prophet Elijah (or the ghost of Elijah, as I interpreted it as a kid). He then proceeds to drink from the goblet of wine that has been left out for him on the table throughout the evening.

(This sounds pretty ridiculous when I write it out like this. But as a child, it is wondrous—and fun. At Pearl's house, the kids used to get out a tape measure to see if there was actually less wine in the goblet after Eliyahu's visit. My sisters recall some fun antics at our house, too, including my father shaking the table to give the illusion of Eliyahu drinking from the cup.)

In the ghetto, my mother went to open the door for this ritual and screamed. There she found a very bony, old-looking relic of a man standing at the door. Was this Eliyahu?

The man was alone and starving. He begged for some food. Moshe Rafael beckoned him inside. There was very little on the table that year, but they invited him to join them. Would there have even been any leftovers? Or did Rachel dive deep into the cupboards to find something else for this man to eat? I don't know where he went after that night, but I am certain he did not live through the war; there is no way a man like that could have survived what came next.

I think of that man every Passover, and so a tiny bit of him remains alive; the man who had the courage and desperation to wait by a stranger's door and beg for something to eat when it was opened by a child for a ghost.

...

The story I have heard from my mother about what came next began as she was outside in the ghetto with her friend Hela who later wrote a memoir about their experiences there. They were running an errand for Hela's father when they were approached by a soldier who ordered them to do some work for the Germans. "I was kidnapped on the street," is how my mother put it to me.

This frightening man in uniform took them to some barracks where German and Ukrainian soldiers would be living.

My mother, a fifteen-year-old girl, who may have seen herself as athletic but was certainly no bodybuilder, was suddenly hauling furniture around as "animals dressed like men"—that was Hela's description—barked commands. Gitla and Hela were ordered to return the next day.

"Were you scared?" I asked my mom during that radio interview.

"Of course," she chuckled a bit here. "Who wasn't scared?"

Gitla went home and found frantic parents. They had been looking everywhere, asking around for her, desperately trying to find their daughter. They were so relieved when she returned.

My mother told them what had happened to her, and that she was supposed to return to this job ("job") the next day. Rachel, her mother, told her not to go. When my mother told me this story, she would say something like: "You know how a mother doesn't want her child to work hard, to suffer like that? That was my mother; she just said oh no, don't go. It's okay. Stay home, my darling, rest."

Staying home was not an option. The soldiers came calling for her at home ("home") the next day, and my mother was taken to go work at the barracks.

Once the barracks were set up with the furniture, Gitla and Hela were forced to move in. My mother was then sent out to labour, her task depending on the day. She would be taken to work—in the fields, in the kitchen, cleaning, but mostly gardening. Given no food all day. Others were beaten, but my mother wasn't, she told me. She worked very hard, this fifteen-year-old who had known no real manual labour her entire life. "If you come back in one piece, you were lucky," she said.

In the absence of details from her about this time, I went looking. I have found awful stories about what the forced labourers were put through in the Radom Ghetto. Labourers who were made to take off their clothes at the beginning of the assignment, set them aside and work naked all day, to ensure they would not escape.

Women who were made to clean toilets or cold floors using their own underwear as their rag. I read about a woman who was forced to put her wet underwear back on at the end of the day and walk home wearing it. She died two weeks later.

On Yom Kippur, 1939, shortly after the German invasion, Jewish men and women in Radom were rounded up by Nazi soldiers and forced to clean windows and remove paint from an armament factory. The Germans did not supply rags for this job; the men were forced to use their prayer shawls, the women their underwear. (What if they were menstruating, I wondered as I read this.) Ladders were not supplied either, despite the fact some of the windows were quite high up. So the Jews formed a terrifying, wobbly human ladder, climbing one on top of the other on that holy day, to get the task done.

Thank goodness my mother was not subjected to such torture. Or, I then start to think, was she? Had my mother really been spared, or had she spared me the details? Was she protecting me from these horrors with her vague recounting of events? Or had the trauma been so horrendous, so damaging, that she had buried it deep inside? Where maybe it still lived when she conceived me, when she raised me.

. . .

This ghetto job was horrible, but it saved her life. There was a group of women as young as thirteen working in that barrack. "We nine children of sorrow formed a league as close and united by our common sorrows as any family," Hela wrote. To think that my mother had a substitute family, this little gaggle of teenage girls, offers a sliver of comfort.

There was not a lot of comfort, though, in Hela's memoir. Her depictions of the freezing conditions, the starvation and the daily view—which my mother would have shared—were haunting. Dead or dying bodies in the streets of the ghetto; women being shot for the crime of asking after their children; and the horrific physical and emotional torture this little group of teenagers, my mother among them, had to endure. Their Nazi captors "delighted in describing with a wealth of details how they had killed babies and they were dedicated to the extermination of our race and how they would do it," Hela wrote.

The friendships saved them, in a way. "My friends and I were so close," Hela wrote. "We lived a monotonous life in our dreary little attic and were most of the time hungry, but we tried to live in our dreams." Years after my mother's death, when I read this, I tried to picture her in that attic, a place she had never really described to me. I had no idea what her dreams might have been, the ones she had to live in.

And then I got to Hela's description of my mother, which I read for the first time nearly fifteen years after my mom died.

"My friend and former schoolmate, Guta Lindzen, was another of the sad battalion," Hela wrote. "We had shared our happy days and now we shared the horror of the prolonged nightmare in which we lived. She was tall, blond, with a generous heart accepting the actual life without any protest, but . . . underneath she felt the well known loneliness. She represented one of the most unforgettable persons for us at that time."

I at first chuckled at this characterization of my mother—who was maybe five-foot-one as a grown woman—as tall. But I thought about myself at a young age. I had also been tall. I was the tallest girl in my class, and then I stopped growing. I'm now five-foot-two-and-a-half and yet I operate in the world as if I had a towering frame; because of that early experience, that's how I feel. I wonder if my mother did too.

Height aside, this depiction of my fifteen-year-old mother was so moving to me. She had a generous heart. She did not protest. Underneath she felt the loneliness.

Hela wrote in her book that she would hear her friends call to their loved ones in their sleep. I thought of my mother, calling out to her mother. Or her father. Hela tried to be quiet when this was happening; she did not want to wake the girls from their brief, dreamy happiness.

...

Years later, Hela's son, Joseph Morder, a filmmaker who lives in Paris, made a documentary about his mother's experiences during the war. Not just hers, but the other women in this sad battalion, including my mother. He called his film *Mes Sept Mères*. "My Seven Mothers," after the seven youngest women in the barrack who had been especially close. Because if it weren't for these other women, he said, his mother would not have lived, and he would not have been born. They were all responsible for his existence.

One of those seven women who appeared in Joseph's film was Nusia. Nusia's mother remained in the ghetto longer than the other girls' mothers and she would have the group of girls over to her place every Sunday. She fed them soup and she gave them soap to wash up with. "She called us all her kids," my mother says in the film. "It's undescribable; it now seems totally normal"—the soup, the soap—"but then, it was amazing."

From Joseph's film, I learned some terrifying details about life in those barracks.

One night, without warning, an officer knocked on the door and chose one of the girls to go with him, one of the youngest. The others were so naïve, they didn't know where he was taking her or why. The two older women who were part of the group of prisoners, however, understood.

Another officer—a maniac, Hela called him—came to their quarters every evening and sat at the table, looking the girls in the eyes. It was his favourite game, she said. He drank a lot of vodka and was lewd, and terrifying. There was one girl, Jakira, whom he chose as his victim, because of her beautiful eyes.

"He used to look at her enormous dark eyes and tell her, 'your eyes, your huge vulgar Jewish eyes are the sort that started all this destruction and death! One of these days I'll pull them from your face with my nails!'" He would hold out his long fingers, curving and extending them toward Jakira's eyes.

"He accused me of being a spy," Jakira said in Joseph's film. "I didn't know what a spy was." They were so young, so innocent; imagine, she didn't even know what a spy was. "He didn't stop telling me that he was going to kill me."

This is what my mother experienced in her teenage years.

There's a point in Hela's memoir where she witnessed some Jews in the ghetto being forced into cattle cars. Children screaming for their mothers; mothers frantic, looking for their children. In her account, everyone was shoved inside, the doors were bolted and eventually there was silence. The cars, she wrote, had been lined with quicklime.

"If it had not been for the warm companionship of my fellow workers in the labour battalion," Hela wrote, "I think I would have killed myself then."

...

The Radom Ghetto was liquidated in August 1942. The small ghetto first, then later that month the large ghetto. My mother was not there. She was in the attic barrack with the other women.

They were not allowed to be in the ghetto during the liquidations; their captors ordered them to stay away.

My mother's sister Ella was not in the ghetto either. She also had been taken to work and live elsewhere—in her case, a large munitions factory nearby. But their parents and little brother were still there.

The *aktion* (the Nazi euphemism for the mass deportation and killing of Jews) in both the small and large ghettos began at night; the giant German floodlights switched on, the SS aided by Polish police, driving Jews from their houses, shooting some, herding the rest into cattle cars, sending them to Treblinka where they would be exterminated in gas chambers.

Reading the writing on the wall, Rachel and Moshe Rafael had hatched a plan for Rachmiel. They may have made a fatal error by not going to Palestine, but they would save their little boy. My grandparents planned to get Rachmiel to their generous friend—the violin player from next-door in their former life—for safekeeping. Blond, blue-eyed Rachmiel could pass as a relative—even the son—of this childless couple.

This, in the horror of it all, was something to hold on to: their youngest would be spared their fate. He would go on to do something—anything. It didn't matter. He would outlive them. He would grow up. Not much of a goal for your child, but in those unimaginable circumstances, survival was a parent's greatest ambition.

The plan was set. But on the day of the deportations, Rachmiel refused. He would not go with the neighbours. He would not leave his parents. Rachmiel was not sheltered by the generous Polish neighbours with the violin. He was loaded onto the cattle car with his real family. The train departed for Treblinka.

Rachel, Moshe Rafael and Rachmiel Lindzen died there in August 1942. It would have been immediate. In Treblinka, there was nothing but death by gas. They would have arrived, the women separated from the men (and boys), all would have been forced to undress, and to run naked down a fenced-in path known as the tube or the funnel to the gas chamber. They would have been forced inside, the entrance sealed, the gas dropped. They would have choked to death in that room, naked.

I don't know if my mother's grandmother, who had been living with them, made it to the gas chamber to die with them too, or if she met her fate earlier in the *aktion*. Or if she had perhaps died earlier, before the ghetto. I don't know what became of my other great-grandparents, of everyone else in her family.

If Rachmiel had been born in 1929, he would have been twelve or thirteen. But in that 1998 radio interview, my mother said he was eleven-and-a-half. I listened to that interview for the first time, many years later, in 2020. When my own son, Jacob, was eleven-and-a-half.

…

At the barracks during the liquidation, all night the young women heard gunfire, crying and screaming, my mother recalled. People were shot on the spot. The ghetto was lit up like it was daytime. The next day the girls were told that the ghetto's inhabitants had been deported. They were instructed to go back to their homes in the ghetto to collect their clothes, whatever they could carry with them, and then come back to work.

My mother returned to the house where she had lived to find the place in chaos. At the bottom of the stairs, she saw her grandmother's wig.

(One of my sisters recently dug up some old notes suggesting our great-grandmother had died before this happened—but I remember the story about her wig on the stairs so vividly. Could it have been my grandmother's wig instead? But my mother's mother had been so against the practice, after what had happened to her beautiful hair when she got married. Whose wig was it? These are the things I can never know.)

The ghettos were empty. Whatever was left—the possessions of the dead Jews, their property—was sold or distributed for free to Polish residents of Radom.

With the ghettos cleared, the regiment wound down. And the work disappeared for the girls. This was a grave development, because work meant life. Fortunately, Gitla was selected to be a slave labourer else-where, at that large munitions factory where Ella worked. Their joyful reunion at the factory was tempered by the deportation of their parents and little brother. They did not know where they had gone. Making ammunition for their enslavers, Gitla and Ella became inseparable. For a time.

One record I found shows that my mother began working at the factory before the ghetto was liquidated. But my mother's description of what she experienced—the liquidation of the ghetto while she was still in the barracks with her girlfriends—was so vivid. I have to believe my mother, over the records.

I heard a talk in Vancouver by Chris Friedrichs, a Holocaust historian, where he discussed an early reluctance—since corrected—by historians to find testimony from Holocaust survivors adequately credible. The academics apparently thought the survivors' stories might be too unreliable to accept for the historical record. Some survivors might mix up a date or a name, or the order in which things happened. But when it comes to emotional truth, they are completely dependable, Friedrichs said in his talk. "Survivors never forget what they saw or what they felt."

I am also not sure if the night my mother recalled was the liquidation of the small ghetto—where her family was—or the large ghetto, which would have been a lot louder and taken a lot longer. Longer than a single night. According to what I have read, that liquidation took three days to complete.

Either way, this work saved her. "It was like an angel for us," she told me.

...

At the munitions factory, the slave labourers lived in barracks, under very primitive conditions, but there was bedding, clothing and food twice a day—some bread, some coffee, some soup. Luxurious compared to what was down the road. Down the train tracks.

The factory was a half-hour walk from the barracks. They worked twelve hours a day in a hot, extremely loud crush of people and machinery. My mother lost her hearing for a while. At the end of these long days, they could have a shower. A small privilege in hell. Ella worked in the kitchen and was able to get a bit of extra food; a slightly thicker soup could have been the difference between life and death in those circumstances, as more and more people fell ill and died.

We found a note in my mother's handwriting years after her death, which indicated that this factory was run by Daimler Porsche and Steyer. In fact, the company was actually run by Steyr-Daimler-Puch. I discovered this only after writing an email to Porsche, asking for information about this slave labour situation. When they corrected the record, I offered a too-cheerful reply: "Well, I guess I'm free now to buy a Porsche!" The woman responded that she hoped I would come visit when I picked up the car. My sister Doris has since schooled me on the Nazi sympathies of company founder Ferdinand Porsche, who was chummy with Hitler. It's all moot anyway: as I write this, I am sharing a ten-year-old Honda with my ex-husband.

On its website, Daimler (which became Daimler-Benz and now Daimler AG) lays the facts bare. By 1941, operations were focused on the manufacture and assembly of military components for the Nazis. The company recruited women—the men were off at war—"in order to cope with the required unit volumes. However, as staff numbers were still too low, Daimler-Benz also used forced labourers."

My mother was one of them. By then, she was seventeen. What was I doing at seventeen? I had a part-time job at the mall, selling scented soap and body lotion.

I contacted Daimler to get some idea of what went on there. A very kind corporate communications person from Daimler in Stuttgart told me that about 2,900 workers in Radom were forced to work in the ammunition factory of Steyr-Daimler-Puch.

"Although the name Steyr Daimler Puch suggests that they were connected to the Daimler-Benz, AG, they were not. The plants of Steyr Daimler Puch were part of the Reichswerke Hermann Goring," this person wrote to me. "Today the company Steyr Daimler Puch is dissolved or let's say scattered in all winds. I don't know where the company archive is housed, or whether it is even still intact."

The emails I received from Germany as I made inquiries like this often held this air of respect and apology to them, the translations sometimes a little bit off, almost poetic. "Scattered in all winds."

...

Something I should say about my mother here: she was a cheerful optimist, always hoping for the best, with a sunny outlook that, when I was an unpleasant teenager, I dismissed as shallow, simple and unsophisticated.

I guess what didn't occur to me was how this way of looking at the world might have saved her life, and that this was an astonishing achievement—maintaining the gift of this perspective—given the horrors she had lived through.

As Hela wrote in her memoir, Guta had a generous heart, and accepted what was, keeping any sort of protest to herself.

But during the war, my mother's optimism left her when her big sister Ella did. After about a year and a half working at that factory in Radom, Ella was sent away. Her destination, unknown to my mother, was first Majdanek, and then Plaszow. Plaszow was the notorious concentration camp in a Krakow suburb made mainstream famous ("famous") by *Schindler's List*, where the Ralph Fiennes character, the real-life Austrian asshole Amon Goth, ran the camp and shot Jews dead for sport. He sure loved dogs, though.

My mother did not know where Ella went, did not know if her sister was alive, did not know if anyone in her family was alive. At this point, she became very discouraged. She had once dreamed of freedom, even contemplated an escape. But no longer.

"After they took away my sister, I said I haven't got nobody, it doesn't pay, to bother to live through. If I live, okay. If not, is not," she said during that Shoah Foundation interview.

"Did you think you were going to survive?" the interviewer asked.

"I was sometimes optimistic about. But usually the people weren't. They were very much pessimistic. Even my sister was pessimistic. But no, I had a feeling that we will live through that. And thanks God I'm here to tell the story."

...

In the summer of 1944, the Russians were approaching and the Germans needed to get rid of whatever Jews were left in Radom—2,500 people at this point from the 30,000 or so at the beginning of the war. My mother was one of about 500 women.

On July 26, they were ordered to march.

Thus began my mother's first long, horrific walk toward the unimaginable. Not a death march, I was corrected by one of the many experts I have spoken to about this, those who study this slice of historic Armageddon. This was considered a transit march.

They walked three days and three nights, slept in wet fields, were given very little food and very little water. It was hot, and dusty, and people were dying. They were shot attempting to escape or even trying to access rainwater for a drink ("not a death march"). Some Polish people along the way tried to help—they had bread they could share—but the German guards would not let the Poles get close to the starving, thirsty, dying Jews.

They finally arrived at a town called Tomaszow, near Lublin, and the women, now separated from the men, were locked up in the local jail. They were there for seven or eight days.

Then relief came, or so they thought.

It was a train.

"They pushed us in, squeezed us in, all beat up. We were without food, without water. I don't remember how long we been there.... It was a long time but I don't remember how long. Because day and night was the same thing," my mother recalled.

"It was very awful, smelly. People were just like herrings.... You couldn't move around."

There was nothing to eat, nothing to drink. No washroom facilities.

They arrived in a place they had never heard of. A place that, before the war, was the Polish village of Brzezinka. In German, Birkenau. Auschwitz II.

...

Auschwitz is so loaded with meaning today that it is impossible to think of a time when it was an unknown, when the name meant nothing. My mother would have arrived, shocked by the horror suddenly surrounding her: men in uniforms screaming, dogs barking, floodlights, watchtowers, barbed wire. Already severely malnourished, probably ill, and close to dying of thirst and grief, my mother would have had to process what this place was. I imagine her dazed in the fog of this vicious commotion, being jostled by the brutality around her. I imagine her staring up at giant smokestacks whose truly unbelievable function she could not yet understand.

"They greet us at the station, in Auschwitz. They came, Dr. Mengele. He made the selection—who should live and who should die." This is how my mother described her arrival at Auschwitz. It was August 1944. (Records indicate she received her prisoner's number on August 19.) The word in that description that makes my throat swell, my stomach churn, is "greet." That my mother should use such a civilized term to describe such barbaric chaos. She did not lose her humanity. Somehow.

On what was known as the ramp, the Nazis were waiting for them. They yelled, *Raus! Schnell!*—Out! Hurry!—forcing my mother and the others down from the train, beating them. She saw people beaten to death.

The notorious Josef Mengele—the devil who became known as the Angel of Death—was on duty, she recalled; his piercing blue eyes haunted my mother for life. She was nineteen and somehow, despite years of starvation and illness, she was sent to the right, to the line for people who would live another day, perhaps.

Surviving the initial SS inspection was against the odds. Of the 1.3 million people deported to Auschwitz, the vast majority—about 900,000 people—were gassed and cremated within hours of arrival. In the spring of 1944, shortly before my mother was sent there, the killing capacity reached unfathomable levels: the number of people murdered and cremated there was about 10,000 a day. The total death toll was more than 1.1 million.

After being sent to the right, my mother endured an hours-long ordeal. The women were stripped of all they had left, including the family photographs Gitla had kept with her over those years—most of the people in those photos, unbeknownst to her, now dead. Her clothing, her hair, her hope. Her functioning shoes. *May you wear them until they fall apart.*

They stood in a lineup, naked, for many hours. The bureaucracy of barbarism moves slowly.

It was very hot—"scorching heat," my mother said. They were forced to walk three miles. To the showers.

Another selection was made. Some women, older women, were taken away.

Then my mother and the other remaining women showered—real showers, but they didn't understand how lucky ("lucky") they were to have water rain down on them rather than gas.

Their heads were shaved, they were treated with some kind of insecticide.

My mother often talked about having her head shaved—it made me think, and perhaps made her think, of the very different head-shaving trauma her mother had endured when she was just sixteen. But my mother never talked about anything else being shaved. Many accounts I have read indicate that the inmates had all of their hair shaved, everywhere. I don't know if this was something that did not in fact happen to her, or if it was a detail she omitted out of shyness, or to protect me, or because she had banished from her mind the memory of a stranger shaving off her pubic hair.

Soon these women would be stripped of their names, branded with numbers instead. She was prisoner A 24751—the number that would remain imprinted in blue ink on her left forearm forever.

They were given ill-fitting prisoner uniforms and the wooden shoes that would ruin my mother's feet for life. It was the daily struggle she limped along with, the only thing I really ever heard her complain about from that time.

Then they were sent to the barracks. Still, no food.

The beds in the barracks were stacked up on three levels. Four to six girls slept together in a single hard bunk—more a shelf than a bed. If one person needed to turn over, the other five had to do the same thing. It was August. Scorching. There were hundreds of women in each barrack and no sanitary facilities—just one bucket for all of them.

One of the women who was with my mother on most of this journey wrote in her memoir that the top bunk was always preferable, because women would urinate in the middle of the night and if you were below, the urine would cascade down onto you.

What a thing to have to do. To be stripped of your humanity, of your ability to move, to function as a human being, to be so weighed down with grief and exhaustion and too many bodies in the bed with you that you cannot move, that you have no choice but to pee the bed.

It was on her second day in Auschwitz that my mother learned about the gas chambers. Some people had been separated from their families after they arrived and they inquired of the woman who was sort of in charge—a *kapo*, I imagine (a prisoner assigned to some sort of supervisory duty). Why couldn't they find their family members? Why hadn't they arrived at the barracks yet?

"So she showed us the chimney, that they went there," my mother said.

...

Joy came a couple of days after my mother arrived, and, also unbelievably, laughter.

In that sea of half-dead women, Gitla saw a familiar face, minus the hair: her sister, Ella.

"We cried and we laughed," my mother told me. Laughed? They laughed, she explained—this was another story I heard many times—because they both looked so funny without their hair. I think I understand now: the laughter must have been an expression of their absolute elation at the miracle of having found each other again, both alive, both in the same place, both bald.

They also laughed at each other's clothing: Ella had been given a very short dress that she could barely squeeze into. My mother was wearing a long dress that hung on her short, emaciated frame. They found this hilarious. Ella managed to switch barracks so that she could be with her sister. They were inseparable from that point until the end.

The girls were also reunited with their aunt, Raisel. Doda Rushka—as she became to me—was already there when Gitla and Ella arrived. During the daily camp roll call, she noticed them and ran to join their cluster, knowingly putting her life in danger. These were her nieces! A guard witnessed this and beat her harshly. But he didn't kill her. He could have, I know.

Raisel's daughter Miriam told me a story—now funny, then not—about something that happened between the women at Auschwitz. Raisel had managed to get her hands on some potato peels—an absolute treasure—and saved them for her nieces. She gave some to Ella and told her to give the rest to my mother. But my mother never got them. Ella traded those potato peels for two cigarettes.

They were so angry with her, furious. But Ella's presence meant everything to my mother. And after the war it turned into a bit of family lore, repeatedly told at gatherings. With laughter.

...

The laughs didn't last. Life at Auschwitz began with a very early roll call—4:30 a.m. in summer and 5:30 a.m. in winter—where they had to present themselves to their cruel enslavers, rain or shine. This could go on for hours while they made sure all of their slaves were accounted for. My mother contracted typhus, and there were days when she was so ill, so weak, she felt unable to get out of bed. Ella forced her out of that bunk, and she and other friends walked her to her spot for that *appel*. Because if she didn't show up, that would be that. Her next journey would have been up through the chimney.

Passing the initial SS selection at Auschwitz in no way guaranteed survival. The average life expectancy in the camp, for those who were not gassed right away, did not exceed a few weeks. Starvation, exhaustion, torture, disease, medical experiments and the harsh conditions of daily life and slave labour were killers. People were executed for any little transgression, like not performing a task to the satisfaction of the guards—who had free rein to work out their frustrations on the prisoners.

The roll calls were particularly dangerous, one of the few things my mother talked about. She remembered how cold it could be, standing there for hours. She mentioned once not saying her name—it must have been her number, surely—loudly enough, and being thwacked on the head for it. Was she punched? Hit with a baton? A rifle butt? I don't know. I do know this: It could have been worse; people could be kicked to death for the crime of being a little late.

Beyond the nasty roll calls, there was a lot of standing around at Auschwitz. If the weather was nice, and sometimes it was, they would sit outside, careful to watch out for the SS. Sometimes the guards would just show up and beat them. No reason given. No reason necessary.

I still can't fathom that such people exist, people who would beat up women, just because. People who would pluck whiskers from an old man's beard. Or is this a quality that lies dormant in some: that given ultimate power with no accountability necessary, given permission to be sadistic with impunity, they become their true selves? If that's the case, there must be people like this, still, who walk among us. I try not to think about this too often.

Some days the women were put to work: cruel make-work projects, carrying heavy boulders from one side of the road to the other. A day that could last eight hours. Then the next day, they would return to the same site. They would spend another eight hours moving the boulders back to the other side of the road.

A difficult task physically—and also for its pointlessness—at any time. But they were doing it under the burden of grief and severe malnutrition. In the morning, they were given hot water with a piece of bread. In the evening, a bit of vile soup. If you didn't move those boulders fast enough, you would be beaten. Sometimes to death. Really, it didn't take much.

I recall my mother saying that she had a friend who worked in the kitchen, who brought her extra food. She was so sick, but Ella and Raisel forced her to eat. There were no cigarette trades this time. They nursed my mother back to health, or whatever counted as health at Auschwitz.

...

About three months after my mother's arrival in the worst hell, the SS announced they were looking for people to be sent to Germany to work. My mother didn't know if it was a trick, but she volunteered. She figured any place was better than Auschwitz. And if it was a trick, so be it. She took the gamble.

(My mother's recollection of having volunteered somehow doesn't square with how things worked at Auschwitz. This is how she told me the story. But I can't imagine it being the sort of place where prisoners would be asked to put up their hand if they wanted to give this new work detail a whirl.)

About three hundred women were selected. The women were examined by doctors to ensure they were strong enough to work, after which they were provided with some actual clothes, one set. They had showers, real showers—and they were off to Germany.

In an account I read by another woman who was also sent from Auschwitz to the same place my mother ended up—albeit for a different transport, in July, not November—this selection process was recalled in horrific detail.

The women had to line up naked; eight hundred were selected. They had to place their clothes in little piles in front of them as they were forced to stand with their arms outstretched, hands in the air. The doctor in charge, accompanied by shouting female guards, pointed to the strongest, then sent them to another location, where they underwent another examination and had to wait and wait, not knowing what was next.

I imagine my mother underwent a similar ordeal.

My mother was transferred, the official records say, on November 23, 1944, to the Concentration Camp Buchenwald/Kommando

Lippstadt, where her prisoner number became 25536. (On this document, her name is spelled "Gitta Linsen.") November 23 appears to be the date of her arrival. She was one of ninety-two women from Poland in that transfer, along with her sister, Ella, and their aunt, Raisel.

Transportation was once again in the form of cattle cars. No food, crowded conditions—although not as packed as on the trip in. The train would stop from time to time so they could have a drink or a wash, get some fresh air.

The Shoah Foundation interviewer asked my mother about the conditions. "They weren't pleasant," my mother responded. "It's not first class." God, I miss her.

After three or four days, they arrived in what is now the North Rhine–Westphalia region of Germany and were sent to a labour camp in Lippstadt. It was a satellite camp of Buchenwald, an ammunition factory—my mother was familiar with those—set up in the forest to avoid detection by enemy planes.

There they worked twelve-hour days doing they didn't know what—some small piece of work on something that would become an airplane, they assumed. Or maybe a gun. Or a bullet. Or a bomb. In fact, as I later learned, the company she worked for ("worked for") produced, among other kinds of ammunition, hand grenades and aircraft parts.

The conditions were an improvement over Auschwitz—the barracks, about a ten-minute walk from the factory, were equipped with double-stacked beds, not triple-stacked like in Birkenau. Only sixty or seventy women to a room. Still two meals a day, but the soup at the end of the day was a little thicker, and there was more bread.

The gamble had paid off.

Perhaps the biggest payoff in the new place (other than escaping the gas chambers) was being mixed in with other people—not Jewish slave labourers, but other foreigners—deportees, refugees: Non-Jewish Poles, Hungarians, French people. A lot of Italians. The Italians in particular were very kind, I have read. They would clandestinely pass the emaciated Jews some of their food, giving away their own dinners. But maybe even more important: they would come over and talk to them, talk to these Jews like they were actual humans.

One of these Italian men kept calling my mother *bella*. Why is he calling me Bella, wondered my non-Italian-speaking mother—who had had some friends who were actually named Bella. My mother kept telling him that her name was not Bella, but he kept calling her that. She thought it was funny, a joke. Eventually, she learned what *bella* meant in Italian. Imagine what that did for her. To be called beautiful, after all that.

The non-Jewish workers were encouraging as well as generous, telling their slave colleagues that the war was going badly for the Germans, that the end was near and they would soon be free—if the Germans didn't kill them first.

To have information, outside contact with the real world, to have any idea of what was happening—this was a gift. Because in addition to food, proper shelter and their loved ones, my mother and the others had been denied information from the world beyond their imprisonment.

I don't want to paint an overly rosy picture. My mother was still a prisoner and a slave, making explosives for her captors. Some of the female slave labourers died from dysentery and cholera. Women who became pregnant were transported back to concentration camps. You can imagine their fates. And the fate of their unborn children. According to the *Encyclopedia of Camps and Ghettos*, the final transport from Lippstadt to a concentration camp included three women and their babies as well as sixty-nine women who were unable to work for sickness or other reasons. One of those babies, according to a former prisoner who witnessed this, was trodden to death by an SS man. It may or may not have been intentional, the witness reported.

This camp, I learned on a rare snowy morning decades later in Vancouver, was making products for two companies: Eisen and Metallwerke AG. It was known as LEM, for Lippstadt Eisen- und Metallwerke.

A bit of Googling revealed that HANSA Metallwerke AG, based in Stuttgart, makes home and office products; the sub-industry is home improvement. "A good feeling starts with a shower," one of its pages declared in bold type.

When I checked in with the company again in the fall of 2021, it was simply called HANSA. "HANSA is dedicated to perfecting your shower moment," its website stated, also promising that its showers have been developed with "multi-generational aspects in mind."

Eisen makes pencil sharpeners. On its company history page, the entry for 1939: "The capacities of the company were impounded by the German weapon industry." One sentence written in passive voice to stand in for the slave labour my mother and her friends were forced to endure. Twelve little words with no acknowledgment of regret or responsibility. When I checked the website again in late 2021, its history page had been altered. For 1939: "The capacities of the company are seized by a defense company." Eleven little words.

I contacted the companies. I wanted to know what it was they were making during the war, maybe find a photograph of their facility at the time, any information at all to add some detail to the incomplete picture of my mother's life. I didn't receive a response from either of them, poetic or otherwise.

My mother was at Lippstadt as a slave for the German weapon industry for about six months, until the end of March 1945. Then she and the others were sent on another march. This time there is no dispute over the correct terminology: it was a death march.

...

On March 29, 1945, the Germans evacuated my mother's slave labour camp at Lippstadt. The Allies were closing in.

The women were told they were going to the "main camp." That would have been Buchenwald proper. But based on the direction they were walking, they were not headed there. They were going to Bergen-Belsen.

"There is no word, no language that can express the awful terror

these two words 'Bergen-Belsen' sounded in Jewish ears," wrote Hela
Morder, who herself ended up there. And this was after she had experienced Auschwitz.

Starvation and disease were rampant in that overcrowded hell,
where about fifty thousand people died, including Anne Frank. Where
rats and lice feasted on piles of human bodies. Where there might not
have been gas chambers to kill you, but typhus would do the job. Or
starvation. One liberator described the corpses—fourteen thousand of
them—as being stacked like cordwood. Even without the gas, nature
took its course.

There were no trains anymore to take them to Bergen-Belsen. This
time, my mother and the other women would walk the whole way.
They walked at night and slept during the day in barns, in an effort by
their captors to avoid detection by the Allies. They took dusty country
side roads, not main roads, always watched over by guards, including
an SS man and his SS guard girlfriend.

The chief guard, the LEM commander, was said to be riding a bike
with a bright light as those starving women marched. A motorcycle?
A bicycle? I'm not sure.

They walked for three days and nights, some seven hundred to nine
hundred women when they departed (there are conflicting accounts of
the numbers). There was no food, no water. Many of the women didn't
even have shoes anymore. They wore blankets as coats. It was late
March—cold, soggy. One woman had to do the work of a horse, pulling the baggage cart—the baggage belonging to the guards. People
were dying by the side of the road.

The sound of a whistle meant the women could stop for a short rest.
Another whistle and they were forced to rise and continue the march—
five across, exhausted, helping each other push forward. The roll calls
continued; meanwhile there was war all around them, bombardment
from the skies.

At about 5 a.m. on what would have been the fourth day of the
march, the group reached the outskirts of a town, Kaunitz, and stopped

on a large patch of grass. The guards were consulting maps, looking for a route or perhaps a place for the women to sleep—a barn or other shelter. The front was closing in. There was confusion everywhere.

Suddenly the guard couple was gone. And then they were all gone, all the guards.

The women were unsure what to do. Do they wait? Do they run? Hide? They remained on the patch of grass. They were so tired. To be able to sit, even amid the chaos, was a relief.

Then: a convoy of military trucks. Soldiers.

Americans!

The U.S. soldiers were on their way to Berlin to conquer the Nazis. But they paused in their military campaign. They made a U-turn and liberated the women. It was April 1, 1945. The fourth day of Passover. Easter Sunday. And these women rose from graves that had been all but certain. Resurrected, given life.

Ella described it in her Shoah Foundation interview. "The most beautiful day what can be after six years."

In my brain, the stories from my mother about her liberation day blend with old black-and-white footage of American soldiers: impossibly fresh-faced boy-men, grinning and smoking a Lucky Strike. *All right boys, let's free these women before we push on to Berlin and beat Fritz once and for all.*

The women prostrated themselves on the ground, kissing the wheels of the tank, according to an interview with a woman who must have been part of the same group. The woman, identified as Anna Kaletska (her real name was Anna Kovitzka) told American psychologist David P. Boder in 1946 that the U.S. soldiers at first must have thought the women were insane, and then slowly understood. Tears rolled down the face of a U.S. soldier as he began to grasp who these women were, what had happened to them. "And they would jump off the tanks and they were kissing us. Us dirty and lousy ones!" Anna said. (She is quoted in Boder's 1949 book, *I Did Not Interview the Dead.*)

These Americans gave food to the women—chocolate, my mother told me. These men were so kind. And probably so young. They did not know what chocolate could do to someone who had been malnourished to the brink of death for so many years.

I have always pictured the U.S. soldiers showering the women with little wrapped chocolates and other well-meaning—but in this context potentially lethal—treats from slow-moving trucks, like Santa's elves on a parade float, tossing out candy canes to the crowds lining the street.

"They were rejoicing with us like little children," Anna Kovitzka told David Boder.

Imagine the hundreds of women there—weeping, embracing, eating. Resting.

The American soldiers told these women who had been starved of everything—including support from any authority figures—to go into the houses; these would have been the homes in Kaunitz, Germany. Take what you want: food, clothing. Find a bed to sleep in. It's yours for now. Don't worry about what the Germans who live there say. Go in, make yourselves at home. Some of the Americans went in themselves to collect necessities for the women.

I loved this detail growing up—revenge on the Germans! Get out of your bed and give it to a Jew!

But as a more mature person, living in my own home, I now feel for those Kaunitzers who had to give up their things to strangers. I think about their kids, having grown up listening to nasty lies about the Jews, and suddenly seeing a bunch of them living in their house, eating their food, sleeping in their beds. That must have been something.

A group of women—about fifteen of them—ended up in the home of a banker, or was it the bank itself? I have also seen it referred to as the Liquor Mansion. Perhaps it was the large home of the local distiller? My mother and Ella were among the group.

There were some Jewish men in that U.S. Army division—or was it a brigade? A platoon? In any case, they had some matzo with them, Ella told me. Anna Kovitzka recalled that matzo "fell from the tanks."

There in Kaunitz, on I'm not sure which night of Passover, they had a Seder. They recounted the story of being enslaved by cruel captors, fleeing on foot, finally liberated and making exodus to the Promised Land. For the Jews, for some reason, it has been ever thus.

I have read many stories from Jewish-American soldiers involved in liberating the camps. Sometimes they would say to the living skeletons, walking corpses (the soldiers' descriptions): *"Ich bin a Yid."* I am a Jew.

Imagine hearing that. I don't know if my mother was one of the people on the receiving end of a sentence like that, but it's possible.

I have thought about those liberators so many times over the years, wanting to know who they were, what they thought. In the absence of that exact information, I got some ideas from the descriptions in the National Museum of American Jewish Military History's publication *GIs Remember: Liberating the Concentration Camps.*

One soldier described the prisoners as almost worshipping their liberators. I believe that to be true; that is the impression I got from what my mother told me. Another recounted liberating Jews so weak that they couldn't walk. "They were glad to know a Jewish person helped liberate them and they blessed me ... made me feel like a Messiah," George Fichtenbaum said. Another was haunted by the sight of prisoners eating whatever they could get their hands on, including cigarettes.

One soldier said his identification with the use of showers to kill Jews stayed with him for years, whenever he showered.

Kaunitz is a village in the district of Verl/Gutersloh in what is now the state of North Rhine–Westphalia, located roughly between Dusseldorf and Hanover. Even now, it's tiny, with a population of less than three thousand. In 1945, despite the hell of the war, it was still a pretty little place, with nice houses, a few stores, a church and a lot of forested land. The air was fresh. The Allies—the British came in and established a military government after the Americans liberated the women—made sure the women were taken care of. They had food, proper clothing, shelter, medical care.

"They supplied us with everything," my mother said. "And then we start to look for families. Then we got the truth."

...

At the beginning of 2006, we celebrated my mother's eighty-first birthday in Toronto at a little Italian restaurant. Then she packed herself up to go to Florida for a couple of months. She had rented the condominium belonging to the family of my best friend, Marsha, in a complex with a beautiful pool and its fair share of Holocaust survivors playing cards at the tables around it, and, wow, did she ever deserve that winter in the sun.

A few days after her departure, on January 17, a week after her eighty-first birthday, I spoke to her on the phone from my desk in the busy CBC Radio newsroom in Toronto. She wasn't feeling well, she said. Just a little virus or something, the doctor had told her that day; she had gone to a clinic to get checked out. He had written her a prescription—antibiotics, I think.

My mother sounded very tired and weak. I made a snap decision: *Mummy, I'm going to come down and visit you.* There was something I had been meaning to do anyway: to spend time with her one-on-one and interview her, in a comprehensive way the Shoah Foundation woman had not, about her life in Poland and her experiences during the war. I wanted to know everything. I would write it all down. I was a writer, for heaven's sake, and an interviewer. This was my job. It was time to turn my reporter skills to the most important story I would ever tell.

I got off the phone, requested some days off from my CBC job, went online, booked a flight. A few days later, I would be down in North Miami Beach with my mother, swimming, shopping, over-eating, and finally hearing—and recording—the whole story. She was so happy I was coming. I was too.

Flights booked, I came home from dinner and a play that night and my phone rang. It was my brother-in-law, Sam—the Swedish doctor, by now living in Hamilton, Ontario, with Doris and their two younger children. He had terrible news, he said. His voice was cracking. I knew what he was going to say before he said it. And yet, all I could blurt out was, "Please tell me you're joking. Please tell me this is a joke."

As if he would joke about my mother dying alone of a heart attack in my best friend's family's condominium in North Miami on a Tuesday night.

It was January 17, 2006. Two days later, still in absolute shock, I delivered the eulogy for my mother.

Had the Nazis shortened her life? In addition to the grief and malnutrition and bad feet and everything else, my mother had contracted rheumatic fever during the war. Which can weaken the heart muscle.

We sat shiva at Rachel and Jack's large Toronto home with its black granite floors and grand circular staircase, overwhelmed with sorrow and comfort and food. Friends and family surrounded us. A couple of ex-boyfriends came.

My former partner Pat, whom my mother had called "Pet" in her thick Yiddish accent, paraded into the house with a huge box of bagels and cream cheese—"Jew food" he called out—a story I would tell at his own memorial ten years later. It was election night. We sat together, the whole family and Pat, and watched Stephen Harper and his Conservative Party win the election. Had my mother voted in an advance poll before leaving for Florida? Had she voted Liberal, as she traditionally had, or did she go for the Conservatives this time, persuaded by their support for Israel? Did she manage to have her say about a government she would not live to experience?

On the last day of shiva, my sisters and I got up from the couch, the luxury sectional that had been stripped of its cushions, as is customary for mourners. We rose from the hard place where we had been sitting and took a walk through the barren, upscale suburban neighbourhood. This is the tradition, how shiva is supposed to end. With a walk outside.

There are so many rituals in Jewish death: the body, never left alone until burial. Burial the next day, with each attendant taking a shovel and pouring soil over the lowered coffin, and the hard, awful ka-chunk that results from those first few shovels of dirt delivered—in that case, on a freezing January day, by my sisters and me. Washing your hands after the cemetery before you enter a home, a cleansing. The seven days sitting shiva, with mirrors covered so you can't be bothered to think about your appearance, and the mourners identified by low, hard seats and a piece of ripped fabric that you wear. The friends and family who come by with food. The endless food. The endless chaos of people, also in shock, telling stories about the person who has been lost, and offering support to the mourners. So that by the final day, when you rise from shiva and take that walk around the neighbourhood, the first time you leave the house in a week (in theory), you are ready to breathe the air and to appreciate it. You are ready to go home and be alone, blissfully. You are ready to reintegrate, a little bit, into the world.

The shiva gives you a week of comfort and love, of food and caring, of a break from the world and its usual daily obligations. And you are so surrounded that by the time it is over, you feel okay about being alone. You crave it, actually.

Getting up from my sister's couch that morning, I was struck by the realization that to grieve is a luxury. That on top of everything else, this was something my parents had been denied in their youth. Not only did they lose everyone, but they had no choice but to go on to the indignities of the ghetto and the boulders of Auschwitz, living on watery soup and bitter fake coffee. Nobody brought them bagels or rugelach or sweet stories about their parents. Just as their parents had been stripped of the dignity of death—gold teeth ripped from their mouths, bodies burned to ash—so my parents had been denied the dignity and comfort of mourning.

This is what I thought about as I strolled past the monster houses in a very Jewish, very peaceful suburb of North Toronto, walking with my sisters. How lucky we were, even in this worst moment.

FIVE

Little Miracles

IT WASN'T LONG AFTER my mother and several hundred other Jewish women were liberated on April 1, 1945, in Kaunitz, Germany, that word of this travelled twenty-five kilometres or so south to Holsen, to the farm where my father was still living and working as Tadek, Catholic Pole. When he learned that some of these women were from Poland, he became hopeful. Maybe his sister, Devorah, was among them. My father set out for Kaunitz to look for her.

Devorah was not in Kaunitz. Devorah had been gassed to death in Treblinka in October 1942. I don't know when Tadek discovered this horror. Perhaps he met someone from Piotrkow on that trip, someone who said to him: *Yes, I saw your sister board the train with your parents. No, we never saw them again. No, we never saw anyone who got on that train, ever again.*

I like to think that he lived with hope a little longer than that. Hope is a powerful drug, no matter how things turn out.

He did learn that another woman he knew, an old friend, was among the group who had been liberated in the area. She was ill, in hospital. He went to visit her.

In the hospital bed next to this woman was another survivor, also a Polish Jew who had recently been liberated. Gitla Lindzen was in hospital because she had been in a motorcycle accident. (What she was doing on a motorcycle, I somehow never asked.) My father's visits to the hospital became quite frequent—and it wasn't his old friend drawing him there.

Part of the beauty of this story—in addition to the randomness of them meeting or the universe interfering to ensure it happened, whichever you want to believe—is that in the hospital, my mother's face was wrapped in bandages. During all of those visits, my father was never able to see what she looked like.

My parents married in a ceremony with their friends on August 20, 1946. I know two things about their wedding, both bummers. One: the photographer produced zero pictures of the event. I'm not sure why; I think something went wrong when developing the film, or maybe his camera broke? In any case, no photos. The other thing I know is that my mother was in charge of the wedding feast—there were no caterers, I take it, in those days—and she made a chicken. But she did not really know how to make a chicken. And she burned that chicken to a crisp, burned it beyond edibility. She wept over that bird on her wedding day.

Doris recalls our mother telling her about the first time she tried to make chicken soup. It was a disaster; she didn't know that she was supposed to add water. Were these different versions of the same story? Or had there been two separate poultry calamities?

In any case, my mother did not know how to roast a chicken or make chicken soup because her mother had never been able to teach her how. Because Rachel was murdered when her daughter was a teenager. Even before Rachel had been hauled away to Treblinka, the opportunity for such a lesson would have vanished. As life became more difficult in the ghetto and food scarce, there would have been almost no way to find a kosher chicken—or any chicken—to cook; no way to afford it even if a chicken could be found; no way for my grandmother to teach my mother how to carry on a family recipe.

Post-war Kaunitz must have been brimming with Jewish life. The liberated men and women found solace in each other. They played cards together at night, our parents told us. Imagine the freedom of being able to play a card game, walk wherever you wanted, do what you wanted, kiss who you wanted.

I also imagine the residents of Kaunitz were somewhat aggrieved. And I can understand that. Their country had just suffered a crushing defeat after years of living through the hell of war. Further, some had had their homes and belongings confiscated for the benefit of these women—Jews, about whom they had been told terrible things for many years. Some of the residents had fled the area when the front moved closer. They returned after surrender to find their homes occupied by Jews. It must have been a shock.

I learned a lot about this time from Andrea Tebart, a German journalist my sisters and I hired at the beginning of 2020 to investigate this time in our parents' lives. Andrea routinely went over and above what I asked of her, sending me information as she found it, translated into English, often with sensitive, contextual, and yes, poetic comments.

After the women were liberated in Kaunitz, Andrea told us, a written directive went out to the residents, signed by a priest from Verl, and the mayor: "Please be kind to the people and give them a roof over their heads until they are picked up again." The priest then wrote by hand: "Please follow!"

I can't imagine what life felt like for these young women. Many of them did not yet know what had happened to their relatives; many did not know how to proceed with life. The last time they had been free, they had been with their families. Children, or just a little older. At the same time, they were meeting nice, understanding men who had experienced a similar hell. It's not a huge surprise that couples were hooking up at a great pace.

This was strongly frowned upon by the locals, Andrea explained to me. This Jewish life with all of its new freedoms encountered a conservative rural population that would have been shocked by even a kiss on a street corner, she wrote.

The military authority—first American, then British—protected the Jewish women. They were allowed to do anything as long as they obeyed the laws.

Andrea speculates that the mayor, who acted as a sort of liaison with the military government, called on that priest to appeal to the locals because the Catholic population probably trusted him more than anyone.

"After what I've read, everything in Kaunitz was turned upside down for a long time," Andrea wrote to me.

She also told me that the priest was probably one of very few people who understood how traumatized these women were.

How traumatized my mother was.

"As far as I personally know about traumas," Andrea wrote, "they cannot be deleted, but 'only' overwritten by good things."

I had to laugh, because that same week I had told a friend that I was worried I would never get over the grief from my divorce. My friend said that I would probably never really be over it until I met someone else.

I think it's time, I told her, *for me to try to meet someone else.*

She pointed out that we were in the midst of a global pandemic. It was maybe not the best time to start dating.

My timing has always been off.

···

Neither of my parents went back to their hometowns after they were liberated. I'm fairly certain I asked my mother why and I always got some version of "We knew there was nothing to go back to."

If it were me, I think, I would want to go back—at the very least to have a look around for some of my things. My parents' things. I don't believe I pressed these points when discussing it with my mother. Maybe part of me was protecting her; maybe I was protecting myself, afraid to crack open the armour she had created with her day-to-day life, and witness what emerged.

A couple of her friends from the Radom barracks did go back. Nusia returned and found her mother and brother, but she could not stay in Poland, she said. Radom was like one big cemetery. The houses were there, but all the Jews were gone. Remember—they had once comprised almost one-third of the population.

Another woman, Freda, also returned.

Freda travelled to Radom after liberation, despite the logistical difficulties in doing so, to see who she could find. But while there, she began hearing about pogroms elsewhere in Poland—in particular, in Kielce, where a mob of Poles killed forty-two Jews who had survived the Holocaust. Imagine surviving that hell only to be killed by your neighbours back home. In Radom, Freda became afraid even to go outside; the streets were again dangerous for Jews, she felt. She made her way back to Germany, and eventually to her new home, Canada.

In Toronto, Freda lived a couple of blocks from us, in our subdivision filled with Holocaust survivors and other immigrants from the Old Country—Italians, Greeks, Portuguese. I knew her my whole life.

...

My parents had a happy life in Kaunitz. Officially Displaced Persons, they were registered in a variety of DP camps, but lived on their own in a little home there.

My father traded goods on the black market; my mother kept house and had a job cleaning, I think, for the British army, which had taken over control of the area from the Americans. On one document I found, my mother listed her trade, occupation or profession as "dressmaker." I'm not sure she was ever actually employed in that capacity. As I recall, she wasn't the best sewer. (On the other hand, she could knit beautifully. I keep two of her sweaters in my closet; one, a cardigan, I have worn on many hard days, especially while writing all of this down.)

On April 12, 1949, Gitla gave birth in nearby Gütersloh to their first child. They named her Sara Rachel. Sara for my father's mother. Rachel for my mother's mother.

As the story goes, my father was so eager for a son, so sure he was about to have a boy, that when the nurses told him it was a girl, he thought they were joking, and refused to believe it. (Sigh.) This story always included the detail that he brought my postpartum mother a gigantic bouquet of flowers, nonetheless. Nonetheless! But he fell hard for his baby girl. Nonetheless.

Tadek, as he was still being called, loved Germany and wanted to stay. He was doing well in business; the black market was thriving. And he had what I have always thought of as a bizarre love for Germany— its culture, its people. I guess it was where he found life again after the hell he experienced in Poland, even if it was German-occupied Poland. Still, it made no sense to my mother. She wanted out.

Guta—this was my father's preferred name for her—initially wanted to go to Palestine, where her sister was living. But Ella wrote to her and told her not to come; it was awful there, too hard, she should wait. "But I couldn't wait because I hate Germany. I hate it," my mother said in *Mes Sept Mères*.

There was some talk of Australia as well, where some of their friends had gone, but it just seemed so far. It was down to North America. My parents waited to see who would give them permission first: Canada or the United States. Canada won out; my mother had a first cousin— herself a survivor—already living in Toronto, who sponsored them.

"I would never think that I [would] be in a free country like Canada," my mother says in *Mes Sept Mères*, chatting with Freda in a Toronto ravine. "To be so free."

On February 28, 1951, my parents and Rachel departed from Bremerhaven, Germany, on the SS *Goya* for Halifax, Nova Scotia. When they docked, after the long journey, they had some time in the city. My father was craving fresh bread. He ventured out to a bakery, dreaming of the fragrant rye bread that had brought him sustenance in Germany, maybe with caraway seeds and some butter spread on top. But the bread he found in Halifax was unfamiliar. What was this soft, flavourless mound? Tadek did not have a taste for white bread. He worried it was an omen: what had they done, coming to this place, with this awful bread?

Upon arrival in Canada, my mother adopted a new name: Jean. I guess she was going for something exceedingly white. My father adopted a Canadian name too: Jack. But almost everyone, my mother included, called him Tadek, or Ted, for the rest of his life.

Sara Rachel got to keep her names, but we called her Rachel, never Sara. (To add to all the confusion with multiple names in our family, for some reason we called her Rochelle for many years. She's Rachel again now.)

My parents arrived with a pile of money but almost no English— and little business or financial acumen. It seems I come by my lack of financial prowess quite honestly.

My father was a furrier, a real estate agent, and eventually went into business with two friends. They bought a seedy hotel in downtown Toronto with a tavern on the main floor, the kind of place with a separate entrance for "ladies and escorts." My father always seemed to get saddled with the rotten shifts, working all hours behind the bar, while his partners wintered in Miami. So it was often my father on the clock when fights would break out. One night, he was injured by flying glass. I think the story was that someone threw a bottle at him. Anyway, not the greatest place.

When they were still living in downtown Toronto in a neighbourhood known as The Annex, they had another daughter. Doris was born in the '50s, when my parents were doing most of their shopping in the crooked aisles of Honest Ed's, the discount department store aimed at immigrants—and stood in long lines for spectacular door crashers. Or travelling a few blocks to Kensington Market, where they had had their first home in Canada, and where all the little Jewish-owned shops selling cheese and meat and other delicacies must have felt so familiar to them. My mother had a job at the post office, and also had a side job where she worked from home, touching up photos.

A story from her time at the post office: the workers had to memorize postal codes so they could quickly get letters into the right bins. They were actually tested on this—and my mother would often get a perfect score on these tests. She would come home and tell her little family; she was so proud of this achievement.

She had a friend at work, Marie. Not Jewish. One day Marie noticed my mother's tattoo on her forearm and asked her what it was. My mother, surprised and scrambling, told her that it was her phone number. She had written it down there because she forgot it sometimes.

It must have seemed very odd to Marie that Jean, who was getting perfect scores on these postal code tests, could not remember her own phone number, to the extent that she had to write it down in some sort of permanent marker on her forearm.

But when Rachel reminded me of this story many years after the fact, it occurred to me: the phone number answer was actually a less crazy explanation than what had actually happened to her, why those numbers had really been branded onto her arm.

Rachel and Doris were good little girls, excellent students, although Rachel reports that she had a bit of an attitude. The girls would roam the downtown neighbourhood with their friends, play hide-and-seek in the grimy laneways; they had a lot of freedom. They, like me, had only a passing knowledge of what had happened to our parents. Their history was like an ominous shadow that hung just beyond reach, and well beyond comprehension.

Ten years and one move up north to the suburbs later, they had their third daughter, me.

The fact that after such tragedy my parents were able to build new lives—purchase and set up a home, go to night school to learn English, buy a business, raise children—seems astonishing to me, as I contemplate it all as an adult. How on earth did they manage to do it, manage to be so normal?

In 1984, at a conference for children of Holocaust survivors, Elie Wiesel told the gathering: "That your parents were not seized by an irrepressible anger . . . remains a source of astonishment to me. Had they set fire to the entire planet, it would not have surprised anyone."

They were too busy mowing the lawn and bringing home the brisket to burn down the planet. And maybe too exhausted, too sad. Anyway, their life, their very existence, was an inferno.

. . .

In my heart, somehow, I always knew I was going to have trouble in the romance department. Self-fulfilling prophecy perhaps. But true. Every relationship I had was troubled. I made bad choices. And I behaved badly.

In my late twenties, I was dating someone who was perfect on paper—Jewish doctor (my mother was overjoyed), very smart, very funny. I thought this was it. I imagined our life together, forever.

But things were going south. He had moved away for school and my insecurity was toxic. I was spinning out.

For the first time in my life, I sought the help of a therapist. I went to her to help me save my relationship. She was more interested in saving me.

She was a Jungian, big into dream interpretation, and it was a retelling of a dream that sparked the lightbulb that has illuminated pretty much everything I have written here.

I had a dream about that Jewish doctor boyfriend: we were on a train, and he was naked.

The therapist was astounded that I did not see the significance, the symbolism in this dream. You're dreaming of your Jewish boyfriend, the one you're afraid of losing forever, being *naked* on a *train* and your parents survived the Holocaust? Don't you see the connection?

I hadn't, in fact. There were no Nazis in this dream. Just the boyfriend.

The Holocaust had barely, if ever, come up in these sessions. I had probably mentioned it in passing when talking about my parents.

Discussing this dream unlocked an astonishing possibility: that my abandonment issues, and contemporary relationship troubles, could in some way be traced back to the Holocaust. This was the first time I had ever considered a connection between what had happened to my parents and my own issues: an often overwhelming sadness— far beyond the moody teenager norm; a pervasive loneliness; my tendency to cling—like at Mothers and Babes; a debilitating homesickness when away from my parents or home. Always, always expecting the worst. The glass wasn't just half-empty; it was half-full of poison. Or Zyklon B.

I started to think about this, re-examining my messed-upness with this question at the heart of it: Could I possibly be a victim of the Holocaust, once-removed? The stories I had grown up with. The naked corpses, the cattle cars, the deadly showers. The uncle who made the remark about the shoes and wound up dead in a gas chamber. My great-grandmother's wig. Or was it my grandmother's? The tattoo on my mother's arm, on her life. Rubbing off on mine.

I am certain that therapist, who was wonderful, would have loved to have gotten into all of that. But the boyfriend wound up dumping me, and my broken heart became the prime focus of my appointments. The hypothesis of the Holocaust as the source of my troubles was all but forgotten.

After the doctor who dumped me, I spent years with Pat of the shiva bagels; we lived in Toronto and Vancouver and then Toronto again. And then there was the man who would become my husband—my soulmate, if I believed in that stuff. I used to say he was the male version of me—as if that were a good thing.

A few weeks after my mother died, on a trip to Montreal meant to help me with my grief, the male version of me got down on one knee in a fancy hotel room and asked me to marry him.

I wore the most beautiful, sparkling ring to dinner that night, and inside I was a hurricane. I was so in love, happier than I ever thought I would be, and yet it was all dulled by my grief and my crushing understanding of what could never be. My mother would never know.

When we returned home to Toronto, we met up with two of my best friends, Shannon and Rosemary, and told them the news. They were thrilled. Rosemary, my closest friend from university, had breast cancer at the time, but she was such a force of positivity; we were certain there would be a miracle.

Seven months after I eulogized my mother, I was back at the pulpit, this time at a Catholic church, eulogizing my dear friend.

There *was* a miracle to come, though. The year after my mother and Rosemary died, I left Toronto for Vancouver permanently, to get married and become a stepmother (I hate that word) to two brilliant, hilarious children. Well, I thought it was all permanent.

Getting married for the first time at forty-one—miraculous. And getting pregnant three months later without even trying—now there's a miracle for you.

I was high risk, a geriatric pregnancy, and I was already doing to my future child what my parents had done to me: cursing him (I didn't know it was a him yet) with really old parents.

I was still a couple of weeks away from leaving my job at the newspaper for that blessed two weeks of maternity leave pre–due date—I had planned to go to movies and get the house ready and nap—when my water broke. I was thirty-four weeks and four days pregnant.

The next day, October 8, at precisely 6 p.m. according to the giant watch worn by the doctor who was looking up into my body, I gave birth to a small, but ultimately healthy, baby boy.

He needed time in the incubator, so he was sent to the intermediate NICU. When my husband and I went to visit him that night, still throbbing with shock and relief, the nurse, warmly welcoming us, told us our son was the loudest baby in the place. This was good, she explained. (Because what did I know?) It meant he was doing well, thriving. She was kind and warm and jovial. A saviour at a scary time. I froze for a moment when she told us her name. Rosemary.

The next day my stepchildren visited their brother in the hospital and we snapped one of my favourite photos of all time: my stepdaughter peering in at Jacob in his incubator; my stepson looking up at the camera with a big smile. This was my family.

The following week, we were in the NICU parents' lounge with a bunch of other worried mothers and fathers, watching the results come in from yet another federal election. I was transported back to my sister's sectional couch, surrounded by family after the death of my mother, watching Stephen Harper get elected the first time while we ate Pat's bagels. Now I was at the hospital after the birth of my son watching Harper get re-elected. I remembered my thoughts about the luxury of mourning rituals. What I was living through now was an even greater luxury. Women in the camps who gave birth—there were no lounges or election night results for them. There was no hope for them or their babies.

I was writing a group email to let friends, family and co-workers know that I had had this baby, that he was early but he was healthy, when I realized that he had been born the same day on the Hebrew calendar as my father: Erev Yom Kippur.

I said over my shoulder to my husband: *The baby was born on my father's Hebrew birthday; isn't that amazing?* It was something I had never even considered happening, because the due date was more than a month later. My husband was quiet for a moment and then he said: October 8 was my father's birthday.

On the rare day that our fathers' birthdays, Hebrew and regular, should collide, our son was born. He felt like a miracle.

We named him Jacob Lederman.

SIX

Circles and Arcs

THEY SAY NOBODY TELLS you how hard it is to have a new-born—the sleep deprivation, the beat-up nipples, the mood swings. But even if they did tell you—and they do, actually—you don't know it until you're in it. And for me, I was in it hard.

My baby had whatever they call colic these days. He cried and cried and cried. He cried through feedings, through walks, through everything. He woke up every hour or, if I was lucky, every two hours, to be fed. He was tiny.

I had no family in Vancouver, nobody to help, to hold my baby so I could nap or shower or go to the grocery store on my own. My sisters and my closest friends were all back in Ontario. I felt like my life had been stolen from me, that I would never be the same. My baby cried and cried.

I thought about families in hiding during the Holocaust. I pictured an underground bunker with my crying baby, having to cover his shrieks with whatever I would have had with me—not a pillow, surely. Did they have pillows in those hiding holes? And what if the baby suffocated? Many did, I know.

Imagine having to smother your child to death so you and whoever else was with you might live.

Even without the triggering Holocaust associations, something felt off. I looked around and everyone was continuing to live their lives—my husband went to work, he took his older kids out for weekend adventures—and I was stuck at home, absolutely exhausted, with a baby who wouldn't sleep and wouldn't stop crying. Other moms looked so natural, casually walking around the neighbourhood with their sleeping babies in their designer strollers and attachment-parenting chest-carriers. I was afraid to take my son anywhere, afraid he would wail and I would be judged. It felt like too much effort to dress him up in the cute outfits people sent, or to even get dressed myself. I lived in alternating pairs of yoga pants and extra-large T-shirts as I shuffled from the bed to the couch to the exercise ball where I would bounce my unhappy baby. Like my baby, I cried a lot. I could not get it together to prepare dinner or clean the house. Or to care about anything. What did the global economic collapse or the election of Barack Obama matter when I did not possess the ability to comfort my baby?

Would my body ever feel normal again? Would I?

I saw a counsellor at BC Women's Hospital, mostly on my own—well, the baby was always with me. The counsellor I was assigned asked me questions and observed me. These visits became a lifeline. We sat in her office and I tried to explain the inexplicable—how I had been given what I knew was the greatest gift but had completely lost myself. I didn't feel like me anymore. This woman listened. She was warm, kind. Almost motherly. Unlike at home, in this space I didn't feel like I was whining or weird. The other mothers in the waiting room must have been suffering too, I told myself. My counsellor offered under-standing, compassion, knowledge—and reassurance. She noted that I was bonding with my baby; that was good. But she also pointed out the obvious: I met many of the criteria for postpartum depression.

I was like a walking checklist for the disorder: the hopelessness, the severe anxiety, the inability to sleep, to concentrate, to make decisions, to care about the things that I, just a few weeks earlier, had cared deeply about. The shame and guilt. I was so tired I fantasized about getting hit by a car so that I could get some rest in a hospital bed. (My baby was always safely at home with his dad in these fantasies.)

The counsellor strongly recommended that I speak to my doctor about anti-depressants. For some reason I don't think I can explain, I refused. Even though the research said it was safe for breastfeeding mothers, I felt like I should be able to push through whatever was happening. Maybe my refusal was another symptom; I was too exhausted— and too depressed—to think straight. But that was my final decision.

So instead, we went with: get outside with my baby every day, no matter what. Get one stretch of at least four hours of sleep each night. Talk to friends and family on a regular basis. And get help with breast-feeding, which was also giving me a lot of trouble.

I made an appointment with lactation consultants at the hospital. They watched me feed my baby and listened to him cry and cry. They weighed him before and after; they told me that he was getting the milk, so that was not the issue. Something else was going on. They said I needed to take him back to the pediatrician as soon as possible. We made the appointment; I would go straight there from the hospital. Before I took off, my baby still wailing, I asked if they wouldn't mind if I left him with them for a minute so I could use the bathroom. "Don't worry," I said, "I'm coming back for him." We all laughed. Well, not the baby.

When I returned from the bathroom to collect my poor suffering preemie, one of the women looked at me and said, "I think you're amazing."

I have never forgotten that. I think about that woman all the time, what she said to me. And I try to remember, when I see a woman in distress, someone who is doing her best in spite of terrible circum-stances, to tell her: *I think you're amazing.*

The doctor diagnosed my baby with acid reflux. That was why he was crying so much. We got him on medication and I took meds to get my milk flowing better. (Funny how I took those without a second thought, but refused the anti-depressants.) I continued seeing the counsellor.

And soon, my sisters Doris and Rachel came out to visit. Then, a few weeks later, my two best friends, Marsha and Lezlee, visited as well. They helped me face my fears: I took Jacob to a restaurant. Nobody died—of embarrassment or otherwise. The day after my friends left, I attended my first Salsa Babies class. Once a week, I danced with little Jacob in my BabyBjörn. I eventually made friends with a few of the other exhausted mothers. I was doing a little better.

I started to re-engage with the world: reading the news—which, as a journalist, had been my life, after all—and returning to some of my interests. Among them, the Holocaust.

I mean, what better topic for someone still teetering on the edge of postpartum depression to dive into?

I remember exactly where I was when I encountered the story that helped me recognize the danger of the topic. I was sitting at the family computer, holding my napping baby (that was the period where he wouldn't nap unless he was held; I was still so tired) when I came across the unshakeable detail. Weirdly, I can't remember if I read the story online or heard it on the radio, coming through the kitchen speakers. But I remember the content as if I heard it yesterday. It was a story about Jewish babies in Ukraine during the Holocaust.

The soldiers were having a laugh, throwing the babies up into the air and seeing if they could spear them with their bayonets. For sport—and to get the job done. Two birds, one stone. How many babies?

It wasn't the first time I had heard of something like this.

In *Night*, Elie Wiesel had written about a similar demonic activity, recalled by a Jewish man who had been deported but escaped back to his small town. He reported to the community that he had witnessed Jewish babies being thrown in the air, used as targets for machine gunners.

When Wiesel himself, a teenager, arrived at Birkenau, he was greeted—to use my mother's word—with a horrific site: a truck pulling up and dumping into a flaming pit small children, babies.

Another horrific detail I had read about in another book: the Germans carried infants out of a synagogue in Piotrkow Trybunalski, smashed their heads, and hurled their bodies into basin heaters over bonfires.

Babies thrown in the air as targets. Babies thrown into a pit of flames to be burned. Babies' heads bashed in. How many more examples were there of this unthinkable barbarism, where there were no survivors to bear witness later on, and no perpetrators who would dare speak of it? Also—what kind of person can do such a thing? And how do you find groups of people not just willing to do this, but to make a game of it? With babies?

No, it wasn't the first time I had heard of something like this, the bayonet story. But it was the first time I had heard it as a mother.

I looked at my sleeping baby and I was overwhelmed. This is what this baby would have been in for, had he been born at another time, not that long ago. I pictured a spear through his heaving little chest, through his gorgeous baby soft skin.

I remember exactly how I felt: I was done with this. No more Holocaust. It was something I had vowed to do in the past—free myself of this unhealthy preoccupation. And I had been drawn back in more times than I could count. But my ongoing project to stop obsessing about the Holocaust had a new weapon: my baby.

I had a real-life boy in front of me, who needed me. Who needed a healthy, happy me. And the ghosts were taking me from him, even if neither of us really noticed it. They were haunting me and I needed to be free. This time I meant it, and I stuck with it: it was time to live in the present. I closed the book on my Holocaust obsession. I was done with it.

It was not done with me.

PART TWO

Trauma

SEVEN

Inheritance

THERE IS A MORNING each spring when the recurring miracle of the natural world makes its presence known to even you, smartphone-addicted multi-tasking working mother rushing crazily through life (and yes, I mean me). That first morning you head into work and manage to notice the scent of the air as you stroll the brief but precious distance from your home to the train station, floating on honeysuckle and budding lilacs.

I remember some of what I was wearing that morning: a stretchy skirt, black, embroidered with green-blue trees. Black tights that showed off the only body part of mine I am a little bit proud of, my calves. And on top, some sort of flowy sweater thing that attempted to mask the body parts of mine I am less proud of.

And at the other end of that train ride, as I marched to my dream job as an arts reporter at Canada's national newspaper, still married and happy, looking forward to sipping my overpriced, overrated, over-milked (non-fat!) latte, a shredding truck made its way into my peripheral view. The kind of mobile unit that goes around destroying confidential, possibly even compromising, documents for businesses and the like. The truck was parked outside the office building where I work.

Back home, Jacob, now a toddler, would have been playing with his babysitter and the other little boy in our nanny-share arrangement. Maybe they were taking advantage of the beautiful morning and had made their way to the playground across the street. Or maybe they were still home, reading books or building Lego. Or playing paper shredder. Jacob, at three, was obsessed with this particular piece of office equipment—an item we did not own—and sometimes as we hand-zoomed his collection of trucks around the living room floor, we would pretend one of them was a mobile paper shredder.

So what might a natural response be to seeing this office-document shredding truck parked outside one's place of business at a time when one's young child holds a deep interest in such an activity?

Perhaps—*Oh, I wish Jacob were here; how delighted he would be! I miss him.* Or, a more neurotic reaction (my specialty) might be something like: *Paper shredding? Is something going on at work that I should be aware of? Are we in trouble? Are we all getting fired today?* Yes, that escalated quickly. I'm good at that.

My response did indeed escalate, but to entirely different highs—or lows. Much like that New Zealand sky that would years later propel me to Auschwitz, I saw that mobile paper shredder and I thought: *Einsatzgruppen.*

Einsatzgruppen was a term I first came across as a high school student embarking on some sort of self-directed Holocaust-related research project. I know it was self-directed because I wasn't taught a single thing about the Holocaust during my public-school education—not a sentence, not a word. Not in the many history classes I took, where it felt like I learned about the French colonist explorers Samuel de Champlain and Jacques Cartier year after year, not in social studies or geography, or anywhere else.

Not until my first year of university, when I was studying to become a broadcaster, did a media and sociology professor—who opened my eyes to so many other injustices of the world—become the first person employed to teach me who said anything about the Holocaust. (Well, not counting Hebrew school.)

Einsatzgruppen, as I learned from the set of encyclopedias that held court across the built-in shelves in my childhood basement, were mobile killing units made up of Nazis—and people recruited from the local population—in occupied Europe and the Soviet Union in the early 1940s. These roving murderers were primarily equipped with guns initially, but some graduated to gas vans. Innocent people would be forced into the backs of the trucks and slowly killed with exhaust gases—precursors to Auschwitz, on wheels.

Reading this encyclopedia entry as a teenager, I came across the names of places where these portable gas chambers had been active. The first use of them had been in Chelmno. Victims, I read, were deported there from, among other places, the Lodz Ghetto. Whoa, Lodz! That, I knew, was the city where my father was born and raised. Had someone in his family been gassed to death in one of these, I wondered, shivering in our walnut veneer-paneled rec room? (The answer, as it turns out, is no—at least nobody in my father's immediate family.)

There were some problems with these special vans, as I learned years later, watching Claude Lanzmann's epic documentary *Shoah*. A Nazi memo about repairs required for the vans indicated that "the merchandise aboard displays during the operation a natural tendency to rush to the rear doors and are mainly found lying there at the end of the operation so the front axle is not overloaded."

The memo also called for enclosures around the lamps inside these vans, to better protect them and allow them to be used at certain parts of the operation. It noted that as soon as darkness sets in, "the load naturally rushes toward the light . . . which makes closing the doors difficult. Also because of the alarming nature of darkness, screaming always occurs when the doors are closed." The memo also called for a sealed drain in the middle of the floor "for easy cleaning of the vehicle."

The merchandise. The load.

Another detail that has stuck with me from my reading about these rolling murder machines was that apparently the men who operated the mobile extermination units had suffered negative mental effects from doing all of that killing, essentially by hand, in such close proximity to their victims. All that screaming, all that scrambling toward the light.

And so not merely in the pursuit of efficiency but also workplace wellness, the Nazis fashioned something more suitable: the well-constructed, built-to-last gas chamber.

Years later, listening to Philippe Sands's podcast *The Ratline*, I would learn the name of an inventor of the mobile gas chamber—Walter Rauff—and that Rauff received refuge after the war in Italy, living in a Catholic monastery, under the protection of an Austrian-born Catholic bishop who made no secret of his love for Hitler. In Rome, that bishop helped establish the ratlines, clandestine escape routes for Nazis such as Josef Mengele, the Angel of Death at Auschwitz.

So back to downtown Vancouver and my springtime strut into work. I see the mobile paper-shredding unit parked outside the building; I think *Einsatzgruppen*. Then I think about my dad and how sad I am that I didn't get to know him better. And then I think: *It's messed up that this is your first thought when you see an office-document shredding truck.* And then I start thinking about deadlines and research and the story I need to write that day for the newspaper. And then I arrive at the bureau, say my good mornings, hit the power button on my computer and get to it.

...

I knew, always, that there was something, if not exactly wrong with me, then something that was not quite right. I felt as though I was less happy than the other children I knew. Or, I was, as my mother and father so delicately put it, "a miserable kid." This was a frequent parental muttering, a repeated accusation—to the point where the word "miserable" is still triggering for me. Even if, upon reflection, they were right. I was pretty miserable. I worried a fair bit, and then when I got to adolescence, things got even darker inside my brain. Life just seemed a little harder for me than it did for my friends.

And it seemed as though my parents could not tolerate any sadness of mine, certainly not anything even approaching miserable.

Perhaps when your family tree has more dead branches than living ones—branches that you do not even know how to identify because the names are lost along with the people, turned to ash—when your own roots sprout from this terrible thing that happened before you were born, which felled this once great tree, that must affect how you grow, what you grow into.

My parents wore their sorrow on their sleeve—my mother quite literally on her arm. Even if what had happened to them wasn't explicitly talked about on a daily basis, it was always present. I was raised on a diet of quiet sorrow. There was a sort of osmosis taking place in my house; the grief of genocide hung silently in the rooms. Sometimes not completely silent, but transmitted in bits and pieces of conversation, or deafening absences.

When parents tell children stories about their lives, it can be a point of connection, a bonding experience. *This is the lullaby my father sang to me. This is the way my mother used to cut my sandwiches. This is one of the books we read in kindergarten.* But the stories I was hearing from my parents concerned death, starvation, hiding, escape—surviving in spite of it all. Even if they left out a bunch of details, the subtext was always there: their lives had been terrible. And the stories about their lives— even the exciting ones, like the haystack—were set among horror. If that's what we were bonding over, what else was going to stick?

This was long before we heard the word "parent" used as a verb, before endless child-rearing guides lined bookstore shelves. I don't think my parents gave it much—probably not any—thought, the impact these stories might be having on my development.

Still, intentional or not, when stories about death and hiding are the soundtrack to your childhood, what does that do to the movie of your life?

My parents just wanted me to be happy. I know this because I heard this sentence on repeat: "We just want you to be happy." It sounds like an innocuous, fairly baseline desire. What parent doesn't want their child to be happy, even in a normal family? But there was so much weight to that wish. My happiness would be a path out of the devastation that had befallen them: a way to erase—or at least alleviate—their supreme unhappiness.

This is not to criticize. My admiration for them could fill volumes. The fact that my parents did not succumb to despair remains a shock and a miracle to me. I would not have done as well, as became particularly clear to me when my own life started falling apart.

A hint that there might have been any connection between my youthful misery and what my parents had gone through were my nightmares. The Nazis were coming to get me, or my mother. I was hiding during World War II or I was hiding in my own bedroom closet; I was running through the forest, being chased by Nazis—or at least men in scary uniforms who were out to kill me.

Fully awake, I had revenge fantasies. I dreamed of kicking Nazi ass. Torturing them, slowly, in jail cells. Teenage me wanted to hurt them, humiliate them. Those subhuman pieces of shit.

It took me many years to understand that my life itself was the real revenge. The fact that I existed, that I walked the earth. I was a testament to the failure of the Nazi project.

The slogan "Never Again" was drilled into us, implying—to me, anyway—that there was always the potential for an again, for another catastrophe. What would we do when the Nazis came back and came for us, like they came for our parents?

This happened to *us*. This could happen to us again. I was one of the us. On some level I believed, from a very young age, that this could happen to me. I understood the need to be on guard, that we weren't really safe. We needed to be on alert. Have a plan.

When I visited Israel on an organized group trip in 1985, the summer I turned nineteen, one of the exercises on the curriculum was a debate about what we were first: were we Jews first, or Canadians? We split up into small groups to discuss the matter.

Canadian, was my answer. I'm Canadian first.

This was apparently not the answer they were looking for. Before the Nazis took control, they reminded us, many German-Jews thought of themselves as being German first. Jews in Austria too. And France. And Hungary. We know what happened to most of them.

The moral of the story seemed to be that the rest of the world—maybe even Canada—viewed us as Jews above all. We would always be something else first.

The point was to drill into us the importance of the State of Israel. Because if the Jewish nation had existed a couple of generations prior, European Jews would have had an escape, a country that would have accepted them. If the State of Israel no longer existed today, we would have nowhere to go should the need arise; if the world once again turned on—or turned its back on—the Jews.

True on both counts. But the exercise scared the hell out of me. Don't be so comfortable in that Canada you think of as home; you never know what could happen. I still resent that little tutorial. I am reminded of it too often, in these divided times.

This strategy of teaching-by-terror was employed on us beginning at a young, impressionable age. That Hebrew school documentary screening that I experienced was not unique.

A close friend of mine, Eileen, told me about a particularly harrowing Sunday at her Hebrew school. The teacher made an announcement to the class. In a rather casual way, she explained that the authorities—she did not explicitly use the word "Nazis"—had come to the school's office and were demanding certain information from each of them. Every student had to write down the name of every family member and list all of the Jewish items in their homes.

It was only after the lists had been shakily written out by these terrified eleven- and twelve-year-olds that the teacher revealed the truth: this was just a drill. A way for the students to get a sense of what it was like, back in Nazi Germany. This is what the Jews experienced, this is what your families experienced.

"And you immediately understand how it can happen," Eileen told me, more than forty years later, when I asked her about that exercise.

The point of the lesson, I take it, was to emphasize how quickly one can be rendered weak and cede power. If I just do what they tell me to do, write out those lists, everything will be okay.

I suppose these educators didn't quite understand the potential damage such an ordeal could perpetrate. But Eileen was shaken to the core.

I was reminded of this cruel classroom exercise years later when I read an essay by Eva Fogelman, a psychologist who established groups for descendants of Holocaust survivors way back in the 1970s and is still active in this area of study and treatment. The day after watching the graphic 1950s Holocaust documentary *Night and Fog* at her Jewish summer camp (fun!), the camp held its morning prayers in a different place than usual—much smaller, more cramped—as a simulation of a concentration camp prayer session. More than sixty kids crammed in, sharing one prayer book. A counsellor was assigned to be the guard. This counsellor guard—who must have been a teenager—took the role-play very seriously and lost control, hitting some of the camper-prisoners. At that point the exercise was halted.

It's hard to imagine what this activity was supposed to teach—or how it was deemed appropriate. But Fogelman's main takeaway surprised me a little: she was angry that the campers' Jewish identity might be forever defined by this state of victimhood.

Boy, did that ever hit home. The state of victimhood is where I live, where for some reason I feel most comfortable. And yet it has brought me so much grief. Reading this story decades after Eva Fogelman experienced it, I thought: *I need a new comfort zone.* And also: *what brought me here?*

...

Eva Fogelman and author Helen Epstein are two of the pioneers of what has come to be known as the "second generation"—often shortened in our world these days to "2G". Children of Holocaust survivors. People like me.

The 2G movement began to come together in the 1970s, when many children of survivors were young adults. Meeting in groups, they began to recognize similarities—things they had not discussed even with their siblings, and certainly not with their parents.

In 1975, a dialogue among children of Holocaust survivors published in the independent journal *Response: A Contemporary Jewish Review* caught Fogelman's attention. She and her colleague Bella Savran decided to hold therapy groups for children of survivors at Boston University. They put up little ads on campus, at the bookstore, at the kosher butcher shop. They held their first two groups in 1976.

Meanwhile, as a student at Hebrew University in Jerusalem during the late 1960s, Epstein had discovered what she has called this "peer group without a sign." These were international students like herself who had little family, spoke two languages and had been raised in two cultures.

As a part-time journalist for the *Jerusalem Post*, and later for the *National Jewish Monthly* in the U.S., Epstein began writing about these people, culminating in her June 1977 *New York Times Magazine* article titled "The Heirs of the Holocaust." The story caused a stir of recognition in the Jewish community.

Epstein explored the issue as a reporter, but also as the child of survivors herself: someone who, when she rode the New York subway at rush hour, would imagine the trains were going to Auschwitz, or when attending Carnegie Hall as a child with her mother, would picture men in black coats bursting in and shooting everyone to death.

"These were important childhood rituals," Epstein wrote in the article, "but it was not until now, not until I began interviewing other children of survivors, that I found the reciprocity I needed to talk about them out loud."

Epstein had been trying to interest the *Times* in a story about this topic for a while, and finally the paper found what we in the business call a news peg—a current event that deals with the issue. In this case, it was a lecture by a researcher at Stanford University Medical School about the trauma of the Nazi concentration camps being re-experienced by children and grandchildren of camp survivors. "The effects of systematic dehumanization are being transmitted from one generation to the next through severe disturbances in the parent–child relationship," said the press release describing the findings of the Israeli researcher, who was on sabbatical at Stanford. Epstein was commissioned by the *New York Times* to write what would become a seminal article.

Eva Fogelman's father, a survivor, had been ambivalent about the therapeutic work his daughter was doing with this population; he would say to her that nobody cared about the Holocaust. But after Epstein's article ran as the magazine's cover story, complete with quotes from his daughter, he came around. "Well I guess America is finally interested in the Holocaust," he told her.

...

Helen Epstein ended her piece with a prediction: "I suspect this article is only the beginning of a long conversation."

It was.

The interest generated by Epstein's report was enormous. For a full year, she received letters from children of survivors—often very detailed confessions. "Some wrote that they had read and reread what I had written for several days in succession, unable to fathom how thoughts that they had believed to be so personal, so secret, so particular to themselves could be shared by others," she later wrote.

Epstein knew she was not done with this topic. She took on a bigger project, a book. *Children of the Holocaust: Conversations with Sons and Daughters of Survivors* was published in 1979.

"There had to be other people like me, who shared what I carried," Epstein wrote in the opening chapter. "There had to be, I thought, an invisible, silent family scattered around the world."

Children of the Holocaust resonated throughout the 2G world. In this
book, when I eventually read it, I found anecdotal stories similar, in
some ways, to mine: fathers who shovelled food down their throats
at mealtimes, not wishing to chit-chat at the table. Children of survivors who dreamed of mutilating Nazis. Children whose survivor parents demonstrated reluctance to feel completely safe and secure in
their new homes in North America. Don't get too comfortable; you
never know when things might turn.

Since Epstein's groundbreaking reporting, countless 2G groups
have been established; there are 3G groups now too—grandchildren of
survivors. In these groups, we can share our experiences and thoughts
and, weird as they are, learn that they're not uncommon with our next-
generation peers. But when *Children of the Holocaust* was published,
this felt like a radical discovery.

Eva Fogelman, the psychologist, was another groundbreaker. Out of
those initial meetings of what they called awareness groups, Fogelman
and Savran envisioned a large gathering of these young adults, to give
them an opportunity for a collective mourning experience. Together
they could memorialize family members who were murdered in the
Holocaust that they had never known, "but were the ghosts with whom
they lived," Fogelman explained to me.

The first conference was held in 1979 in New York, which galva-
nized 600 children of survivors across the U.S. Many participants
went back to their local communities and started organizations and
awareness groups.

In Israel in 1981 at the World Gathering of Jewish Holocaust Survivors, the second generation formalized the idea.

A few years later, in 1984, Elie Wiesel was one of the speakers at
what was called the First International Conference of Children of
Holocaust Survivors. That's when he made the remarks about the irrepressible anger survivors should be, must be, harbouring.

"It was you that the enemy sought to destroy," Wiesel also told
the children of survivors, the people like me, in that speech. "We"—the

survivors themselves—"were only the instruments. You were the ene-my's obsession. In murdering living Jews, he wished to prevent you from being born."

...

We, the enemy's obsession, have become an area of great interest for academics. Beginning in the 1960s, there have been hundreds of stud-ies conducted into the impacts of intergenerational trauma on chil-dren of survivors. There may be, as it turns out, some science behind my *mishugas*.

Not that it's straightforward. The findings, one prominent researcher, Natan Kellermann, wrote in a 2019 article summing up decades of research, have resulted in "extensive and sometimes confusing find-ings on the intergenerational transmission of Holocaust trauma in survivor families."

Like Kellermann—an Israeli clinical psychologist who is one of the leading researchers in this field—many of the people doing this work are members of the second (and now third) generation, as one of the researchers, Vancouver psychiatrist Robert Krell—who has his own Holocaust history—pointed out to me.

"It is a study of ourselves, so to speak. When you think about it, who the hell else would tackle it? Seriously. What person who enters psychology and does a PhD thesis actually wants to pick Holocaust survivors as their topic? Unlikely. And so this is a large literature gen-erated by seekers of answers," Krell told me.

As I began a study of my own self, the more I have read—in Epstein, Krell, Kellermann and far beyond, in the many books and articles I have consumed on the subject—the more I have recognized myself in the other children of survivors.

Our conditions, our preoccupations, our issues—our quirks, if you will. Anxiety. Stress. Depression. Hypersensitivity. Suspicion of others, of the world at large.

Overprotective parents. Revenge fantasies. The nightmares.

And the impossible ever-present question: Our parents survived, but would we have been able to if it was us in their shoes?

...

Some of the earliest research in this field was conducted in Canada, by psychiatrist Vivian Rakoff, who published an article about the issue in 1966 after he and his colleagues at the Jewish General Hospital in Montreal noticed high rates of psychological distress in children of survivors. "Too many" adolescent children of survivors were coming in for help.

"The parents, the actual victims in these cases, are not conspicuously broken people," Rakoff wrote. So what happened to their children?

This first article looked at three cases, children of survivors who had sought help.

One girl had fainting spells and suffered what appeared to be psychosomatic paralysis, and also suffered from a debilitating case of imposter syndrome. The smartest girl in her class, she approached an exam certain this was going to be the time she was found out.

There was something common in the family dynamic that was preventing the children from developing a sense of identity, Rakoff found. The children, all born after the Holocaust, displayed severe psychiatric symptoms. "It would almost be easier to believe that they, rather than their parents, had suffered the corrupting, searing hell," he wrote. (His work can be found in the University of Toronto Archives.)

Rakoff ended the article with a haunting line. "With the accumulation of knowledge and the growth of the concentration camp experience through the damaged generations one may fairly ask if indeed there were any survivors."

Another 1966 article co-written by Rakoff noted that the consequences of the survivor parents' preoccupation with their traumatic experiences left them with few emotional resources for coping with their children—whose "requests for attention and care are either ignored or dealt with as unfair demands."

He found a lack of true emotional engagement, homes where the rules were either too rigid or chaotically ineffectual—"but rarely related to the needs of the child."

The children themselves displayed apathy, depression and emptiness; they were receptacles for identities they did not understand. "In effect they are deprived children because the parents are so involved with their own depressive pre-occupations that there is little left to give to others."

These articles were written based on people coming into the clinic—so families that were troubled enough to seek help. Still, I recognized a much more severe version of my own family dynamic in some of these descriptions.

"The natural involvement with life's ongoing activities—a hallmark of youth—is present in these children in only minimal quantities. Their parents were just not able to respond to the natural curiosity of a growing child, to tease it out, to make its expression a rewarding experience—and so it was often destroyed."

In 1973, Rakoff contributed to a more comprehensive article that came out of these clinical observations; what was described as the first systematic study of children of survivors. The authors found that children of survivors experienced greater feelings of alienation, exhibited more dependence on their parents, and had more difficulty coping.

This study suggested that the children of survivors reported "an anxiety stirred in them by their perception of their parents' unconscious rage . . . that forces the children to cling for reassurance." That sounded an awful lot like me—with my parents (I thought of how I had literally clung to my mother at that summer camp Mothers and Babes), in my relationships, and especially in my marriage. As it was falling apart, I was holding on for dear life.

I didn't realize until many years later that Vivian Rakoff's daughter Ruth was one of my group leaders on that Israel trip—although I should say I don't think she was in any way responsible for the curriculum or that specific exercise. He was also the father of one of my favourite writers, David Rakoff, who died in 2012. Vivian Rakoff himself died in 2020. I met him briefly in 2005, at a literary event in Toronto. Dr. Rakoff sought me out after I interviewed his son David onstage—along with Jonathan Safran Foer—to deliver a compliment about how I had conducted the event. I remember thinking: *He didn't have to do this, he didn't have to find me.* It stayed with me, this kindness. I now wonder: Could he tell by my questions, by my demeanour onstage with those two famous authors, that there was something off about me? Did I remind him of his damaged 2G patients?

...

In the years since the early research, studies have found that survivors' relationships to their children could be detached; that survivors were suspicious of the world around them and imposed their beliefs that the world was a dangerous place; that children of survivors suffered from guilt, anxiety, depression and low self-esteem. Depression was a primary response to stress of any kind. Children of survivors are conflict-averse and want to change frightening situations into pleasant ones. "Denial is prominent where aggression-provoking situations are represented, especially when they are confronted with separation and death," researcher Hillel Klein found in a study published in *Survival and Trials of Revival: Psychodynamic Studies of Holocaust Survivors and Their Families in Israel and the Diaspora.*

All of this was excruciatingly relatable. The suspicion that my parents displayed. My low self-esteem. The guilt, the depression. The denial in the face of terrible events—like a husband going emotionally AWOL. The desperate need to turn a frightening situation into a pleasant one.

In their 1982 book *Generations of the Holocaust*, Martin Bergmann and Milton Jucovy concluded: "It is not possible for a child to grow up, without becoming scarred, in a world where the Holocaust is the dominant psychic reality."

...

In Vancouver, Robert Krell was also working with survivors and their children. Krell, now professor emeritus of psychiatry at the University of British Columbia, comes at this from an interesting place: he is both a child survivor of the Holocaust—taken in by a non-Jewish Dutch family during the war—and the child of survivors, as both of his parents, separately from him, miraculously survived. This has given him a particular kind of insight.

In the mid-1970s, local Holocaust survivors started bringing their children to his clinical practice. "They had all the usual problems," Krell explained to me. "Childhood depression, ADHD, learning disabilities. And they all carried one other problem: the Holocaust. They were surrounded by Holocaust memory, Holocaust imagery."

He heard two things again and again: that the parent-survivors talked too much about the Holocaust—or, conversely, did not talk about it at all. These children intimated that they did not know what was going on in the shadows of their own homes, he told me in an interview.

Krell started writing about this issue, in spite of the ambivalence of some of his peers, who questioned the importance of this area of study.

"It appears that the effects of the Holocaust experience are transmitted by survivor-parents to the children," Krell wrote in a 1979 article. He warned that children of survivors seeking help for any psychological problem—related to the genocide or not—required a professional with an "acute awareness of the unique problems of these families."

Often, he told me later, the parents or children did not make the connection themselves.

Krell cited work that suggested the transmission of the concentration camp experience was inevitable, and identified two reasons for transmission: survivors being ever vigilant, ever on-guard; the survivor parents mourning, with rarely a day going by when they did not experience a nightmare or terrible memory. And yet here were their children, tangible evidence of their survival and therefore incredibly precious. "It is into this ambivalence and despair and anger that children were born," he wrote.

Among the examples he used in this article were some I very much recognized: constant, often daily references to the Holocaust on the part of the parents (check), partial stories and oblique references (check), children told to appreciate something they don't like because the parent had been deprived of that item for years (liver and onions, check).

"Veiled references are made by survivor parents to the odds against them surviving the death camps and having children," he wrote. "Sooner or later the child experiences his or her existence in the same fateful manner, for by all odds, neither the parent nor the child were to exist. That recognition gives the child the feeling of a survivor."

Oh my God, I thought, reading this more than forty years after he wrote it. *I experience the world like a survivor.* No wonder I'm always waiting for things to fall apart, certain that they will. And when they do, no wonder I am so deeply affected. As if divorce, for instance, were some kind of death camp.

...

In 1983 Krell identified the obvious: that the survivor parents were not equipped for parenting the way others were. Not only had they been robbed of their adolescence and education ("their classroom was the concentration camp") but they had been deprived of crucial parenting experiences during their formative years as adolescents and young adults.

My mother couldn't cook a chicken. How would she know how to raise a child? (I should state for the record that she did eventually become very skilled in the kitchen and learned to make a mean roast chicken. I, on the other hand, am still working on this.)

"For the second generation," Krell wrote, "the Holocaust remains an intimate event lived with its eyewitnesses."

It is accepted that the trauma experienced by the survivors was so great that inevitably the second generation "picked up the vibes," as Krell told me during one of our conversations. "And a preoccupation with what had happened to their parents and the mystery of it. Did my mother prostitute herself? Who did my father kill to live? Mysteries. And which of those people actually did those things is not the issue."

I was shocked when he said this to me. Shocked because I had never once even asked myself these difficult questions about my parents. Had my mother had to submit to rape to survive? Had my father actually killed anyone? I don't think so, on either count, truly—but the fact that I did not even ask myself what, given the context, were in fact quite reasonable questions, was about more than naivete, I think. The explanation for this was not so much about a noble story that I told myself, the myth of my heroic survivor parents. I think this was my protection for them, taken to another level. They did not deserve to be submitted to such a line of inquiry, even silently, in my brain.

...

Not every study has concluded that children of survivors are more messed up than their peers.

I spoke with another Canadian researcher, Morton Weinfeld, who conducted years of research on this issue, working with John J. Sigal, and published the findings in their 1989 book *Trauma and Rebirth: Intergenerational Effects of the Holocaust.*

"The negative psychological consequences of prolonged victim-ization, be it for ethnic, racial, economic, or other reasons, need not be transmitted to a large proportion of the members of subsequent generations," they wrote. "Indeed psychological impairments may be compartmentalized, coexisting with normal activity and even possi-ble benefits."

Their study, also based in Montreal, found no difference or a neg-ligible one in psychological outcomes between the children of survivors and other Canadian Jews of European descent.

"It could be that all Jews are comparably neurotic," Weinfeld, a McGill sociologist, told me in an interview, while I was trying to wrap my head around their findings and how they fit in with the giant pile of other studies on this topic.

He pointed to the conclusion of his book: the effects of the Holocaust were not homogeneous for the survivors, or their descendants.

Helen Epstein, the journalist who began looking into the scientific literature on this topic in the 1970s, also became uncomfortable with the homogeneous treatment of the issue, referred to sometimes as "survivor syndrome." The term has been applied not just to Holocaust survivors but to other survivors of mass horrors: the nuclear attacks in Japan, the wars in Korea and Vietnam, the Armenian genocide.

The term "survivor syndrome," Epstein wrote, "seemed to imply that a defective human mutant had been created, intrinsically different from you and me. Children of survivors knew that the truth was far more complex."

EIGHT

Trauma Baby

I WASN'T READING STUDIES about Holocaust descendants in the 1970s, and certainly not in 1966, when Vivian Rakoff started publishing his work on children of survivors—that was the year I was born. I wasn't even reading them in the 1980s, when I was graduating high school, starting university and becoming obsessed with U2 and all things Irish. Or in the nineties, when I began my journalism career.

I started looking into this area of research as my life was falling apart in 2015. Something had changed at home. My husband was not really present, seemed very unhappy. He wouldn't say what was going on. Was it me?

It was.

I learned when I was five years old in that conversation with my mother in our kitchen that asking questions about very hard things can lead to answers you do not want to hear. Those German showers. And now my marriage—gassed.

It was a shock. I had thought we were solid. I thought things were good. I thought this was for good. Forever. I had allowed myself, in spite of my nature, to feel secure.

A mistake.

When I was fighting to save my marriage and then dealing with its dissolution, I felt like I was living a double life. At work, I was prolific, breaking stories and earning respect from readers and the arts community. (I was also making enemies, but that comes with the territory.)

At home, I felt like I was drowning in insecurity.

At the same time that my husband's distance had become irrefutable, I landed what was for me the interview of a lifetime: U2, the band whose music had been central to my life since I was fifteen.

"Central to my life" sounds like a bit much, I know, but it's a valid description. My interest in this band provoked in me a deep and abiding interest in Irish politics, history, literature and art. In my early twenties, I got myself an Irish work visa, a place in Dublin and a job at a little organization there that collected royalties for record companies (and, ultimately, for U2, I gleefully told my starstruck self). It was one of those foundational experiences that helped shape everything that came afterward. I could easily trace a through-line from my adoration of this band to my career as an arts journalist.

I also believe that my interest in the persecution of the Irish on their own land helped me understand the persecution of the Jews—without the tricky personal aspect. It started with "Sunday Bloody Sunday," a catchy tune about a tragedy. It led to a life-long investigation that was fundamental to my understanding of my own history.

So this interview was a very big deal.

In a circular booth at the back of a lively Vancouver restaurant, I sat sandwiched between Larry Mullen Jr. and Bono, the man for whom I had harboured a schoolgirl crush for more than thirty years. On the eve of Bono's fiftieth birthday, we talked about everything—his children, his wife, the band's history, the state of the world. He urged me to partake in the appetizers that arrived at the table. He said "Cheers" and clinked my wine glass. When the publicist said it was time for the interview to end, Bono said no, let's keep talking.

It should have been the best night of my life.

But when I came home on that Saturday night, floating on air, my not-yet-physically-absent husband was absent. He did not come downstairs, sit with me at the kitchen table and relive every single moment, listen to the tape of the interview, revel in my insightful questions, tell me it wasn't so bad when Adam Clayton bristled at my use of the term "nostalgia" in discussing the Innocence + Experience Tour, which the band was about to launch in Vancouver. Maybe pop a bottle of champagne at the fulfillment of my lifelong dream. Perhaps figure out how to help me turn Bono's "Cheers" into my ringtone. No, my husband stayed upstairs, asleep. Well, maybe he was asleep.

A year later, I was living a different kind of double life: actual separation, which I told almost nobody about. Early on, before I understood that this new marital situation would be my future, my sister Rachel was getting answers about our past. She had hired a Polish researcher, a man named Jacek, and was trying to find out whatever she could about the Ledermans of Lodz. I couldn't bring myself to pay very close attention. I was reeling from my own little mysterious tragedy, and exhausted with the work of keeping it a secret—from everyone, including the kids. It was hard to care about anything else.

On a Monday in April, I received an email forwarded by Rachel with the subject line "Your Grandfather." I was walking a few blocks to meet a new friend for a drink, where I would go to great lengths to not reveal anything about what was actually happening with my life, and while waiting at a red light I quickly glanced at the attachment. It was a photo I had never seen of my father. But it didn't really look like him.

And then I realized: my God, this was *his* father, *my* grandfather. It was the first time I had ever seen a photo of Moshe Aron. He was handsome, well dressed—it was an official identification photo, probably for the Nazis—and he looked at the camera with tired eyes but a slight, steely smile under that moustache, as if to say: *You cannot take away who I really am.*

The other thing that struck me? His ears. They stuck out quite prominently—just like Jacob's had when he was born. My baby got my grandfather's ears. What else had he inherited from him? What skills? What interests?

What trauma?

The next day, in the afternoon, I visited my former partner Pat, he of the election night bagels, in palliative care, and showed him the photo. Pat was bone thin and very, very tired—but he understood what a big deal this was. We had spent years together; he knew my shtick. That evening, I was called back to the hospital. Pat was not doing well. He died that night, surrounded by people who loved him—including his son, his former wife and me. My first in-person death. It was not a good spring, 2016.

…

As it turns out, the year my life began unravelling was a very busy time in the study of the intergenerational transmission of trauma. The field was moving into new territory: research looking into the possibility that the transmission of the trauma was about more than parenting style; it was about biology.

The work of one researcher in particular attracted a great deal of attention. Rachel Yehuda, professor of psychiatry and neuroscience and director of the Trauma Stress Studies Division at the Mount Sinai School of Medicine in New York, had found that the transmission of Holocaust trauma from survivor to child could happen at the cellular level due to something called epigenetics.

Her 2015 study made waves—and headlines. "Study of Holocaust survivors finds trauma passed on to children's genes," *The Guardian* announced. "Descendants of Holocaust Survivors Have Altered Stress Hormones," read the headline in *Scientific American*, followed by: "Parents' traumatic experience may hamper their offspring's ability to bounce back from trauma."

Having a very hard time bouncing back from personal trauma myself, I was skeptical, but also fascinated by the possibility of a connection.

It was intriguing to think that maybe my inability to handle my marital crisis wasn't all my fault. That maybe it was in my genes.

I didn't understand everything I was reading, but the gist of it seemed clear.

The research seemed to suggest that trauma experienced by earlier generations not only had an impact on their own epigenetic mechanisms but could also influence the genetic operations of their descendants, making those descendants more likely to switch on negative responses to stress and trauma, making them—making me—more vulnerable to stress.

I set out to read everything I could find about this. Searching for more information about Rachel Yehuda and her work, I came across an interview she did with Krista Tippett on the radio program and podcast *On Being*, where Yehuda explained the basics of epigenetic transfer in language even I could understand.

"People say, when something cataclysmic happens to them, 'I'm not the same person. I've been changed. I am not the same person that I was.' And we have to start asking ourselves, well, what do they mean by that?" Yehuda said to Tippett in the 2015 interview, which I listened to sometime later during one of my sad, post-separation walks around the neighbourhood, trying to escape the gloom that had settled inside my little house.

For someone—me—who felt like I was not the same person after my own cataclysm, this was a wow.

She talked about environmental influences that are so overwhelming, they force a major constitutional change, an enduring transformation.

Children of survivors, Yehuda found, were three times more likely to develop post-traumatic stress disorder (PTSD) than Jews of a similar demographic whose parents were not Holocaust survivors, if they were exposed to a traumatic event—especially a traumatic experience that involved some kind of an interpersonal component.

Reading this was deeply unsettling and deeply comforting all at once. I was in such a dark place, and it was unsettling to think that if there was science behind it, maybe I wouldn't be able to cheer myself up out of it. But it was also comforting to think that my inability to accept what had happened and bounce back maybe wasn't totally my fault.

In this radio interview, Yehuda talked about setting up a clinic in New York for Holocaust survivors, who back when they had arrived in the U.S. had not been graced with much in the way of psychological help. But the survivors weren't coming. Their children were.

The children of the survivors were coming in with problems, and Yehuda noted commonalities. For instance, she said: "They had difficulty in any kind of a separation circumstance—divorce; those kinds of things."

Divorce. Had she really said that? My stomach did flips. I re-read that part of the interview again. I re-read the whole transcript again.

Difficulty dealing with divorce. PTSD after a traumatic interpersonal event.

This was personal. This was me.

...

Bear with me while I try to write about something scientific. It has taken me a while to wrap my head around this, and people much smarter than me have helped.

Epigenetics, a developing field, is the study of the molecules and processes that control expression of the genes carried on our DNA. To take a step back, the human genome is the complete assembly of DNA. The epigenome is made up of chemical compounds and proteins that can attach to DNA and direct actions to the genes—telling them what to do. They can activate or silence genes. So epigenetics controls the program that turns genes on or off.

Epigenetics is critical to growth and development and can alter genetic operations inside our cells as we go through life. Consider the fact that most of our cells have the same DNA, but most of our cells do not behave the same way. Some become skin cells, others muscle or nerve cells thanks to epigenetic tags that control which genes are activated and which ones are silenced in each tissue. Different tissues have a different repertoire of genes that are expressed, giving each tissue its uniqueness. So the breast and lung would have a very different set of genes expressed, although both carry exactly the same genome or complete set of DNA.

When epigenomic compounds attach to DNA and modify its function, they have "marked" the genome. These marks do not change the sequence of the DNA, but they change the way the cells use the DNA's instructions.

Epigenetic alterations can be triggered by our environment and experiences. Extreme stress, for instance, can affect how some genes behave—while not changing the gene (or the DNA) itself. This is an amazing feat of nature; it allows us to adapt to our environment. But it can also be damaging.

By way of explanation, I have come across a computer analogy a few times: if a cell's DNA is the hardware, the epigenome is the operating system, controlling the cellular operations.

Another good analogy that has helped me comes from the National Institute of Environmental Health Sciences in the U.S.: Epigenetics focuses on the processes that help direct when individual genes are turned on or off. The cell's DNA provides the instruction manual, but genes need specific instructions. Epigenetic processes tell the cell to read certain pages of the instruction manual at distinct times.

Recent studies have looked at trauma and epigenetics. If trauma can leave a chemical mark on a person's genes, can that trauma be passed on epigenetically? Meaning, can parents pass on not only their genes to their babies, but how their genes are expressed?

Findings like Rachel Yehuda's raise the tantalizing and potentially world-changing possibility: that this change might indeed persist through the process of meiosis—cellular division and reproduction. *Reproduction*—meaning the change can extend to the next generation.

Yehuda found that epigenetic alterations in the way genes are expressed in the initially affected person were also present in the descendant. A biological scar—or memory or imprint, if you don't want to be negative about it—in both the parent who experienced the trauma and their child.

Wow, did this ever hit me: a trauma experienced in someone's lifetime can create epigenetic changes that also show up in that person's offspring.

Also, Yehuda and her team have found that descendants of Holocaust survivors have different stress hormone profiles than other Jewish adults of the same age. Their systems are more responsive.

This makes sense when you think about it: the body is preparing offspring for an environment that is similar to what the parents had endured: an environment without enough food, enough water, and far too much stress.

Yehuda found that cortisol—the stress hormone—can be more reactive in response to a social stressor. A divorce would be a definite social stressor.

These findings seem like a huge development with extraordinary implications, especially for trauma babies like me. Not only could this explain a few things, it was also a gift in terms of how I could think about my upbringing.

If the trauma experienced by Holocaust survivors had been passed on to their children at the cellular level—and not simply through problematic parenting—I could let my parents off the hook. Their disinterest, their less-than-happy baseline mood, the constant references to the war—behaviour I have wondered about in terms of its impact—might not be the only driver of my emotional foibles. It had been easy to blame my parents for my own unattractive tendencies: to be morose, pessimistic, terrified. Maybe "easy" is the wrong word—because this is actually a very hard thing to contemplate. But if the trauma was wired into me biologically, I could lay the blame elsewhere.

"This is the first demonstration of an association of preconception parental trauma with epigenetic alterations that is evident in both exposed parent and offspring," Yehuda's study concluded, "providing potential insight into how severe psychophysiological trauma can have intergenerational effects."

Yehuda's study led to that flurry of—perhaps oversimplified—reporting in the mainstream press at around the time that I was looking for answers to my own misery. I would be up half the night, going over theories about what was going wrong with my marriage. During the day, I moved through my eggshell-floored house in a daze. Different house, different century. But same me: morose, pessimistic, terrified.

The mental health playing field was not even and I was the one getting the raw deal. I worried about a separation being even harder to endure for me than for the average wronged wife. And then an even scarier thought: Did what had happened to my parents actually cause the breakdown of my marriage? Was I impossible to live with because of the hell my parents had been through?

And then, the scariest thought of all: Does this cellular baggage continue to the next generation? How hard was it going to be for Jacob to deal with adversity in his life? Because all signs pointed to serious adversity coming his way: his parents separating, him having no control over his life blowing up.

And the implications were much wider, beyond whatever marital issues I was having.

Was I doomed before I was born? Before I was even conceived?

Was Jacob?

...

There is a great deal of research being done into epigenetics—focused on not just the psychological piece but the implications for physical health as well. And there is a ton of interest in the issue of inherited trauma; this idea that our ancestors' trauma can show up in our bodies. Because it's not just about the Holocaust, of course. Too many of us humans can point to trauma in our ancestry; too many of us have been the targets of enslavement, vicious colonization, and genocide, in one form or another.

But there is no real consensus on the issue. Not yet.

In 2019, Natan Kellermann sent me that overview he wrote summarizing and analyzing what he called the currently available knowledge on Holocaust trauma transmission.

In the comprehensive article, Kellermann traced the shift in the field of study from a psychosocial to a neurobiological focus—from the Rakoffs and Krells to the likes of Yehuda, essentially (there are many others, of course)—making it clear that no definitive answers have been found to some central questions: Who is more likely to transmit, what is transmitted, who is more susceptible, where and when is it more likely to happen, and how does such a transmission transpire? Is it like a virus, he asked in the article, contagious from the survivor to the offspring? Or is it like other hereditary traits passed from parent to child?

Only a few offspring of survivors meet the criteria for mental disorders, he explained. Many more have occasional Holocaust associations from time to time. *The paper shredder*, I thought. *The starry New Zealand sky*.

"Some also struggle with stress-related problems and a lack of emotional resources when faced with adversity."

Ah, yes. When it appeared my marriage was in trouble, I did not soldier on, strong and confident. I crumbled. I felt unable to function. It was all sorrow all the time. I did not know how I was going to survive.

Even when the stakes are much less high, when I encounter a problem at work, for instance—an impossible deadline, an error in an article I've written that requires correcting (ugh), an angry reader or person I've written about—I am a mess. My whole world is taken over by this issue. It is impossible for me to compartmentalize my work problem and not let it bleed out, colouring everything else in my life with a coat of gloom.

This sounded like the kind of living environment that might drive a loving husband away. Did my struggle with stress-related problems and lack of emotional resources when faced with adversity cause the worst problem of all?

In his article, Kellermann wrote about vulnerability markers that can lay inactive and do no harm for years, until being suddenly switched on in a threatening situation.

Like a divorce, I thought. Because I was feeling under threat. My life as I knew it was in danger.

Environmental transmission had to be considered as well, he stressed. Kellermann called it tacit communication.

"The child is trapped in a closed setting where it adopts a threatening world view that regulates thoughts, feelings and behavior."

I misread "closed" as "closet." And I was immediately transported back to those nightmares, to my bedroom closet. The Nazis were still after me, closing in on me, while I tried to hide. This time, I was wide awake.

···

I had always been burdened with something dark, something I didn't really understand.

I was preoccupied with these Nazis, with worry, with a sense of injustice, with a sadness that did not seem to have a cause—my childhood weighed down with a prehistory that wasn't actually so far back in the past. That was still walking around, in the form of my mother and father—victims and witnesses to history, my protectors, responsible for me and my well-being.

Many scholars, many studies, have pointed out that children of survivors were more than children to the survivors. We were symbols of rebirth, of life, a fuck-you to the Nazis (the studies didn't put it exactly that way). We represented lost families—parents, siblings and, in the worst cases, children; the brothers and sisters we would never meet. Our presence was the result of vast absences.

So of course the facts of our parents' lives—sometimes well known to us, sometimes only hinted at—would weigh on us as their children. There was mystery and drama attached to our parents. They had been hurt, severely.

Would it happen again? And what would it look like when it happened again? These were things I thought about all the time. I needed to be prepared.

If they came for us, if we were deported, what would I take with me? Which photographs? Would I dig a hole in our backyard and hide precious things there? Would there be time? What would I have put on Eileen's list? Normal people think about what they'll take from their house if there's a fire. I was preparing for the SS to burst through my front door.

When I read the title short story in Nathan Englander's collection *What We Talk About When We Talk About Anne Frank*, I immediately recognized the issue suggested by the title: When the Nazis rise again, who will protect us? Which neighbour will hide us in their attic, behind a swinging bookshelf? This is what the couple in the story talks about when they talk about Anne Frank. I too have had this conversation, but with myself. When you go through your list of non-Jewish friends, of very close friends, and ask yourself this question, you get a bit of a sense of what it was like for the Jews of 1930s Europe. The betrayal they must have felt. I can't imagine these people, these friends who are like family to me, not doing everything in their power to help me, and Jacob. And yet.

...

In his article, Natan Kellermann touched on an important paradox: the coexistence of both vulnerability and resilience in the offspring of survivors. Rachel Yehuda has also studied the resilience of children of survivors. We function well, achieve so much—and yet do so while struggling with emotional stress symptoms throughout our lives.

I could give a million personal examples of this: interviewing literary stars onstage to a wildly appreciative audience (well, "wild" by book festival audience standards), then weeping in my car, all the way home, because I was afraid of the brick-wall welcome I would receive when I got there, if there was any sort of welcome at all.

When my colleague and role model Elizabeth Renzetti went on a leave of absence for a fellowship, the newspaper asked me to take on her high-profile Saturday column—a huge leap for me in terms of profile and achievement. It was scary and exciting and the best. Readers wrote to me, shared my columns on social media, praised me or offered considered (and, sure, sometimes nasty) critiques. I got emails from people I hadn't seen in years—colleagues from my early days in tiny radio newsrooms, friends I went to school with, even teachers, and children of my parents' friends. *You've done so well*, they gushed. *Your parents would have been so proud.*

A few months into the temporary column assignment, my husband moved out.

I had to stay cheerful for our son, run the household on my own, continue doing my job. I could not sleep. I kept writing my columns and covering the arts. I had trouble getting out of bed. I kept writing. I felt like I wanted to die. I kept writing.

...

There is something beautiful and literary about much of the scientific writing about intergenerational trauma.

Zahava Solomon, head of the Multidisciplinary Centre of Excellence for Mass Trauma Research at Tel Aviv University, has written extensively on the topic. "Psychic trauma may be likened to a stone thrown into a pool of water. It creates ripples that affect not only the victims themselves, but also those who are close to them," began one of her research papers.

While working with the Israeli military, Solomon found that combat soldiers whose parents were Holocaust survivors did not recover as well from PTSD as their peers. These were soldiers who had been tested beforehand and found to be healthy and suitable for combat. It was only the trauma of war that unmasked this latent vulnerability. The psychopathology created by their parents' trauma emerged with the new trauma, the one they experienced first-hand.

Perhaps, she hypothesized, this was because of overprotective parenting. Or perhaps these soldiers were conflict-averse—something associated with children of survivors—so being on the battlefield was more difficult for them.

Solomon almost stumbled upon this result; she had not intended to investigate this question. "This was not the focus of the study clearly, but being who I am, I always asked about Holocaust background," Solomon, a 2G, told me. "So this was not something that anybody would have anticipated."

She faced some skepticism when she began looking into this at the time, but she was acting on her instincts. "I had some sort of a hunch that vulnerability is something that is actually intergenerationally transmitted," said Solomon, who is the former Head of Research in Mental Health for the Israeli Defence Forces.

I wondered what it was like for her to learn that. Her hunch had paid off, which was a professional win—but the implications seemed huge and personal. I asked her, when we spoke, if she was surprised by what she found.

"Oftentimes the body remembers," she said during a late-night Pacific time interview. "The body keeps score of experiences. So it just stands to reason that that would be transmitted as well."

But, of course, it was fraught. She told me a funny ("funny") story about how the study had come to the attention of her mother—who was born in Lodz, like my father, and had survived Auschwitz, like my mother.

Her mother first read about it in the newspaper. "Is it true what is written in the paper?" she asked her daughter. *Yes*, Solomon said. Her mother told her, "Well, I'm extremely disappointed." *Why?* Solomon asked. Her mother answered: "You mean to say that Hitler was so successful that he even now rendered you guys more vulnerable in the face of trauma?"

Imagine hearing that from your mother; oy.

Solomon believes there might be a genetic component to this transmission, but whether that comes to be fully expressed has to do with the interaction of genetics and environment. You can't look at one—nature—without the other—nurture.

My mother's cells, my mother's sorrow.

After that initial study, Solomon, working with another researcher, found that veterans of Israel's 1973 Yom Kippur War who were children of Holocaust survivors were *less* likely to suffer from PTSD and related conditions years after combat than other soldiers. Among the possible explanations was that children of trauma survivors may have acquired coping mechanisms from their parents that helped protect them from suffering in their own lives, and thus did not experience their own trauma the same way "trauma virgins" would have.

As Kellermann wrote: extensive and confusing.

...

As I have read more studies and books about intergenerational trauma, I have continued to find bits of myself eerily reflected.

It is not uncommon for children of survivors to live in a state of hyperarousal—where we are easily triggered by any perceived threat.

I am the queen of hyperarousal, always on the lookout for perceived slights. For signs that I am being demeaned, unappreciated, that I am less than fully loved. If this is exhausting for me—and it is—what is it like for the people around me? I wonder how many men in my life ran from this. Is this what my husband ran from?

As well, having overprotective parents who constantly remind their children of the dangers in the world—check—leads their children to develop cynicism, phobias, lack of trust and feelings of victimization.

I have major issues with trust, I tend to identify as a victim, I am extremely cynical.

Many survivor parents view luck as the reason they managed to live through the war. Their children view life as precarious and unreliable. Check, check.

Another common theme for 2Gs is that of rescue. This has always been a big one for me: the fantasy that I could be rescued from a difficult situation. Not necessarily by a Righteous Gentile who hides me in their attic from the Nazis. But maybe by a kindly university professor who understands my potential and rescues me from a life that does not live up to its promise. Or the proverbial handsome prince who rescues me with a kiss, I'm a little ashamed to admit.

Watching films, it is always this idea of emotional rescue by an outsider that gets to me. When Judd Hirsch's therapist character in *Ordinary People* finally gets through to the young man played by Timothy Hutton—the boy whose brother, their mother's favourite, did not survive a boating accident—and assures him that the tragedy was not his fault. When the townspeople in *It's a Wonderful Life* rescue George Bailey from being thrown in the slammer on Christmas Eve by donating cash from their pockets and piggy banks. This idea of people coming to your rescue who aren't obligated to do so; this is a plot point I connect with on a very deep level.

This idea of rescue is so central to my way of seeing the world. When I was a kid, I wanted to be rescued from my family, from my life, from my misery.

...

Holocaust researcher Yael Danieli, founder and director of the International Center for Multigenerational Legacies of Trauma, has identified four adaptational styles of survivors which she coined as: the Victims, the Fighters, the Numb Ones and "Those Who Made It."

The Numb Ones have been depleted by the stresses of what they've experienced and are emotionally detached and intolerant of weakness in others; they probably don't say much about the Holocaust. The Victims are depressed, anxious, emotionally volatile and suspicious—worried about a possible recurrence. The Fighters are tough and defiant. "Those Who Made It" are socio-economically successful; they made it big. Holocaust, Shmolocaust—look at me now.

At my house, the one I wanted to be rescued from, we were victims. The descendants of victims, Danieli has found, can have tendencies toward generalized anxiety, depression and PTSD.

Was this my inheritance?

Nobody wants to mope or worry their way through life—or out of their marriage. And yet, reading this material that felt like it could have been written directly about me was weirdly soothing. This information provided a different sort of rescue operation. *I'm not the only one who lives this way. It's not my fault.*

. . .

Not everyone is comfortable with the term "inherited trauma." Even Rachel Yehuda, in a co-authored study from 2018, noted that "terms such as 'inherited trauma'. . . obfuscate rather than clarify what is being transmitted and how—indeed, how can an experience be inherited? It is clearer to frame the discussion around how the *impact* of a trauma occurring to the parent can affect the offspring," she wrote (emphasis hers).

And the idea of epigenetic transfer of trauma is by no means universally embraced. Yehuda herself has since declared that that particular study was over-interpreted—the findings blown out of proportion by all those tantalizing headlines.

And there is a lot of skepticism expressed by others working in this field. In fact, it would be fair to call this area of research controversial. Some suggest the findings have been way over-blown by people (researchers, journalists) eager to find such a connection.

One question that has arisen: how can you separate the nature from the nurture—the impact of the horrors that children of survivors like myself heard from our parents versus what we may have inherited biologically?

Kellermann, in his 2019 article, wrote that "There is insufficient evidence of the assumption that massive stress exposure in parents can influence the risk of stress-related mental problems in their children.

As a consequence, there is no tangible evidence for the epigenetic inheritance of . . . Holocaust traumatization."

In some of her other work, Yehuda has shown that resilience can also be passed down intergenerationally—a different epigenetic event than what she has found with the intergenerational effects of PTSD.

"We have been saying that both are possible for years," she told me in an email. "It depends on what you measure."

Research is ongoing. At McGill University, for instance, studies in rodents have found that offspring of mothers who received more maternal care (more licking!) had a gene switched on that reduced the amount of the stress hormone cortisol that is released when the offspring rat is under pressure.

Also in Montreal, Morton Weinfeld, one of the early researchers into the psychosocial transmission of Holocaust trauma, remains skeptical. "Where do these allegedly negative effects end?" he asked me. "Does it go to the fourth generation? When does the stuff run out of gas?"

...

In any case, for me, discovering Yehuda's work, that incredible interview, this whole field of study at a time when I could not get past my own little tragedy opened a new way of thinking, new possibilities about what was wrong with me as I struggled in my own life. And maybe, just maybe, it offered the possibility that I could get past it.

What we have to do after an adverse event, Yehuda said in that radio interview, is to take stock and not be so hard on ourselves or set expectations. She said we should "just listen to our bodies and give ourselves the space to be quiet and to heal and to see, to ascertain what has been damaged and try to counteract that by putting ourselves in the most un-stressful, healing environment that we possibly can have, to counteract some of that and promote a biological and molecular healing process that might forestall some of the epigenetic and molecular changes."

A month at the spa, I thought.

Yehuda also emphasized that this epigenetic transfer was not a wholly negative phenomenon.

"Who would you rather be in a war zone with—somebody that's had previous adversity, knows how to defend themselves, or somebody that has never had to fight for anything, but might be very advantaged in many other social and cultural ways?" she said in that interview.

I thought of the "possible benefits" Sigal and Weinfeld wrote about in *Trauma and Rebirth: Intergenerational Effects of the Holocaust*. Not being a trauma virgin sounded like a possible benefit.

There is a wisdom, Yehuda continued, in our bodies. Think of these generational markers not as scars, but merely as effects. She would like this information, she told the host, to be empowering.

"It's very important that although you can't change what happened to you in the past, there's this whole future that you might be able to do something about."

...

Researchers into intergenerational trauma have not focused solely on the Holocaust. Studies have examined offspring of survivors of other catastrophes and found similar links.

Rachel Yehuda studied pregnant women who were at or near the 9/11 attacks on the World Trade Center, and their children. Her team found that pregnant women who survived and subsequently developed PTSD had significantly lower levels of the stress hormone cortisol (which helps the body deal with stressful situations) than pregnant women who had been similarly exposed but did not develop PTSD. Then a year later, the cortisol levels of the children born to those women were also checked. The children of the women who had developed PTSD, the women who had lower cortisol levels, also had lower levels of the hormone. This more sizably affected the children of mothers who had been in their third trimester when the attack occurred.

A study out of Bar-Ilan University in Israel examining the effects of the Rwandan genocide on the descendants of the Tutsi survivors found that the offspring of survivors who had suffered from CPTSD—complex post-traumatic stress disorder—themselves suffered with nightmares and thoughts about the genocide, and felt less equipped to handle adverse situations. "We need to understand that genocide and massive trauma can leave their mark not only on survivors who were directly exposed, but also on their offspring and probably on other family relatives, as well," study co-author Ben Mollov, a political scientist, told *Science News* in a 2019 report on the study.

In Canada, Ojibway scholar and researcher Amy Bombay has been studying the intergenerational effects of the Indian Residential School system. A small but growing literature has provided consistent evidence of the enduring links between attendance at residential school in the family (which was forced by government policy) and a range of social and health issues in their descendants. Bombay, an associate professor at Dalhousie University's Department of Psychiatry and the School of Nursing, is also interested in the role epigenetics plays in intergenerational trauma in Indigenous communities.

In their book *Lay My Burden Down: Suicide and the Mental Health Crisis among African-Americans*, Harvard Medical School psychiatry professor Alvin Poussaint and journalist Amy Alexander have written of "posttraumatic slavery syndrome" and the physiological risks this legacy has created for contemporary African Americans: high rates of heart disease, hypertension, and other stress-related illnesses. And a reluctance among many of them to seek the health care they need.

A 2018 study in the U.S. concerning the Civil War found that the sons of Union Army soldiers who were prisoners of war were more likely to die young than the sons of soldiers who had not been prisoners—and had therefore been spared the brutality that the POWs had experienced. The sons had been born after the war.

Canadian researcher Brent Bezo at Carleton University has been studying the transgenerational effects of the Holodomor—the intentional famine in Ukraine in 1932 and '33 that killed millions of people. In interviewing three generations of fifteen Ukrainian families, Bezo found that coping strategies employed by survivors were transmitted to their children and grandchildren. The transmitted behaviours and effects included horror, fear, mistrust, sadness, shame, anger, stress and anxiety, decreased self-worth, stockpiling of and overemphasis on—even reverence for—food, as well as an indifference toward others, social hostility and risky health behaviours. The parent–child role reversal that is so prevalent in Holocaust survivors and their children—where children feel a responsibility to protect the parents—was present in the children of Holodomor survivors as well.

In his interviews, Bezo found the second and even third generation offspring had thoughts that would wander to the 1930s catastrophe. If they had a piece of bread, for example, a normal, everyday piece of bread, they might wonder: How many people would this have saved in 1932 or 1933? The bread takes on an almost sacred meaning, Bezo told me during an interview from Ottawa, where he lives.

"The thing that surprised me the most," said Bezo, as he was working on his PhD thesis on this subject, "is how a mass trauma from decades ago can affect a person's life decades and decades later."

...

Brent Bezo's use of the term "mass trauma" was important for me because I had been wondering why the Holocaust, as horrific as it was, would cause the sort of intergenerational trauma I was reading about, when there was so much else in our history to consider. What about everything that had happened to the Jews before that? Hundreds of years of displacement, exile, forced conversions, pogroms.

Anti-Semitism is a persistent tragic state of being for the Jewish people. So, was the Holocaust really the root of the intergenerational trauma, or were these issues percolating in the bodies of Holocaust victims too?

Following this line of questioning takes me to the next place: Aren't humans all descended from people who have undergone traumatic experiences? Don't we all have trauma in our histories?

When I mentioned this to Zahava Solomon, she agreed that yes, most people have some trauma in their family, of course. "But it's very, very different if you've experienced concentration camps, if you witnessed the execution of other people, if you were deprived of your daily needs, if you were humiliated on a daily basis, if you were starving," she told me. "It's of a different magnitude. The effects are of a different magnitude."

...

For many Jewish people, the Holocaust defines our Judaism.

Canadian Jews were asked in a survey published in 2018 what they think is essential to Jewish life. Remembering the Holocaust received the second-highest rating, ahead of celebrating Jewish holidays with family, ahead of being part of a Jewish community. It came second only to leading an ethical and moral life. Respondents to a similar survey conducted in the U.S. in 2013 put remembering the Holocaust at the top of the list; it was number one.

What a thing: for your cultural and religious identity to be wrapped up in calamity. For grief and mourning to be the baseline of how you identify yourself in the world. If your sense of identity, not just as a Jew but, in my case, as a daughter—a person—is inextricably linked to devastation, how could it not do a number on you?

It isn't so easy, being a Jew. A whole bunch of people hate you for some reason you cannot understand. Sometimes you get called a name, which feels bad. "Oven-dodger," a term I first heard used by Mel Gibson, comes to mind. But sometimes people literally get shoved into those ovens, or must live for the rest of their life with the knowledge that their parents and big sister and little brother got shoved into those ovens, and yet they must go on, somehow. Or you grow up in a house where these horrific deaths become the facts of life, and you must figure your way through it, even before you understand how unusual it is, how damaging.

It colours everything. One Thursday morning, Jacob and I came downstairs to find glass everywhere—on the floor, on the couch, on the bright red recliner that had been a pandemic impulse-purchase. All over the fuzzy sweater Jacob had tossed on the chair after coming home from school Wednesday afternoon. Had our cat, Lucy, broken something overnight? No. I soon discovered the source of the jaggedy mess: a rock had been tossed through our front window. We figured out that it had happened on Wednesday night—Jacob had heard it after he went to bed and checked the time; he thought I had dropped something. I, having taken a quarter of a muscle relaxant for a bad back, had slept through it.

And then I remembered something about Wednesday: it had been International Holocaust Remembrance Day. A terrible coincidence? Or something more sinister—a tiny little Kristallnacht in my East Vancouver living room? People generally know I'm Jewish and know where I live. A mezuzah hangs next to my front door. Could it be? Even the possibility—remote though it might have been—left me shaken. Dangerous shards all over my window seat, poking at my suspicions.

· · ·

In an essay, Mark L. Tykocinski, former chair of the Department of Pathology and Laboratory Medicine at the University of Pennsylvania and also the child of survivors, wrote that the ability of survivors to compartmentalize and tolerate the fractured realities of their lives was often passed down, a survival tool. This was his experience.

Me, I dreamed of the ability to compartmentalize. When my life was falling apart, it would have made all the difference: not to be dragged down by the horrible mystery of what was happening in my marriage no matter where I was, what I was doing, who I was with. So I guess we're not all the same. Happy families are all alike. Unhappy families of Holocaust survivors are messed up in our own ways.

More than anything, I wanted my kid to grow up in a not-messed-up family.

But I worried it was too late. Divorce, I knew, was not the ideal context for not-dysfunctional child-rearing. I wanted to make the bad stuff stop, for Jacob to get the best possible upbringing, even if his parents had split, even if my upbringing had been lacking in some areas. Especially because mine had been lacking.

There was an inescapable feeling of doom that was palpable in my childhood home and in my life, and it remains still. So when something terrible happens, like, say, a divorce, I can nod sagely and tell myself: You see? You were right. Things don't turn out well for the likes of us.

I did not want to pass this difficult way of living, this negative-skewed way of seeing the world, to my child. I wanted to protect him from this. To pre-emptively rescue him.

My inclination was to protect him by keeping him from finding out what had gone on in our family history. At some point it became clear that he had some idea of who Hitler was—okay, that's in the zeitgeist—but I worried so much about him making the connection between Hitler and his own life. Would it rattle him the way it had rattled me when I was a kid?

I told him very little, almost nothing, about this piece of his history. He knew that I, like him, had grown up without grandparents, but I don't think he knew what had happened to them. He knew that my parents had been Holocaust survivors—but he didn't really know what the Holocaust was. I was not going to do to him what had been done to me when I was far too young.

When he mentioned that they were learning about the Holocaust at Hebrew school, which I had signed him up for in advance of his bar mitzvah, I panicked. Would he make the connection between whatever it was they were learning and himself? Would he begin to fear for his life, make lists of what he would save, of who might save him? Would he be plagued by the nightmares I was still having?

I was afraid to ask him anything about what exactly he was being taught; afraid of what I might stir up.

But as I learned, protecting my son to allow for healthy development was not the same thing as protecting him from the actual information that had caused all the grief to begin with, two generations before him. This was something Robert Krell eloquently pointed out during one of our conversations.

"The trauma is passed on to a degree in the stories . . . but so what? So what should they not know? It's a trauma that you have to deal with in a sense to be aware of what's possible. That's why we have Holocaust education. So why not have education within the family?" Krell told me.

"I wouldn't want in [the next] generations of children to try to help them forget by not giving them any input on all of this because I think it leaves them vulnerable and naïve and defenceless and complacent. I think they should know. So the question then becomes: in what manner? How should they know?"

Certainly not that gas showers explanation that my mother had offered, certainly not those bulldozers in black and white I had seen at Hebrew school.

The stakes are so high. I understand this as someone whose life has been shaped to some extent, I think, by this event, and, perhaps by the ways I was exposed to it in early life. If I needed to pass on this information to my child, I did not want to pass on the burden with it.

We don't show them *Night and Fog* when they're seven. We don't make them write down a list of Jewish items in their homes when they are eleven. We don't make teenagers choose between being Canadian and being Jewish.

"You are concerned about your son," Eva Fogelman said to me, expertly picking up on my anxieties during our conversation.

He'll be fine, she assured me. If he grows up in a happy household.

NINE

Denial

I EXPERIENCED ONE OF the worst days of my working life when I was twenty-seven, employed in commercial radio in Toronto. There were no boulders involved, but Auschwitz was very present in that recording studio. It was 1993 or '94, and I was interviewing a man who insisted with a sneer that the prisoners of the notorious concentration camp didn't have it so bad at all; they were, for instance, served ice cream, he told me.

Another of the worst days of my working life, almost twenty years later, was the morning an artist I revered shocked me by using the phrase "so-called Holocaust" during an interview and said he had read that "the rooms with the gas were actually delousing rooms."

In that first case, at the radio station, I had been prepared for denial; that was the point of the interview. In the second, I had been expecting a conversation about art, with a celebrated photographer.

One of the best days of my working life was the afternoon that Pulitzer Prize–winning graphic novelist Art Spiegelman became the second person, after my husband, to learn that I was pregnant.

My father's career aspirations for me, a student with impressive marks who wrote books in my spare time from the age of six, were not exactly in line with my abilities. Or my interests. My dad had determined that I would make an excellent legal secretary. Not a lawyer—an assistant to a lawyer. The main goal attached to this aspiration had nothing to do with the legal profession itself or my ability to navigate it, but with the exposure such a career would offer. His real dream for me was that I would meet and marry a lawyer.

I was not interested in law. I was interested in telling stories. But I was also trained, child of war survivors, to seek a steady income. And I loved school, loved learning things. So instead of doing the thing my heart really dreamed of—studying literature and giving fiction writing a go—I pursued a career in journalism. I would be a constant student (this is true), I would get to write for a living (a truth that still thrills me) and journalism could offer a regular paycheque (something that is becoming less and less true—a hugely concerning development not just for the financial stability of my colleagues and me, but for democracy).

My journalistic ambition was more than a practical back-up plan to becoming a novelist. It wasn't just that I wanted to learn stuff and write about it for a living; the democracy piece was significant. While I understood almost nothing about the workings of government at the time, I did have a grasp of my own family's history. And I was developing a belief that journalism could have changed the game, could have saved the family members I never got to meet.

If I could not go back in time and prevent what had happened, I told myself that as a reporter, I could play a role in ensuring it would not happen again, to us or to others.

Because of another great love of mine, performing, I landed on broadcast journalism as the right avenue for me, and I was accepted into the Radio and Television Arts program at what is, as of this writing, called Ryerson University—but was then a polytechnic institute, and is now to be renamed.

A more academic setting would have been a better fit, evidenced by my heightened interest in the electives my classmates mostly saw as a chore. English, philosophy, sociology. These classes were far more exciting to me than the ones where I learned about the ins and outs of the Canadian Radio-television and Telecommunications Commission, for instance, or how to edit reel-to-reel audiotape.

One class that bridged the liberal arts with the study of broadcasting turned out to be a personal favourite, and foundational for me, opening my eyes to the world and to possibilities. In that course, which was called something like Media and Sociology, our professor—the one who opened my eyes to so many injustices—showed us *Night and Fog*. He also showed us Nazi director Leni Riefenstahl's *Triumph of the Will*.

Triumph of the Will—considered a masterpiece of propaganda—is pretty persuasion for ugly convictions on a massive scale. Hitler in the clouds. All those parallel outstretched right arms, endless Nazis in strict formation, euphoric crowds at the periphery. The rigid geometry gives way to soft scenes meant to illuminate the ideology. Little girls offering flowers to Hitler, their grown mothers leaning lustily toward the madman as he rolls by on parade.

Then, in Alain Resnais's *Night and Fog*, we learn what was on the flip side of the cheering crowds—the human cost of tyrannical fanaticism. Scenes from the concentration camps. What the absolute adoration for—and collaboration with, even simple apathy toward—a demagogue can lead to. Did lead to.

In Resnais's 1955 documentary, the abandoned sites of Auschwitz and Majdanek, now tranquil fields, are contrasted with the horror of what had happened at the concentration camps a little more than a decade prior. The naked women, waiting to be executed. Marks of fingernails on the gas chamber ceiling. The lifeless bodies afterward; those bulldozer scenes. "The endless, uninterrupted fear."

The short film—it is just over thirty minutes long—makes time to mention the contributions of people beyond the core Nazi regime. "A concentration camp is built like a grand hotel," the narrator explains. "You need contractors, estimates, competitive offers." Companies—people—had bid on this project, and profited from it.

"The leisurely architects plan the gates," the narrator continues. "No one will enter more than once."

The contents of both films sickened me, but the contrast achieved my very smart teacher's objective. He was trying to show us the impact of the image, the influence our careers could wield. We had the potential to change the world and this professor found a powerful way to demonstrate that to us.

I felt a real affinity for this man, especially after he showed us those films, and I confessed to him one of the secret reasons I had chosen journalism as a profession: that had reporters known about what the Nazis had been up to with regard to the Jews before and during the Second World War, the newspapers could have exposed it and stopped the whole thing. Maybe I would have a grandmother. Or parents with stories about their lives that weren't so tragic.

The class was assigned a big project that year: to go back and look at media coverage of a historic event and recount, with 20–20 hindsight, how fair the reporting had been, whether it had been influenced by bias (I now understand he meant establishment bias; he was a committed leftist) and whether it had effected change.

And so, I attempted, in the pre-Internet age, to determine: Could journalism have saved the Jews of Europe? I was nineteen, hunting down examples of substandard newspaper reporting about what the Jews were experiencing under Hitler—reporting that maybe minimized what was going down. Please understand that I was attempting to accomplish this by searching through piles of microfiche at the central branch of the Toronto Public Library, not really having a clue what I was doing.

I found almost nothing—certainly not enough to wrap a thesis around, never mind expose a catastrophic failure on the part of the international media establishment.

My teacher—seeing that this was perhaps not the ideal project for a first-year polytechnical student en route to becoming something like a radio newscaster—came up with a Plan B. Figuring it was Jews I was interested in, he suggested I write about coverage of Julius and Ethel Rosenberg, accused of and then executed for being Soviet spies in the McCarthy-era United States. Did anti-Semitism play a role in the news coverage and, perhaps, even their conviction?

I cared less about the Rosenbergs than I did the Holocaust; in fact, I had never heard of them prior to this conversation. But that class, including that assignment, confirmed to me what I had suspected when I signed up for this line of work: that journalism has power, that journalists have power, and that we can change the world by reporting on it.

There were times that year when I was tempted to decamp for a proper university and focus on English literature and my other true academic loves, but that class convinced me that I was on the right track, that the stories we decide to tell can lead to profound change. I couldn't save my own family, but there were other families who still needed saving.

If the Internet had been around, I would have been able to tackle my original idea, at least to some extent. I would have been able to unearth stories leading up to the war written in North America, such as those published by *The Dearborn Independent*, founded by automobile magnate Henry Ford, a notorious anti-Semite who had accused the Jews of starting the First World War (German-Jewish bankers, to be specific). Ford's paper ran articles with headlines such as "Jewish Power and America's Money Famine" and published an entire pamphlet titled "The International Jew: The World's Foremost Problem."

I also would have learned that more respected, mainstream newspapers did in fact report on the Nazi campaign against the Jews. As early as December 7, 1939, the *New York Times* published a report from Paris, coverage of a World Jewish Congress demonstration. They were protesting against a Jewish "reservation" in the Lublin district of Nazi-occupied Poland, where inmates were exposed to starvation and inhuman treatment, forcibly taken without money or sufficient clothing. The article described it as enormous and isolated, sixty miles long by fifty miles wide. The article stated there were about 50,000 inhabitants suffering from lack of food, clothing and shelter. And that more than 1,000,000 additional deportees were expected.

On Wednesday, May 10, 1944, the *Times* reported that the Nazi puppet government of Hungary was planning to use "gas chamber baths" to kill about one million people. And that in Poland, "scores of thousands of Jews, including women with babies in arms," had already been murdered using this method. The article stated that the Jews were taken there from all over in cattle cars, sent to the fake baths under the pretext they would be relocated to Ukraine afterward. And that 5.5 million Jews in Europe had been killed by the Germans since the war began—proof that mainstream papers were reporting on the catastrophic death.

On the same page as that 1944 article about the five-and-a-half million murdered Jews in the gas chamber baths, I noticed a slew of ads for pretty dresses—"a Debonnaire peplum frock with its own necklace of simulated pearls"; a delicate black rayon dress "for significant summer evenings"; cotton dresses in checks, stripes, prints and plaids. "Washable? Of course."

...

There was not much world-changing going on in my early jobs reading news at small- and medium-market radio stations. A lot of car crashes and police blotter stuff, news from City Hall, any time a local politician said something of even minimal interest.

To give you an idea of the level of journalism I was practising: At the radio station I worked at in Barrie, north of Toronto, one of our responsibilities was to broadcast the daily death notices—The Deads, as we employees called this particular feature among ourselves. They ran each day between 5 and 6 p.m., but absolutely had to be recorded in advance; to read them live was to risk breaking out into fits of laughter mid-obituary. We were very young.

Our newscasts did include stories from faraway lands, such as the strife in Bosnia-Herzegovina and the breakup of the Soviet Union. But these were just words on the rip-and-read wire copy, and I probably pronounced many of them incorrectly. I certainly had no first-hand knowledge or even real understanding of the issues. And even if something I said in one of those newscasts struck a chord with one of the few dozen people listening, I'm fairly certain it would not have made any dent in the tragedy.

But in 1993, I got my shot. The radio station I had started working for that year—I had hit the big-time, Toronto radio—ran a news-magazine show weekday afternoons, and the host, who was also the news director and my boss, came to us looking for proposals for documentary series.

This was exciting—my chance to do something with my platform beyond reporting on mill rates and murder cases. I pitched a five-part series about the Holocaust, which was entering the public consciousness in a big way with the release of Steven Spielberg's *Schindler's List* at Christmas that year.

It was for this documentary series, which I called *Hate and Heroism: The Holocaust 50 Years Later*, that I learned about the women being kicked to death by Nazi SS guards for showing up late to those *appels* at Auschwitz. Judy Cohen, an Auschwitz survivor, told me about that during our interview. The roll calls, she remembered—just like my mother had—were horrific.

"That was when bodies were collected—the dead, the not-quite-dead," she told me. "There were these wagons that were drawn by men instead of animals. And as they gathered the corpses, they were throwing them on these wagons like logs, like inanimate objects. And the terrific tragedy of it was that many of them were not dead yet. We could see them move. Their arms, their heads, their eyes were pleading, they couldn't talk, they were too weak, and they were all naked, they stripped the clothes off them. And it was just a horrible sight to see. Many times we could see people we knew among them. And that's how they dragged them away. We understand they went straight to the crematoria; even those who were still partly alive were not gassed first."

Judy Cohen had provided me with more details about Auschwitz the first time I met her than I had ever received from my mother. But those details—no wonder I didn't ask.

...

One episode in my week-long radio series dealt with an issue that had been rearing its ugly head around that time—well, which I suppose has never stopped rearing its ugly head: Holocaust denial. One of the people I interviewed was Bernie Farber, whose work in this area had made him a local hero in the Jewish community. At the time, he was in a leadership position with the Canadian Jewish Congress, an out-spoken critic of anti-Semitism in general and Holocaust denial in par-ticular. Everyone in the community knew about him; everyone knew the fight he was waging against these racist thugs. He spoke to the media, testified in court. He was determined, eloquent, respected. And he was also the child of a survivor. His father's first wife and two children had been murdered in the Holocaust.

We met in his office in a building next to the Jewish Community Centre in northern Toronto, where I had attended summer camps, taken gymnastics lessons, embarked on my first tentative strokes of the front crawl when I was seven. I was a little intimidated by Bernie Farber—you might even say starstruck. I knew his voice would add credibility to my project; he was the leading local authority on Holo-caust denial and almost poetic in his angry passion.

He called the issue the "knife-point and the cutting edge of modern-day anti-Semitism," during our interview. "All Holocaust deniers are anti-Semites.... And they are all in fact racists and bigots," he said.

One of those racists and bigots was also on my list of interviewees for that episode—the notorious Holocaust denier, very active at the time in Toronto, Ernst Zundel. This loud anti-Semite, in his trade-mark construction hardhat, called the Holocaust a giant Jewish lie. He had already been convicted twice in Canada of publishing hate literature, including the infamous pamphlet *Did Six Million Really Die? The Truth at Last* and one he co-authored under a pseudonym,

The Hitler We Loved and Why. (Both convictions were later over-turned.) Among his ludicrous pronouncements was that Anne Frank's diary was a hoax.

When I told Bernie Farber about my plan to interview Zundel, he urged me not to. *Please don't*, he said. I shouldn't give Zundel's abhorrent views a platform; he didn't deserve the credibility that a media interview would bring him. I explained that I would be in absolute control, the interview would be edited, Zundel would not get the better of me, I would expose him for the fraud he was, I would interview credible experts to counter Zundel's wacko, anti-Semitic views. This was journalism: I needed to explain the issue in order to debunk it and the best way to do that was to go to the source. Bernie pleaded with me. *No, no, don't*, he urged.

But I did.

"A lie repeated six million times doesn't therefore become a truth," Zundel said in the opening minutes of episode three.

Right after that, I played a clip of Farber, saying the deniers were taking after Joseph Goebbels, propaganda chief of the Nazi regime, "who said if you tell a lie enough times, no matter how big the lie, people might start believing it. And that is what Holocaust deniers are attempting to do: to tell the lie over and over and over again, with the hope that people will believe it."

Holocaust deniers were liars, Farber made clear. And their followers? "No sane person believes a Holocaust denier. You'd literally have to be insane to believe a Holocaust denier."

Zundel? "An evil liar," Farber said.

The series was, I think, a success. I heard from quite a few listeners about how I had opened their eyes to this tragedy, asking why they hadn't learned about it in school—people who were deeply moved by the stories of the survivors I interviewed. I felt like I had made a contribution. And when Bernie Farber congratulated me on a job well done, and the documentary series later won an award, I felt pretty pleased with myself. Clearly, I had made the right decision.

But I had not. I know now that I was wrong.

"I'm not a hateful man," I let Zundel say on the airwaves. "I'm not a hate-monger. I'm a truth monger. That tells some uncomfortable truths." Zundel boasted in the episode about the hours of prime-time TV attention his legal battles had garnered him. "Fantastic," he said.

"The trial was good publicity, huh?" I said, my contempt palpable.

"It certainly got my message across. I convinced millions and millions of people. Eighteen million Americans no longer believe the Holocaust ever happened," he responded, citing some study.

"How does that make you feel?" I asked.

"Wonderful. Truth will set us free."

The prisoners were treated pretty well, considering there was a war going on, he told me. There were swimming pools. Ice cream! It's almost funny, how outrageous that lie was and that Zundel actually had the nerve to say it to me during that interview. *At Auschwitz, the prisoners were fed ice cream.* I remember telling my mother about it later that day. Ha, she said—meaning, as if. She made a weird joke: something like if they were served ice cream, it had shards of glass in it.

And swimming pools. How stupid did he think I was? Then again, other twenty-seven-year-old emerging journalists might have believed him. He declared it all with such authority.

The thing is, it's an appealing argument: that what these Jews have described is simply not possible. How on earth could so many people go along with such a plan? Or watch from the sidelines? If this kind of crazy thing was going on, surely somebody would have spoken out, would have stopped it. It's only logical, right?

These arguments are often presented by self-styled historians in pseudo-scholarly books or fake-news research studies filled with bad science. In pamphlets printed in dark basements decorated with portraits of Hitler and Swastika flags, like the stuff Zundel published. Lies that might just plant the seed of doubt in a vulnerable, unsophisticated brain. At-risk youth looking for a place to direct their anger.

People with German ancestry looking to alleviate family guilt. Racists with anti-Semitic leanings to begin with.

The arguments are outlandish and the flaws obvious—unless you have an interest in believing them. If you want to believe the Holocaust denial, reading this stuff will help you find your way.

Certain language is used in this realm to cushion the hatred, mask the anti-Semitism: *We do not deny the Holocaust; we are simply raising questions around accepted facts.* That's what historians are supposed to do.

But these are not historians. They are manipulative liars, to borrow from Bernie Farber.

And Bernie was right. I could have easily explored the issue without giving the source of the denial the credibility that came with airtime and my attention. Rather than hear the lies from the jackass's mouth, I could myself have explained some of the go-to Holocaust denial or so-called revisionist arguments.

I did not need to present in my documentary series any such bullshit from the mouth of the bullshitter. To lend it legitimacy. I could have just explained it myself, said what needed to be said, without going into unnecessary detail or having to expose radio listeners to his sneering, piece-of-garbage voice.

To my great shame, I played parts of that interview with that vile man in the same episode in which I ran clips from interviews with not just Bernie Farber but actual survivors of the Holocaust.

"This is the worst thing that can happen to a survivor, to hear somebody deny the whole thing. I mean, he denies your very being. He denies that you ever had parents or family," said one of the survivors I interviewed, Howard Chandler. "And I just don't understand why these people are doing it. Unless their motives are to repeat the whole thing again."

Zundel, who is now dead, was eventually deported to Germany, where he was born, and convicted under hate crime laws there. He was sentenced to five years in prison.

He did not deserve the airtime, the few minutes of space I gave him. But more haunting to me is the space taken up in my psyche not just by that awful encounter with its preposterous ice cream at Auschwitz story, but by another detail, one of the great regrets of my professional and personal life. I have thought about it with disgrace and disgust for years: that when Zundel waltzed into the studio for the interview, he held out his hand, and I shook it.

···

Even as I began to focus my career on arts journalism, I still sought ways to write about marginalized communities and persecution. To tell stories that would highlight injustice and provoke change.

Often these stories revolved around the art, culture, history and marginalization of Indigenous communities and people living in Canada. I also told stories, through the lens of art, about the Syrian refugee crisis, the civil war in Somalia and other global conflicts and persecutions. And, yes, I still wrote about the Holocaust. All of these stories took on an elevated importance to me. Even if I hadn't become a war correspondent or a top political reporter or a renowned social justice warrior, I could still write about egregious actions and events and maybe, in some way, inspire some change or, at least, awareness.

After years in commercial radio, I worked for the CBC and then miraculously, got a job at *The Globe and Mail*, Canada's national newspaper, as its Western Arts Correspondent. The thrill of this was divine, and terrifying. My well-developed imposter syndrome reared its familiar head.

But I also felt so proud. I thought about how my mother had taught herself to read English after she moved to Canada: by getting a subscription to the *Toronto Star* before she was anywhere near fluent. The newspaper would arrive every afternoon, and she would work her way through as many articles as she could, understanding more and more of what she read over the months and years. And now here I was, working in the B.C. bureau of the venerable *Globe and Mail*—"the paper of record," we liked to say. I was getting paid to write—me, the daughter of Holocaust survivors, two people who couldn't even speak English when they came to this country.

I wished my mother had been alive to witness this. She missed it by a year and a half.

During my first year at *The Globe*, before I had my baby, I arrived at work very early to try to get as much done as possible in my quiet cubicle before the office got busy. The B.C. editor used to show up early too. He was also from Ontario and we would chat about all sorts of things. One morning we were talking about the establishment, for some reason, and I said something to indicate that the establishment was a whole separate entity from who I was. And he said: "I have news for you. You *are* the establishment."

That sounded so weird to me, someone who absolutely identifies in the world as an underdog, who set out on a scrappy little career in journalism hoping to bring about social change. But of course, he was right. As a reporter for *The Globe*, I was not just associated with the establishment, I was part of it. It's still an odd, uncomfortable place for me to sit. I see myself as someone who achieves things in spite of where I came from. The child of persecuted immigrants, refugees. Survivors.

...

The story that would define my career for many years, the one more readers approach me to discuss than anything else I've written (closely tied, perhaps, with my 2010 account of getting bedbugs) was an arts story I wrote for *The Globe*. It was not supposed to be a story about politics or injustice, the Holocaust or Holocaust denial. It was supposed to be a story about visual art, about one of Vancouver's most respected artists, who happened to be a personal favourite of mine as well.

Fred Herzog's colourful photographs of Vancouver in the 1950s and '60s are renowned. I had been a fan of them—and him—for many years when the opportunity to interview him, finally, came my way in 2011. A new book was coming out, *Fred Herzog: Photographs*. I wanted to write about it for the newspaper.

The book was filled with some of Herzog's most iconic photographs and several essays dealing with his pioneering career in colour street photography and his life, including his wartime experiences in Germany and his immigration to Canada in the early 1950s. No doubt his photographer's eye was influenced by his position as a new immigrant, an outsider, the highly respected art critic and curator Sarah Milroy, a former colleague of mine, wrote in her contribution to the volume. Another essay addressed Herzog's interest in expressing social and political issues in his work.

It was a Friday morning and, though I was twenty years into my journalism career by this point, I had professional butterflies while driving up to Herzog's westside home—modest by most standards, but worth a fortune in the Vancouver real estate market at the time. I was greeted by Fred and his charming wife Christel, who made me coffee and served me cookies, hovering in the kitchen, listening to our interview.

He showed me around and I took note of which of his prints were hanging on his wall. It was a pinch-me morning, getting a guided tour of Fred Herzog's photographs by Fred Herzog himself, along with illuminating commentary, in his own living room.

It was a good interview, and an efficient one. I had what I needed after less than an hour, tour and cookies included. There was time to spare. I could leave early—or spend more time with this man I revered, throw in a few extra questions so we could continue the conversation.

For all my preparation, I'm never sure where questions come from, where an interview will take me. The questions often emerge from my own curiosity, areas of interest, and the research I have conducted. I had been reading the essays about Herzog's life in Germany and life in Canada post-war, his political and social interests, his status as an outsider. I am also always interested in the issue of racism. I wondered whether he had his own experiences as a victim of prejudice.

I asked whether, as a German living in post-war Toronto, he had encountered any racism. I noted that his employer at that time was Jewish.

Herzog told me that he had gotten along well with his employer, who had had a furniture business in East Prussia before the war that he must have sold at a comparatively low price, given the circumstances.

"He never complained to me about that," Herzog told me. "That marks him as an unusual person, because even now, many of the people I know, many doctors, are Jewish. And there isn't one who spares me hearing about relatives who were, you know, treated badly during the war and the so-called Holocaust."

Shock is not the right word for what I felt at that moment. It was more a stunned disbelief. *The so-called Holocaust.* The complaining Jewish doctors. Surely this man, this sensitive, perceptive, intelligent artist, could not mean what it felt like he meant.

But he continued in that vein.

"The business with the Germans rounding up the Jews and putting them into cattle cars is true, there's no doubt about that," he went on, unprompted. "But there were other factors why there were so many undernourished people in the end, because the low-flying fighter bombers made it impossible to supply these camps with food, so there were many people very emaciated from not eating."

At this point, reeling, I was able to ask a question: "You think that's because they couldn't get food supplies?"

"You couldn't," he said. He told me he saw trains shot up daily with his own eyes. "Which means train traffic came almost to a standstill. And, of course, the trucks on the road were shot up too. And how can you supply a camp with several thousand people? And German people in many parts also didn't get food."

I was still having trouble digesting what he was saying. "So, do you believe that the Nazis would have fed the Jews better in these camps had the Allies not been bombing the area?" I asked him.

He said he wished he knew all the facts, but this is what he had read. What exactly had he been reading? I wondered.

I asked him what he meant by "the so-called Holocaust" and why he had used that phrase.

Herzog, who had a tendency to ramble, began to answer, stumbled over his words, took another moment, and then said this:

"The Holocaust, I should perhaps not say 'so-called.' Here's what it is: I have, I'm interested [in] what went on, but I don't see how statistics were made or arrived at. The number of six million apparently was decided at a meeting in New York in 1945 or '46. And so, I don't know whether it was six million or not. And here's what I say: If something is that awful . . . you don't have to exaggerate it. That there was a principle"—or did he mean "principal"?—"injustice. And [that it was] indefensible by any standards—that, I have no trouble about. But that people were in such numbers gassed and gotten rid of—that is disputed, depending on where you come from. I don't dispute it, because I have a relative in Germany who used to be the personnel manager of the city where I come from, and he says he has seen the evidence, that he's seen the hardware that was used to gas people.

"But there were other books I have read which say much of this was actually delousing. The rooms with the gas were actually delousing rooms, because lice were one of the biggest problems and the biggest killers of Jews in the camps. So, it's something I'd like to see a little bit more carefully, you know, collected: evidence and how the numbers are arrived [at]. That people were needlessly killed, there's no doubt. That people died on trains being transported is fact. That people died of hunger at the end of the war is fact. But many people, nine million Germans, were thrown out of wherever they lived. Nine million, and with no place to go. And many of those died of hunger and whatnot."

The question of the numbers being exaggerated, the delousing rooms.

Typhus—transmitted by lice—was indeed rampant, but because of deliberate neglect and horrific conditions the Jews and other prisoners were subjected to by the Nazis. Also, to state that lice (or typhus) was among the biggest killers of Jews in the camps immediately after asserting that the rooms with the gas were actually delousing rooms is obviously deeply problematic.

I was flabbergasted. Never in a million years had I expected to hear these words. Certainly not from this man—this beloved, distinguished artist.

He asked if my tape recorder was running and I told him it was.

"It's personal," he said. "And I'm not against anything that is being said except that I would like to see it better documented."

Herzog was very clear that the Nazis "were absolutely mean toward Gypsies and Jews in a totally mean and stupid way," and that he did not like Hitler. "I have no love affair with the fascists. But I'm trying to find out the cause. I'm interested in facts." He pointed out that his wife's best friend, and his best friends, were Jewish. "So, we're not against Jews," he said.

Christel, who had served me the coffee and cookies a little earlier, came back into the living room from the kitchen and sat down, listening.

"I thought this was going to be about art," she would say to me later. Yes, so had I.

Somehow, I steered the conversation back to art. At that point I wasn't sure what my strategy was going to be when it came to writing about this interview. I was doing my best to think on my feet, trying to salvage I don't know what—the interview? The story? My relationship with this man? His reputation?

But it was Herzog who returned to the subject.

"I cannot convincingly say I think everything about it was the way it's being described. That's why I say 'so-called,' and I should not have said that. But what it says, there are some doubts in my mind that the real story is being told. And that is augmented by what happens between Israel and Palestine. The same lack of justice that the Jews experienced in Germany is now experienced by Palestinians in what used to be their country."

Another classic red flag: shift the blame to Israel. The country's treatment of the Palestinians is a separate issue from the Holocaust.

Fred Herzog would have had no idea when he said all of this to me that my parents were Holocaust survivors; it wasn't something he would have known without doing some research into my background, and I don't believe he had done so. At the end of the interview, as I was getting up to leave, I told him.

"I have to tell you about my family," I said. "My parents are Holocaust survivors. My mother was in Auschwitz . . . and all my grandparents were murdered in gas chambers."

It was Fred Herzog's turn to be shocked.

"Even those who worked were never well-fed?" he wanted to know. "I stand corrected. I stand corrected," he finally said. He went searching in his basement for a book of photographs by Roman Vishniac, whose pre-war photos of Jews in Europe comprise an important archive. He insisted I take it home with me.

A Vanished World is a beautiful book, difficult to consume knowing as you look through it that almost every person in it was likely murdered. In one picture, Vishniac's daughter stands, eyes cast downward, in front of a plastometer, a device for measuring the difference in size between Aryan and non-Aryan skulls. The photo was taken in Berlin, in 1933.

Another photo features a Jewish couple, walking through Warsaw, looking worried. "After twenty years with one firm, he has been fired because he is a Jew," the caption reads. "The boycott committee demanded it." This was Warsaw in 1937. Two years before the Germans invaded.

On the next page, a storekeeper stands in front of his locked store in Lodz, my father's city. Because of the boycott of Jewish merchants, he could not pay his rent and his landlord locked him out. The photo was taken in 1938.

Then, a few pages later, a different shopkeeper passes the store that used to belong to him; he was also forced out by the boycott. In the photo, it is being renovated by the new, non-Jewish owner. This photo was taken in Lask, near Lodz, in 1937. Were the Ledermans having boycott troubles at their kafehouse too?

I held on to Vishniac's book—with "Fred Herzog" in what I assume is his handwriting at the top right-hand corner of the first page. I keep it hidden from view. I cannot stand the sight of it—for its contents, and because it is a reminder of that day, and all that happened consequently. But I could never discard it, either. It is an important archive—a glimpse into what millions of people endured. It is also an artifact of that painful interview, evidence of what I endured. I'm stuck with it.

...

At his doorway as I was leaving, Fred Herzog offered explanations for what he had said. He seeks statistics in any matter; he is in search of the truth, always, he told me.

It is also my job to search for the truth. I wonder: How does a man reach the age of eighty-one, a German man, a brilliant artist, and not know the basic facts of this major event in world history—in his own history? His question: "Even those who worked were never well-fed?" They weren't getting ice cream, that's for sure.

This was the only time in my life that I have experienced the phenomenon of mental levitation; I felt like I had floated up to the ceiling and was watching myself experience this bizarre and shocking encounter. I was watching myself hear this great artist use language that I knew from my own work to be the language of Holocaust revisionism—or denial. And I was watching myself with a pounding awareness that there would be a huge decision to make once I left his house.

I was shaking when I drove away, still not quite believing what I had just heard. It all happened so fast, and was a total surprise. Had I got it wrong, misinterpreted?

I was also very aware that I now had a great deal of power, as I stood at the fork in the road all reporters face at the end of any interview. What to include, how to frame it? What to say? And what not to say.

I could write the interview as I had expected to, up to that thirty-minute mark where we talked about his art, his life, Vancouver. If I didn't tell anyone about the rest of the interview, nobody would have to know. Ever. Not my editor, not my husband, nobody. This, I knew, would be the easiest to carry out, professionally, of the three alternatives that stood before me.

I could opt not to write the story at all. I could explain the reason to my editor, or say something vague about things going off the rails, and I knew he would be fine with it. He trusted me, and I was a bit of an over-producer of material as it was. He had been on the fence about the story to begin with; we had written about Herzog before. But I had pushed to write it because I was such a fan. So I knew I had the leeway to abandon the story with no real consequence.

Or I could write about what actually happened.

That evening, I played the interview for my husband and two friends who were over for dinner, one of whom was also Jewish (my then-husband is not). Their eyes widened at all the right places. I had not imagined it.

You can't not write this, they said. *You have a responsibility.*

...

I called Fred Herzog a few days later; I needed to do my due diligence. I had to confirm that I had heard what I heard, to give him a chance to walk it back.

"I'm more focused actually on what's happening now," he said—we had been talking about the environment, an area of grave concern for him. "I have people who are very educated who say even if we did the right thing now, mankind cannot be saved. I just want to state that to you, because it has to do with an orientation that's forward-orientated rather than backward-looking. So, if I haven't fully understood the injustices of the Holocaust, it was probably because I just didn't want to read about it. I've seen the pictures and I know that it happened, but I did not research it and attach guilt to myself."

What about those books, I asked him, the ones with those delousing theories—which I knew to be among the common tropes of the Holocaust denial movement. How did he come to read them?

There was one book published in Switzerland, he said, a gift years ago from a housepainter, now dead. "It presented a different view, which I know now is incorrect."

He said what he had been hearing about the Holocaust—from

Jewish friends, including his ophthalmologist—was having an impact. "It's gradually been sinking in that this actually happened the way it's being described. But I'm the kind of person who, as I told you, would like to see how the numbers and the statistics were arrived at."

And he told me that our discussion had affected him. "You changed my point of view, to some extent."

Was it the trauma of living through the war at such a young age that had led to that point of view? This was the theory I was floating to myself, to try to understand it, even justify it, in my own mind.

"What has shaped me is growing up without parents who love me, more than anything else," he said. "That was what made me street-wise. Almost nothing else, not even the war, did that."

Herzog's age and his tendency to ramble had me wondering if he might have been experiencing cognitive issues. If so, this could account for what he had said, and I could scrap the story. I would not publish such obviously explosive comments if they had been uttered by some-one who was suffering from something like dementia.

I contacted a couple of people who knew Herzog well and asked whether perhaps he had dementia or some other ailment that would have led him to say something like this. No, no, I was assured. He was still sharp.

After these calls, feeling a little bit sick but determined nonetheless, I wrote to my editor and formally pitched the story.

The story I initially wrote was a straight-up account of the inter-view, and included only one line, in parentheses, about my own family. "(Both of my parents were Holocaust survivors.)"

But that story never ran; it was spiked at the last minute by a high-level editor who felt it needed more attention. Then the story was delayed for months as the newspaper's arts editor left his position and the hiring process for his replacement stretched on.

When the new arts editor was finally named, many months later, we met on the phone—he was in Toronto and I was in Vancouver. We had a get-to-know-you conversation, me and the new boss, and at the end of it, I brought up the still-in-limbo Fred Herzog story. Could he read it please so we could discuss how to proceed?

He read it and got back to me promptly with his decision: we should not publish it. It had been so long since the interview, what was the point, the ramblings of an old man, etc. I put up a bit of a fight, and then left it. His decision would save me a lot of grief, I knew.

…

A few months later, Fred Herzog opened a show at Equinox Gallery, which represented him, in Vancouver. The opening led to a feature interview on *The National*, the CBC's main evening television news program. The work, the man, were lauded. My stomach turned.

I went back to my new editor. We are withholding information about a major public figure in Canada, I told him, allowing this celebrated artist to go unchallenged for views that are controversial at the very least, abhorrent and racist at the worst. My intention was not to end his career, but I did not feel comfortable deliberately suppressing this material.

My editor came around. But he had an idea. He said what was really remarkable about what had happened was that of all the interviewers to be on the receiving end of those comments in that living room, it would be me, the child of Holocaust survivors. That had to be a key part of the story, he told me.

I rewrote the article to include this aspect, my own family history. But also to examine Fred Herzog's victimhood. He was a survivor too, his childhood had been shaped by the horrors of war, and I understood that. I understood also that if you were confronted by the facts of atrocities perpetrated by your own people—perhaps your friends, neighbours, family—it might be natural to look for a different set of facts, a more palatable perspective.

Of course, I didn't know if that was what was going on. But it was what I was thinking. Hoping.

I called Herzog again, all those months later. Again, doing my due diligence.

"I have thought about the conversation a fair amount," he told me. "I think the main thing, I was just unprepared for that question at that time. I was so overloaded with other issues that I could not have a level appreciation of your question."

I did not remind him that my question was simply whether he had experienced racism as a German person in post-war Toronto. I wasn't looking for apologies. I believed he was sorry about what he said. What I wanted to know was why he said it.

"I was in a state of shock," he said. "When you brought it up, I reached into something that I no longer believe."

What did he once believe and where did that belief come from?

"The reason I gave you the wrong answer to the Holocaust. . . . To begin with, when I grew up in Germany after the war, nobody ever talked about the Holocaust. Nobody. Not my boss, not the other employees. Nobody there ever talked about the Holocaust. It was actually a seamless denial. And it was only after I had left Germany, I think there were some trials in West Germany where the Holocaust problem was driven home to Germans in such a way that they could no longer ignore it. . . . I remember reading right after the war that there were six million Jews killed and I talked to people about that and most people said they had no idea. And I think on the other hand some people must have had an idea that bad things were happening but simply put their head in the sand."

He was right; there was a gap of time during which the Holocaust—a term that was not then widely used—was not discussed with any great frequency, if at all. Certainly not in Germany. And if that was something that had happened in my own country, perpetrated by my own people, I too might want to put my head in the sand.

After all, I had earned a degree at a post-secondary school named for Egerton Ryerson, an architect of Canada's residential school system for Indigenous children—and I had completed that degree not knowing a single thing about residential schools. I learned all kinds of things about Canada at Ryerson and in my public-school education before that, but not what Indigenous children and their parents had been put through by this racist government policy—not even that those schools had existed. Still existed, when I was at Ryerson.

Aside from the pain the conversation with Fred Herzog had caused, it was also a fascinating thing: this iconic artist had flirted with ideas that had come out of writing presented to him that suggested the Holocaust was not what it was. And he had said this to me, of all people. And rather than walk back what he had said in later conversations, he acknowledged it and discussed it with me, quite openly.

I went back to my story and rewrote it. The child of Holocaust survivors goes to interview a German-Canadian artist and they wind up in a wholly unexpected discussion that included tropes common to Holocaust denial. Two different perspectives on a shared history from so far away, so long ago.

We called it "The Collision."

...

The story was published in May 2012. Social media was not then what it is now. Back in those days before Twitter domination, the hatred exploded in the online comments attached to the story. And that hatred was aimed primarily at me.

Get over it already. Whiner. Opportunist. I was accused of having gone in there with the express purpose of skewering this poor old man about the Holocaust. An ambush! I had written the piece, some commenters accused, only because I wanted to get my family's story into the newspaper.

A man, a revered artist, had suggested—no, said—that lice was the biggest killer of Jews in the concentration camps, and yet I, who reported the words verbatim, was the one who was vilified. Not by everybody, to be sure. I also received quite a lot of support. But even as people came to me privately, quietly telling me they were not surprised by what I had written, I was attacked by many others who would be considered movers and shakers in the Canadian art world. I was the bad guy. Should have kept quiet. They might as well have said: she should have kept her big Jewish mouth shut.

...

Journalists are easy targets. We take a lot of anonymous abuse—back in the old days, in handwritten letters, then in phone messages, then in the comments section of the online article ("Never read the comments" we always tell each other—and yet we do). Social media has made this abuse not just easier to deliver—and with anonymity, but also very public. When people tweet malice at you, the whole world can see it. Or at least the part of the world that looks at Twitter.

Journalists who are women are much more likely to receive this kind of abuse. BIPOC (Black, Indigenous, people of colour) journalists, and other journalists who belong to what we would have once called a minority—gay and Jewish journalists, for instance—have it even worse on this front. Many of the attacks I have weathered over the years have referenced both my religion and my gender, whether relevant to the story or not.

On my first day back from a vacation a million years ago at the radio station where I worked, the one where I had made the mistake of interviewing Zundel, I checked my voicemail. One of the messages went something like this: "I see you're on vacation. Probably having an abortion. Actually, no. Because no man would ever want to sleep with you." The call, I should add, was from a woman.

Still, the response to the Herzog article was more gutting than anything I have dealt with in my career. Because it was so personal. I had bared my soul. And this was no takedown: I had written sympathetically; I had tried to see it from his perspective. And certain elements of the Canadian art world circled the wagons. They were having none of it.

...

Holocaust denial takes many forms. There is the outright outlandishness of Ernst Zundel and others like him. Political candidates, self-styled historians, even teachers have spewed this garbage.

Political leaders and government officials in countries that include Iran have espoused theories as outrageous as the idea that Zionists funded the Holocaust, or that the Holocaust has been exaggerated to create sympathy for Zionists and the State of Israel. The Shoah, they claim, is a myth, it's a lie. At the very least, an exaggeration. A school district administrator in Texas informs teachers that if school libraries contain books about the Holocaust, they must ensure books with "opposing" views are also on offer.

So-called revisionists will present themselves as historians and ask all sorts of red herring questions: Can you *prove* that six million Jews actually died? And that their deaths were deliberate, not a result of the common everyday malnutrition or disease that comes with war? Can you prove that these deaths were the result of a systemic campaign? That they were ordered and overseen by Hitler?

Why the ridiculous questions? Because the biggest deterrent to anti-Semitism in our time is the Holocaust. The Shoah is horrific proof of the potential consequences of anti-Semitism. If you eliminate that obstacle and declare it a hoax or yet another Jewish conspiracy, boom: you can be as anti-Semitic as you like! With impunity. Bring on the Jewish jokes. The stereotypes. No need to dog-whistle with veiled references to George Soros or international bankers. Just say it out loud: the Jews exaggerated the Holocaust so that we would feel bad for them, Germany would have to pay them reparations, and they would be handed Palestine so they could establish a Jewish state.

The Holocaust denial movement and the fringe creeps who belong to it are so pathetic that among those who have stepped in to correct their theories are actual former Nazis. An Auschwitz guard, responsible for collecting money from the suitcases brought to the camp by Jews who were promptly gassed to death, explained in a BBC documentary that he saw it as his duty to face up to what he had done and to speak out against the Holocaust deniers. "I have seen the crematoria, I have seen the burning pits," Oskar Groening said.

He recalled in a separate interview a song from his childhood that included the refrain "When Jewish blood begins to drip from our knives, things will be good again."

When he was in his nineties, Groening, who became known as the bookkeeper of Auschwitz, was convicted of being an accessory to the murders of three hundred thousand Jews. He was sentenced to four years in prison but did not serve this time; he died while in the process of fighting the sentence.

I read a lot of this coverage. He testified at his 2015 trial about a horrific incident he witnessed while on ramp duty at Auschwitz. He heard a baby crying, saw another SS soldier grab the baby by the legs and smash the baby's head "again and again" against the iron side of a truck until it was silent.

The dead babies, again. These monsters.

When what these Holocaust deniers say provokes the people who actually worked at the camps—in this case collecting zlotys and francs and lire from dead Jews' suitcases—to step up and say actually, you're wrong, we *did* do this, how do these despicable fools bother to go on with their outlandish theories?

Then there is the get-over-it-already crowd—which is more dismissal, I suppose, than denial. But it is denying something: the absolute horror of what took place, and the lasting impact. The one my parents lived with. The one I am living with, in some small measure.

...

There is another type of denial that you will find predominantly in parts of Eastern Europe: a historical denial of collaboration. That the discrimination, torture and murder of Jews was something the Germans imposed, while the locals—who were also victims (and they were, of course, that part is true) stood by, aghast. Helpless. Certainly not helping their occupiers.

If only this were the case, understanding this chunk of history would be much simpler. And so many more Jews would be alive.

Consider Vishniac's boycott photos from Poland. One photo in his book shows a street crowded with men, women and some children: It is an anti-Semitic demonstration by members of Poland's National Democratic Party. Some of them are giving the Nazi salute. The photo is from Warsaw, in 1938. The Germans invaded in 1939.

There was a law approved in Poland in 2018—a most insidious type of denial: a Holocaust law. The Amendment to the Act on the Institute of National Remembrance would have made it a criminal offence to accuse Poland of being responsible for or complicit in the war crimes of the Holocaust. After great outrage from survivors and the government of Israel in particular, the Polish government backtracked somewhat and made it a civil offence—so, no jail time for breaking this particular law.

The Poles did not cause or initiate the Holocaust, of course. But once the Germans came in, there were some people there who saw it as an opportunity. Anti-Semitism was already rampant; here was a chance to get rid of the Jews—and to take their property.

That Polish law—criminal or civil—makes honesty about this reality very tricky; it's a slippery ramp down to silence, under threat of prosecution. And that seems to be the point. It suppresses legitimate, unpleasant histories.

In February 2020, two historians—Jan Grabowski with the University of Ottawa and Barbara Engelking with the Polish Centre for Holocaust Research in Warsaw—were ordered by a Polish court to apologize to a Polish woman who claimed they slandered her uncle (now dead) in a scholarly examination of Polish behaviour during the Second World War. The book they co-edited, *Night Without End: The Fate of Jews in Selected Counties of Occupied Poland*, includes a paragraph about the woman's uncle, a prominent Polish man in a particular town who had betrayed some hidden Jews. The passage relied on testimony by a Jewish woman who had survived the Holocaust—this man was her rescuer, in fact.

In August 2021, an appeals court overturned that decision.

Still, I can't help but wonder as I type these words what legal consequences I might face myself. Will I never be able to visit Poland again?

With survivors dying out, it's now on us, the second generation, to take up the mantle. What we say may not have the same effect as the survivors telling their stories of the Polish anti-Semitism they experienced, but soon there will be no survivors left. So it is our job, their children, to remind the world of what blind hatred can lead to.

Were Poles victims of the Nazis? Of course—horribly so. It is estimated that about two million non-Jewish Polish civilians lost their lives during the war, many in the most brutal circumstances. Did some Poles save Jews? Yes, many did—with great bravery and kindness—while risking their own safety, their own lives and the lives of their families. Did some Poles point the Jews out to their oppressors, give up their hiding spots, profit from property and positions confiscated from Jews? Yes. Did some Poles attack and murder Jews themselves? Yes.

While this legislation specifically states that it is illegal to blame the Polish government or nation (which ceased to exist, the law explains, during the German occupation) rather than individual Poles, the law is crazy-making for its intent and for the hurt it causes.

It brings to mind the many Polish-Jewish survivors who told me over the years that they would visit or had visited Germany—a country that had sought reconciliation and provided restitution as far as it could, that educates its young and erects memorials. But that they absolutely would never walk on Polish soil again, could never forgive the Poles. Their former neighbours who turned on them. In the place they called home.

As Daniel Jonah Goldhagen wrote in *Hitler's Willing Executioners: Ordinary Germans and the Holocaust*, while the commission of the Holocaust was primarily a German undertaking, and while non-Germans did not supply the drive and initiative and were not essential to the perpetration of the genocide, had the Germans not found

European—specifically Eastern European—helpers, the Holocaust would have unfolded differently and Germany would likely not have succeeded in killing as many Jews.

There is a great deal of sensitivity around this matter in Poland—understandably. But some of the actions that arise from this sensitivity leave a terrible taste in my mouth. God forbid you write in an article about a wartime atrocity that happened in Poland—you risk getting called out by the Auschwitz Museum's Twitter account for not explicitly stating that these events happened in *occupied* Poland, as if whoever is reading anything about Auschwitz is unaware that the Nazis had invaded Poland and were in charge at the time.

This insistence serves, whether intentionally or not, to deter people from speaking out about some of the more horrific incidents that took place on Polish soil—yes, during the occupation, but also afterward (and before). All of this contributes to a campaign to rewrite history, or at the very least, to suppress it.

In Poland, hundreds of Jews were murdered in pogroms during and after the war. By Poles. Maybe people who had been infected with the virulent anti-Semitism of the Nazis. Or perhaps with the anti-Semitism of their Polish parents and generations before them. Or their priests. Or maybe they just wanted to protect their new acquisitions—some nice clothes, silverware, a better apartment than the one they had had before the war. What happened to my father's bicycle?, I wonder.

Most notorious of these events was that pogrom in Kielce that had rattled my mother's friend Freda when she heard about it while elsewhere in Poland. Jews from Kielce who had somehow survived the Holocaust returned home only to be murdered by their neighbours. Forty-two Jews were killed in an action overseen—even initiated—by the Polish police and military. The townspeople were in a fury and the violence went on for hours. Jewish men and women were beaten, stabbed with bayonets, thrown into the river. The dead included a newborn baby and a woman who was six months pregnant.

This was in 1946, a year after the war ended. The Nazis were long gone.

Polish anti-Semitism cannot be denied. Nor should it be generalized or considered absolute or eternal. Or a Polish issue only. The Poles weren't alone in this; anti-Semitism had been rabid before—and during—the war in other places, such as Ukraine and Lithuania. Poland is of particular interest to me because it's where my family comes from. So I have done a lot of reading, too much reading, about it.

"In Poland, the Holocaust is long over and there are almost no Jews. But the Jewish question lives on," Mort Weinfeld, co-author of *Trauma and Rebirth: Intergenerational Effects of the Holocaust*, told me. He compared it to the Civil War in the U.S.: history still felt in the present, the wounds and divisions remaining. A few months after he said this to me, right-wing insurgents stormed the U.S. Capitol.

...

Germany has done the work when it comes to acknowledging its Nazi past and educating the next generations. There has been a great reckoning along with the restitution. There was a reckoning through the justice system too, and convictions. But I often think about the guilt of others: not the people in charge, but everyday, ordinary Germans.

When you talk to people of German (or Austrian) descent, you often hear a version of the same story: their grandparents were staunchly against Hitler, active in the resistance, a partisan, or what have you. So where are the grandchildren of all those adoring throngs, the Austrians welcoming the Anschluss, the loyal Nazi soldiers in formation, the concentration camp guards whipping my mom and her friends, or sending my grandparents to the ovens? Because there were a lot more of them than there were German resisters performing clandestine acts of sabotage.

Hitler had a primed population to work with. Anti-Semitism was rampant in Germany; it helped him get elected to begin with.

Rabbi Judith Schindler has recalled (in her essay in *God, Faith & Identity from the Ashes: Reflections of Children and Grandchildren of*

Holocaust Survivors) her father telling her about his math lessons from elementary school in Munich as a child, before the war. "If you have ten Jews and kill three, how many are left?" his teacher would ask. (I wonder if there were bonus marks for the student who answered "too many.")

Toward the end of the war, the concentration camp Dachau, near Munich, was liberated by the U.S. Army. An American soldier, who had been one of the first to arrive there, was assigned to lead a group of five locals on a tour of Dachau, to show them the horrors that had gone on at the camp. His group included a German school teacher and a banker. "I showed them the gas house," recounted Abe Cheslow in *GIs Remember: Liberating the Concentration Camps*. "It was like taking them to Disneyland. They were laughing and giggling. When we came to the ovens one of them said: 'a great place; I'd like it for my mother-in-law.'"

...

I am not good around Holocaust denial. I'm not up for any sort of debate about this. I don't want to trot out these facts when I'm accused of unfairly describing a conversation that I took part in (and recorded), or of dwelling on the past, not being able to just get over it already.

I am not good around conflict, period, but I am especially not good around this kind of conflict. It hits too close. The preposterousness of such arguments is hard for me to take, and why should I bother? What is the point of going down that road? My grandparents were gassed to death at Treblinka. My mother was a slave labourer in Auschwitz. My father was a slave labourer in the ghetto. Is the suggestion that all of these people, these survivors, made up these stories? That these family members whom they mourned for the rest of their lives didn't actually exist? That the torture that haunted them didn't really happen? Or wasn't so bad, actually? That at Auschwitz, they were served ice cream—rather than a bit of foul watery soup that might, on an exceedingly rare lucky day, contain a sliver of rotten potato peel?

My response in the face of this is to shut down and quietly boil inside. I'm not up for the fight. I can't handle it. It's a weakness, I know.

Or perhaps it's partly a result of what happened the one time I did stand up and say something. When I was called an opportunist, a whiner, my journalism and my credibility questioned. Not just by people on the fringe, but by prominent figures in Canadian visual art, moving in to protect one of their own—from his own words.

...

I have often chastised myself for not following through on my original journalistic ambitions—to make a difference, to prevent disaster, to shine a light on grave injustice. I think back to my first-year assignment at Ryerson, the one I abandoned: What could journalism have done to spread the word, to stop the massacre?

Years later, I was confronted by the difficult truth: people knew. Of course they knew. They knew in parts of Europe because it was all around them—houses in Lublin, Oswiecim and beyond that shared a neighbourhood with an extermination camp, chugging out ashes of dead Jews at all hours. How could they not know?

Jan Karski, a Catholic Polish diplomat, smuggled himself into the Warsaw Ghetto in 1942, disguised himself as a Jewish resident and tried to report what was happening to the Allied leadership. He was ignored.

And, in North America, those newspaper articles. In his book *Were We Our Brothers' Keepers? The Public Response of American Jews to the Holocaust 1938–1944*, Rabbi Haskel Lookstein points out that by the end of 1942, American readers of the *New York Times* or of any Jewish newspaper at the time would have known about the murders of millions of Jews in Europe.

It wasn't simply a matter of apathy. Anti-Semitism was also rampant in North America. Maybe not throw-them-into-gas-chambers rampant, but still. There was an infamous Madison Square Garden Nazi rally in February 1939. Attendance: twenty thousand. There were swastikas, armbands, white Americans in brownshirt getups. Arms raised in the Heil Hitler salute. One of the posters at the event read "Stop Jewish Domination of Christian America." Onstage, German-American Bund leader Fritz Kuhn ranted about the "Jewish-controlled press" and called for a "white, Gentile-ruled United States" and "Gentile-controlled labour unions free from Jewish Moscow-directed domination."

When a Jewish protestor ran onstage, he was attacked mercilessly, his pants torn off. The crowd laughed and cheered; behind him, a young boy, one of the drummers onstage, rubbed his hands in glee. A giant picture of George Washington looked on. In disgust, I like to think.

During that same period, President Roosevelt was mocked, called President "Rosenfeld," for appointing Jews to prominent offices in his administration. Some referred to his life-changing safety net program, The New Deal, as The "Jew" Deal. Surveys taken between 1938 and 1941, according to David Wyman's book *The Abandonment of the Jews*, found that between 33 per cent and 50 per cent of the U.S. public felt Jews had too much power in the country.

Surely such attitudes kept what would have been life-saving doors shut tight to the desperate Jews of Europe.

"It wasn't Hitler who killed the Jews," one person said at a workshop I attended for children of survivors decades later in Vancouver. "It was all the other countries that wouldn't let them in." Including the U.S. and, to my sorrow, Canada.

Would those newspaper articles I was not able to dig up back at university, the kind I like to think I would have written, really have made any difference? What would those art world poobahs who called me shameless and opportunistic over my Fred Herzog story have thought had they lived in the 1930s and read an article about Jews being mistreated over in Europe? Would they have accused those Jews of maybe overreacting—you know, with their tendency to complain? Or of distorting the facts? Or, if they spoke to a reporter about it, of being opportunistic? Hoping to get their family story in print?

...

Holocaust denial is denial of historical fact, and it is not just a historical issue. It is contemporary, and it is raging.

A survey of U.S. adults between eighteen and thirty-nine released in September 2020 found a shocking level of ignorance: 63 per cent of respondents did not know that six-million Jews had been killed in the Holocaust; 23 per cent believed the Holocaust was a myth or exaggerated or they weren't sure; 12 per cent said they had definitely not heard of or didn't think they had heard of the Holocaust.

Anti-Semitic incidents—many of them online harassment (I have been at the receiving end of a few of these)—have increased in the U.S., Canada, the U.K. and particularly horribly in France and Austria. The Holocaust provokes resentment in Central and Eastern Europe.

All that attention, I suppose—the inability to let it go already.

Chris Friedrichs, Professor Emeritus of History at the University of British Columbia, in arguing for a partnership between historians and survivors to get the truth of the Shoah amplified, explains that some Holocaust deniers are contrarians, conspiracy theorists. Others are anti-Semitic. (You can be both.) The biggest challenge, he has said, is Holocaust indifference. "So what? Lots of bad things have happened. Why focus on this one?"

I imagine people who might be inclined to think this way wonder why the Holocaust gets so much attention. Is it because of those noisy, pushy Jews? Who can't stop complaining? You think this is the only bad thing that has ever happened in history?

The truth must be remembered so it is not watered down, Friedrichs told us.

A nation tried to eliminate an entire race from human existence. And so many people pitched in, cheered it on, or turned away.

. . .

Journalism can be a force for good—but it can also be used to further evil agendas. Propaganda was a key tool in the Nazi campaign against the Jews, and Nazi-controlled media were used to deliver that message. Here is how *Der Führer*, the local Nazi newspaper in Karlsruhe, Germany, reported the events of Kristallnacht in November 1938, as recounted in Nora Krug's graphic memoir *Heimat: A German Family Album*.

"Entering the Jews' houses during the arrests was enlightening: There were the Jewish money magnates with their feudal homes, with their silver, gold, and antique German art objects, amassed in greed; and then there were the Galicians with their greasy, bug-ridden, verminous junk stores. Both kinds were equally insolent during their arrest. They tried to . . . escape by coming up with all kinds of excuses. . . . They tried to threaten, they pleaded in whiney tones, they put on submissive faces and acted as though they carried all of the world's pain on their shoulders . . ."

It's easy to dismiss out of hand this description of how Jewish people reacted to having the windows of their homes and businesses smashed during a terrifying night, to being robbed, to being beaten. Ridiculous. Obvious propaganda. Today's consumers of media are critical thinkers, too smart to believe such out-and-out lies.

But consider the crazy fabrications that the followers of QAnon believe, and how these people have become indoctrinated. I detest the "fake news" label that became ubiquitous during Donald Trump's presidency. But fake news is a serious problem. Wacko conspiracy theories flying around the Internet have been embraced by an alarming number of people. We should be very concerned about the kind of "information" being directed, successfully, at uncritical thinkers—perhaps a retiree who spends the entire day watching and reading this baloney on their iPad; perhaps a curious teenager, targeted by insidious algorithms; perhaps someone who does not have the intelligence or education to be able to critically discern truth from made-up stories. It adds up to too many people believing awful, often racist, insane fictions—from 9/11 conspiracy theories to Pizzagate and everything in between. COVID-19? Made up. The vaccine? Unsafe. Trump's 2020 election loss? A fraud. Let's storm the Capitol.

There was a time when anti-Semitism seemed so fringe, unconditionally unacceptable. Certainly, the Holocaust had shown the world the potential consequences of anti-Semitism—consequences beyond comprehension. In my formative years, I believed this was still the case. I was safe. The world was done with anti-Semitism.

But that has dissipated. Again, I see Jews portrayed as wealthy, greedy bankers and media moguls, secretly controlling the world.

For a time, the blame for all sorts of troubles in the U.S. was placed, almost comically, on George Soros—a billionaire American philanthropist who supports progressive causes and who was himself a Holocaust survivor. (The day I wrote this sentence, a Canadian member of Parliament—from the Conservative Party—tweeted out a photo of Soros with the recently appointed finance minister, a Liberal, from an interview the minister had conducted with the billionaire when she was a financial journalist; the Conservative MP wrote that Canadians should be "alarmed." She later deleted the tweet.)

In 2021, a Republican congresswoman in the U.S. suggested that wildfires in California were caused by Jewish-owned lasers from space. She put the blame on the Rothschilds, another anti-Semitic trope.

Either way—Rothschild, Soros—it's code for "Jews." The Jews remain a target, an acceptable target. Somehow. And if you justifiably respond to anti-Semitism, you open yourself up to more criticism. (God forbid you piss off the Jews; you know how touchy they can be. Plus with all their money and all those Jewish lawyers, they'll probably sue.)

In the spring of 2021, I watched legitimate criticism of Israeli policies regarding the Palestinians turn into a general "blame the Jews" vibe. Ubiquitous and absolutely socially accepted. I felt scared, really scared.

Dehumanization of the Jews was essential in carrying out the Holocaust. But so was anti-Semitism to begin with. Years of it, generations. It floors me that we are back here. Even after the gas chambers, after the crematoria. The bayonets and the babies, the little bashed-in skulls. All these excruciating lessons, and still—why?

They say the first stage of grief is denial. As my own life was falling apart, I became well acquainted with this strategy. I came up with a million reasons why things had become weird at home—none of them the real reason, the one that was staring me in the face, or steadily avoiding me. My marriage was ending. Denial was the easiest way to deal with it, for a while. I understand the temptation.

...

Something happy now. Another interview for the newspaper with an artist I revered. In the spring of 2008, Art Spiegelman was in town for an exhibition he'd co-curated at the Vancouver Art Gallery. For me, this was another pinch-me career moment; Spiegelman's *Maus*, a graphic novel about his parents' experiences in the Holocaust and his experiences as their child, is transcendent. The Pulitzer Prize–winning book had spoken to me in a way few other works of art had. A reflection of a version of my own life, told with such precision, insight and humour. A masterpiece.

To be able to interview Spiegelman was a career highlight, less than a year into my miracle job at *The Globe and Mail*.

I happened to be in the process of another miracle: I was forty-one—and about three months pregnant. I hadn't started telling people because of the risks that came with my geriatric pregnancy. But that day, I had to tell Art Spiegelman.

Spiegelman was a notorious chain smoker, unable to go very long without a cigarette. The interview was taking place in what must have been one of the last remaining hotel rooms in the city that allowed smoking. And so, shortly after we began the interview, he lit up a smoke.

What to do? Do I say something to this esteemed, world-renowned artist, ask him to put it out? What if that sets him off, creates a hostile interview environment? Or, worse, what if he shuts the interview down altogether? But there was a fetus growing inside of me and I was not going to put this fetus at risk with all of this cigarette smoke in an enclosed room.

I had not told anyone that I was pregnant other than my husband. But at that moment, I knew I had to tell Art Spiegelman, to get him to put out his cigarette. To be honest, I kind of loved that the second person I would be telling about this miraculous event was, like me, a child of survivors. But a really famous one, who had made great art from the pain. Still, it was a hard thing to do, to speak up with this request.

Spiegelman was lovely; I'm pretty sure he congratulated me—but he also informed me that he would not be able to do the interview if he could not continue to smoke.

We came up with a compromise: it was possible to crack the windows open in that room, so he sat by one of them and smoked out a slit through the window while we carried on. "Everything I know," he said during that interview, "I learned through comic books." He happened to know a fair bit about caribou, he told me—because "caribou" had come right before "caricature" in the encyclopedia.

We talked about 9/11 as well—a subject he tackled in his work *In the Shadow of No Towers*. He told me that he literally thought he and his family were going to die that day. They were right next to the World Trade Center; the building they were in was shaking. They couldn't see what was going on, it was chaos all around, and they thought that was it. "And at that point," he said, "one of several thoughts that went through my head was, 'Schmuck, you should have done more comics.'"

Four years after I told him I was pregnant, Art Spiegelman was back in Vancouver, this time for a solo exhibition at the gallery. He and I met outside for our interview this time—for obvious reasons—on the gallery's rooftop. "I've been thinking about death since I was fifteen," he said that afternoon, a few days before his sixty-fifth birthday. After the official part of the interview was done, I reminded him of our previous encounter, and told him I had given birth to a healthy baby whom I named Jacob, after my Holocaust survivor father.

Spiegelman had zero recollection of that previous interview—who can blame him?; he must do a million of them. But he listened to my story, and then, when I asked him to sign my copy of *Maus* for the son who had been growing inside me during that first interview (something I rarely do, ask an author to sign a book, but this was special), he quickly sketched out a Maus figure on the title page. And in a speech bubble, he wrote: "For Jacob and the future, such as it is . . ."

TEN

Connections

SOMETIMES A SINGLE CONVERSATION can change your life. Or, the way you see life. And maybe the way you choose to live as a result.

I get to have conversations for a living. I talk to people and then process what they've told me, transcribe the interviews, which sometimes last hours, and then I write about it. I often say I have the best job in Canada (other than the transcribing). And I mean it; I know how fortunate I am.

Each story I get to tell is a gift. I am completely aware of how sappy that sounds, but I don't for a minute take for granted the fact that people take time to tell me important things about their lives and trust me with their stories. Each article I write transports me for a time into another world—a sculptor's technique, a filmmaker's influences, the thrill of the office worker who writes novels in their spare time and finds themselves on the bestsellers list.

Each story is interesting and important. But in daily journalism it all goes so fast: you do the research, the interviews, the transcribing (ugh), write the story, edit the story, hit your deadline and file, then move on to the next thing. There's barely a chance to pee, never mind reflect.

But some stories, my God. They cut into your life and stay with you.

In 2013, I travelled by ferry to Victoria, B.C., to meet master carver Carey Newman, who, on his father's side, is Kwaguilth from the Kwakwaka'wakw Nation and Coast Salish from the Sto:lo Nation, and whose traditional name is Ha-yalth-kingeme. I was nervous in the particular way I get when a story of great consequence awaits and I am the one who gets to tell it. The part of my brain that is nice to me wants to make sure I live up to the opportunity and tell it the best way I can. The less helpful part of my brain puts it a little differently: I had better not blow it.

I knew what this artist was doing was of national importance and absolutely critical. I was excited to meet him, to see his work, to learn his story. But I had no idea about the bomb of connection that was about to go off for me.

Newman was in the early stages of creating something he called The Witness Blanket, an enormous installation to memorialize and call attention to the atrocities of the residential school system. It would be made up of hundreds of artifacts that had in some way borne witness to the national tragedy that continues to affect so many lives.

The federal residential school system was established in 1883, in collaboration with churches that were already running such schools. Indigenous children in Canada were removed from their homes and families and sent away to residential schools, where they would unlearn their culture and language and learn how to be good little Christian, English- or French-speaking children.

"If anything is to be done with the Indian, we must catch him very young. The children must be kept constantly within the circle of civilized conditions," wrote politician Nicholas Flood Davin in his 1879 *Report on Industrial Schools for Indians and Half-Breeds*, which was commissioned by Prime Minister John A. Macdonald.

The report makes for maddening, sickening, reading. Little can be done "as far as the adult Indian is concerned," it states, citing the example of the U.S. He can be taught to do a bit of farming "and to dress in a more civilized manner"—but not much else. The child has an "inherited aversion to toil" that day schools can't fix.

With this kind of racist thinking as the justification for forced assimilation, residential schools were set up across the country. The first day schools opened in the 1860s, the Indian Act was passed in 1876, and in an 1885 report, again to John A. Macdonald, deputy superintendent General Lawrence Vankoughnet concluded that residential schools were necessary in order to remove children from the influence of their homes; the only way "of advancing the Indian in civilization."

In 1920, under an amendment to the Indian Act, attendance at school became mandatory for all Indigenous children aged seven to fifteen.

The removal of children from their homes could be forced, against the will of their parents.

Duncan Campbell Scott, an admired poet (somehow it is even more disturbing that a poet was among those responsible for this) who was also the deputy minister of Indian Affairs, was an architect of the system. "I want to get rid of the Indian problem," he said in 1920 in his very unpoetic remarks to the Special Committee of the Indian Act. "Our object is to continue until there is not a single Indian in Canada that has not been absorbed into the body politic and there is no Indian question, and no Indian Department, that is the whole object of this Bill."

The Indian question.

The schools—the official term "residential schools" was adopted in 1923—were operated by the government and various religious orders. There the children were not only isolated from their families and culture—abusive in and of itself—but they were also physically, sexually, verbally and emotionally abused. They were neglected. They were tortured. Some were deliberately starved as part of a government-sanctioned experiment—research ("research") into malnutrition. Tuberculosis was a scourge. In 2021, the Tk'emlups te Secwepemc First Nation revealed the horrific news that it had detected the remains of more than two hundred children on the grounds of the Kamloops Indian Residential School in British Columbia. Large numbers of unmarked graves have since been discovered on many other sites.

While no firm statistics exist, we know that about 150,000 Indigenous children were removed from their families to attend residential schools. And that thousands of those children died.

According to Justice Murray Sinclair, former head of Canada's Truth and Reconciliation Commission, the government stopped keeping track of these deaths around 1920, after a medical officer at Indian Affairs suggested children were dying at an alarming rate. The medical officer was fired after raising these concerns. Note that 1920 was the same year the schools became compulsory.

The last federally run school closed in the 1990s. I was in my thirties.

This is not my story to tell. But my connection to it is irrefutable; as a Canadian, I feel ashamed and angry. I feel embarrassed that I have learned this history so late in my life. And as a human being, I'm disgusted. And just so sad.

Reading that term "the Indian question" was particularly unsettling; it hit very close to home. Familiar but different.

In 1919, Adolf Hitler issued a statement about "the Jewish Question." He defined Jews as a race rather than a religious community, using the term "race-tuberculosis of the peoples." He said the ultimate goal of a German government "must be the removal of the Jews altogether."

That 1939 *New York Times* article, the way it had described a concentration camp: a Jewish reservation.

...

On that first visit with Carey Newman, we met in the basement studio of his suburban Victoria home. He explained what he was planning: a large-scale installation with multiple panels, upon which he would "weave" artifacts from residential schools and related institutions that had witnessed the atrocities: the church, but also Indigenous structures, to represent the resilience of Indigenous people. He had a team travelling around Canada, collecting these items. He carefully brought a few out to show me, explaining where each came from and what was known about it—sometimes very little. One of these precious items, stored in a Ziploc bag, was a child's shoe, small and crumbling. It came from the woods near where the burned-down Chooutla residential school once stood in Carcross, Yukon. Whose shoe was it? How did she lose it? What happened to him? Did this child ever make it home?

The shoe was found by Rosy Hartman, the project coordinator. While on a gathering trip—looking for artifacts to include in the piece—Rosy was walking with an elder who kicked at something in the woods. The shoe.

"It was like a living organism—there was moss and little mushrooms and things growing out of it. It had just been living in the forest for a hundred years," Rosy told me.

After the studio visit, Carey and I went upstairs for the formal interview. There was a large box of Tim Hortons donuts on offer in the immaculate kitchen and his young daughter's toys scattered in the cozy living room. We sat down on the couch.

There, he told me his father's story, some of it, anyway, and I could feel a strange bridge forming between us, in that space where vastly different experiences meet shared sorrows.

Carey didn't hear a lot from his father about his time in residential school. But there was one particular story his dad, Victor, did share— about how he was expelled from St. Mary's Mission and Residential School in Mission, British Columbia. Victor and some friends had stolen some sacramental wine and were drinking it under an apple tree. Later, when the priests discovered that there was wine missing, they announced that everyone would be punished if the guilty didn't confess. Victor came forward and took the punishment on his own.

But remarkably—or maybe not—Carey had not learned the detailed story of his father's residential school experiences until his dad testified at the Truth and Reconciliation Commission hearings in Victoria.

Victor Newman was seven or eight when he lost his own father— by way of being separated from his parents, removed from his family.

Home was Alert Bay, B.C. The residential school was far away, in Sechelt, on B.C.'s Sunshine Coast.

Arriving there in 1944 or 1945—the family isn't exactly sure when this happened—away from his mom and dad and his home and language and everything he knew, Victor lost another part of himself pretty much immediately: his hair was shaved off.

"They took away his clothes and his hair, and essentially his identity," Carey told me, breaking down.

And there I was, back in Auschwitz; my mother's arrival. Having all of her hair shaved off. It was late August 1944, maybe the same year Victor Newman experienced his trauma in Canada.

Carey and I were both suffering in a next-generation way at a time when I didn't have the language to understand it.

That shoe, too. On its own it was upsetting enough. But for me it triggered a gutting memory: visiting the museum at Majdanek, the concentration camp that is now the backyard for some suburban homes in Lublin, Poland. In the museum, you walk from barrack to barrack, looking at artifacts—things taken from the victims before they were gassed. The most painful, most vivid memory of Majdanek, for me, had been the multiple barracks filled floor-to-ceiling with shoes, shoes of dead people.

Fifteen years after that trip, I was in Victoria, B.C., looking at a tattered shoe in a Ziploc bag, and thinking about parallel traumas.

...

In 2014, the Witness Blanket was nearing completion and I travelled back to Victoria to see it and write about it once again. It was breathtaking by any measure, and once again it was hard to keep my human response separate from my professional reporter response.

That day, Carey showed me what would be the installation's most personal artifact: two braids belonging to his sisters. Ellen and Marion Newman had grown and grown their hair, then cut it off at a family ceremony near that apple tree in Mission, where Victor and his friends had drunk the sacramental wine, an adventure for which Victor had later faced the consequences.

Ellen and Marion grew their hair so they could contribute their braids to the artwork, in recognition of what their father had gone through as a little boy under a stranger's razor. On the installation, the braids are wrapped around a branch from an apple tree the family collected from the Mission orchard.

"Losing your hair for the first time wasn't a very nice thing," Victor told me that day. I was able to interview him, as well as Carey's sister Ellen. I met Carey's mother too.

Victor was clearly moved by it all—the monument his son had created, the braids his daughters had grown for it, the ceremony they had held in that orchard.

"It was a way to honour our dad, but a way to honour all the children . . . because it was just a universal experience," Ellen told me.

Meeting the Newman family was profound on its own, and it revealed much about the shared experiences of descendants of trauma. It also made me wonder: why have our two communities not come together to examine our parallel pain and help each other heal? There have been a few exceptions, times when Indigenous people and Canadian Jews have held dialogues and forums. But none that I had known about; it took some Googling to find them. What a shame, I thought. We have so much to talk about. So much to share. So much to grieve.

. . .

Holocaust survivors, in new countries away from the land of their suffering, have managed, many of them, to thrive. Coming to Canada was an invitation to a new beginning. They started families, built businesses large and small, and created legacies. With a geographic separation from the place that had been their hell, they created a new story. That's not to say they weren't traumatized—oh, they were—but I believe that distance helped. Not just time, but geography.

Indigenous people were traumatized on their own land, land stolen from their ancestors and now called Canada. While many were forcibly uprooted from one place to another, they remain in the same colonial construct we call a country. What does that feel like? Without the geographic escape, it must be a daily reminder of the torture their parents, grandparents and the many generations before experienced, and the continued effects of that—not to mention the appalling conditions on some reserves, some that still do not have safe drinking water, as I write this—and the continued discrimination Indigenous people face.

When I travelled to Germany in the 1980s and '90s, I would look around at people of a certain age and wonder, accusingly: Where were you? What did you do? Today I might wonder: What did your parents do? Your grandparents? A German accent can set me on edge—which I am completely aware is unfair, racist.

It's a torment that comes at me from unexpected places. I watch a German team win Olympic gold in some sport and I look at their faces and their joy and triumph and wonder about their great-grandparents: What did they use their speed and strength to achieve? Gold-medal winner, did you get to the top of the podium with help from the genes you inherited from murderous Nazis? I watch the TV coverage and think: maybe your ancestors killed mine. It's awful, I know, but I can't help myself. It is almost a reflex. I have tried to stop it, but with little success.

Imagine having to do that at home, every day. Your neighbours, your teachers, the politicians elected to represent your interests. The stores where you shop.

...

The final report of the Truth and Reconciliation Commission mentioned a youth panel in B.C. that promoted a cross-cultural dialogue; panelists included intergenerational survivors of the residential schools, the Chinese head tax, the internment of Japanese Canadians during the Second World War, and the Holocaust. That term, "intergenerational survivor," really struck me.

Every time I hear or read (and, occasionally, write) a story about the residential schools tragedy, the missing and murdered Indigenous women and girls, the Sixties Scoop (during which Indigenous children were taken from their families and adopted out to white families), the Truth and Reconciliation Commission, I feel a kinship. This unexpected connection is not the commonality I would wish for with anyone, but it has helped open my eyes in a new way to the treatment of Indigenous people who live in Canada and to the continuing consequences. Intergenerational trauma from residential schools continues to undermine the well-being of contemporary Indigenous people.

I am guilty of giving not nearly enough thought to this for most of my life. We must remember, we must discuss what happened. And by "we," I mean all of us—not just the people who were victimized. Many of these events may be historical, but the consequences remain. Look around you.

The burden of this knowledge leaves me with an unsettling contradiction: Canada became my parents' refuge. Even if they experienced discrimination when they arrived, and probably for many years, with their thick accents, these little humiliations would barely have registered, given what they had experienced back home ("home"). My parents loved Canada and I do too; I feel an immigrant's patriotism for the place. Play the national anthem and I will stand and sing, maybe even choke up.

But as I learned about this shameful aspect of my own country's history—something I should have learned about long ago, at school— I didn't know what to do with these new, conflicted feelings about my home. Canada was my family's safe haven. It also perpetrated terrible wrongdoing against others. I love it. I hate what it did. And I am painfully aware that what it did still manifests itself in the lives of people around me.

...

More than five years before the gutting discovery of unmarked graves at the site of the former Kamloops Indian Residential School and many others around the country—those poor children, and, oh God, their parents—the final report of the Truth and Reconciliation Commission came out. It used the term "cultural genocide" to describe the experience of Indigenous people in Canada. This was late 2015.

In 2019, when the *Final Report of the National Inquiry into Missing and Murdered Indigenous Women and Girls* was released, it went a step further, declaring that what had happened amounted to a race-based genocide. "This genocide has been empowered by colonial structures," the report stated. Residential schools, the Indian Act, the Sixties Scoop, breaches of human rights that have led to increased rates of violence, death and suicide in Indigenous populations. Canada had committed genocide.

Some Canadians expressed strong opposition to the use of the term "genocide"—among them, politicians. The then-head of the federal Conservative Party said it wasn't the right word. There were newspaper editorials, ugly debates on social media, outrage: *This was not genocide! This was not state-sponsored, systemic murder. There were no gas chambers. This was not Auschwitz; this was not Rwanda. The use of the term diminishes* actual *genocides that have occurred.*

A number of people, knowing my own history, asked me what I thought. *Does the term apply? Can we really call this genocide?*

The term genocide was coined by Raphael Lemkin, a Jewish lawyer who escaped Nazi-occupied Poland and eventually joined the U.S. War Department as an analyst.

His 1944 book *Axis Rule in Occupied Europe* documented Nazi atrocities, what we now call the Holocaust, and introduced the word "genocide." The term does not necessarily mean the immediate destruction of a nation, he wrote, but is intended to signify "a coordinated plan of different actions aiming at the destruction of essential foundations of the life of national groups, with the aim of annihilating the groups themselves. Genocide is directed against the national group as an entity."

Genocide, he explained, involved deliberate persecution and destruction.

Lemkin proposed a treaty against genocide to the United Nations in 1945. In 1948, the UN defined genocide as intent to destroy, in whole or in part, a national, ethnic, racial or religious group. That can include killing, but also inflicting harm in ways such as rape, depriving the group of necessities of life such as clean water, and removing children to schools where their language or culture is prohibited.

You have my answer.

...

In October 2019, a number of people were called to a Big House on Vancouver Island to witness a historic ceremony. Responsibility for Carey Newman's Witness Blanket was to be shared with the Canadian Museum for Human Rights, where it would live. It was an unusual, landmark agreement: The Winnipeg museum does not own the piece; legal rights are vested with the artwork itself. It made Canadian legal history—the first time a federal Crown Corporation had ratified a legally binding contract through Indigenous traditions; written documents and an oral ceremony were to be given equal weight in the contract.

I was invited to that ceremony as a witness.

When Carey called to tell me about it, he made it clear that he wasn't asking me to come as a journalist; I was not expected to write about it—although that would be fine, great. Either way, he wanted me there to see this important step in the Blanket's life, since I had written about it so many times and documented its progress from concept to work of art and piece of history. He just wanted me to be there.

"Normally this kind of request would leave me conflicted," I stated in the article I decided to write about it after all. "I am supposed to be an observer, a reporter of stories. But this story has been a special one for me. I wanted to witness this part of it."

At the Big House, warmed by the fire blazing in the centre of the large room, beautiful carvings around it and Indigenous people in ceremonial dress, we were told that we weren't there just to witness the event, but that we were becoming traditional witnesses. With our presence came a responsibility—as legal witnesses and as story-keepers.

"Now there's a whole bunch more of us who carry that responsibility for making good decisions on behalf of the Blanket and the stories it carries," Newman told me after the hours-long ceremony.

Once the handover was complete, everyone in attendance was called down to dance on the earthen floor around the fire. I hesitated. This was not something I normally do. I'm a reporter: I observe, I write about the story. I don't become part of it. But I stood up. I thought: *No, today I'm more than an observer. I'm a witness.* And I made my way down to the floor and I danced. I moved around the fire, fuelled by joy and responsibility. It is a beautiful weight to carry.

In a documentary about the March of the Living, Holocaust survivor Judy Cohen—the woman I had interviewed for my radio series—tells the teenagers on her bus at the beginning of their trip: "As soon as you listen to a witness, you're a witness too."

And now, reading about this, you are too.

I have written this chapter with the permission of Carey Newman and his family.

As I say, this is not my story to tell. But it is my story to learn. We all have a responsibility to know what happened, what continues to happen, and to make it right, to whatever extent we can. Truth. Reconciliation.

ELEVEN

Zahor

WHEN YOU OWE YOUR very existence to the actions of the people honoured on a particular holiday, you take that day seriously. I owe my life to Canadian and Allied soldiers, so Remembrance Day is more than a day off work, more than a minute of silence at 11 a.m., more than a plastic poppy worn on my lapel.

I had taken Jacob to the November 11 ceremony at the cenotaph pretty much every year of his life. I had explained to him, age-appropriately, how important this day was—that these former soldiers had fought for my parents' freedom and so we had to thank them.

Then came the first year since the family had broken apart that Remembrance Day fell on a Sunday. It was the third Remembrance Day since Jacob's dad had moved out. Jacob, who spent Saturday nights and Sundays with his father, would be with his dad and brother and sister, and I would be on my own. I still needed to pay my respects, and I planned to walk to the cenotaph by myself to do so.

But I couldn't. I couldn't face the families together, the children, the couples, I couldn't do it. And so it happened that at 11 a.m. on that Remembrance Day I was in the shower listening to the ceremony on the radio, feeling terrible about letting my little heartbreak and narcissistic self-consciousness stop me from doing the right thing and being where I should have been. And I thought: I'm in a shower. I can do something while I'm here.

I turned the nozzle all the way to the right. Cold water. Not gas, but freezing. I let it spray over me. For a minute, an entire minute, only a minute, a long minute. And I was frozen and crying and remembering and imagining.

What was it like to be in a gas chamber, where most of my family had been murdered?

Now a whole other chunk of my family, my immediate family, was gone. It's not even close to a comparable loss. But here I was, comparing. Because this rupture was so real to me, so awful, so personal. This family, mine, was no longer here. They were at the cenotaph together. I was alone in the shower.

Everything was cold and dark. I could not drag myself back from that place—the floor of the tub, the not-cenotaph, the fear and sorrow that came from being without the family I thought I had built for life.

I like to say the key to happiness is low expectations—expect the worst and even something a little less than the worst will feel like a win. I wonder if, in my case, there's more to this pessimism-as-defence-mechanism. I have often thought about the detail of my grandparents not leaving Poland for Palestine, with those visas in hand. The more stories about this time in history I read, the more I understand that those who responded to the dire warnings of what was to come—even if they seemed ludicrous—were the ones who got out and survived. Believing the worst, and acting on it, became an act of survival. I wonder if this might be at the heart of my well-honed pessimism. If so, its roots were deep. Cultivating a happier existence would be a challenge.

When I got married, I forgot about this method of self-protection. I, for the first time, had expected, really expected, the best. I had let my defences down. And look what happened.

...

It was the milestones I dreaded the most. My fiftieth birthday had been spent at a bright, loud Italian restaurant with my whole family— husband, stepchildren, child. It was a bright summer evening and I was still in the dark, my husband keeping radio silence about the future. He remained at an Airbnb, four months after he took refuge there, but he still hadn't told me he wasn't coming home. That was the worst time: when I still had hope.

Happy occasions were less happy. World tragedies felt lonelier— as I communed with strangers on Twitter rather than with a partner on the couch next to me. Denial no longer an option, I got down to some practical business around the house.

Late that fall, I took the closet that had been my husband's, empty now of his suits and ties, and made it the home for my off-season clothing: flowy skirts, silky cardigans for summer evenings when a chill takes hold. Hidden behind them lived a repository. All the happy family photos I had taken down from the wall, the bag of wedding photos I had never gotten around to placing in an album, the CD-ROM with the originals—I stuffed them all at the back, a museum behind a pile of sandals.

Photographs were so hard—the ones that had been on the walls, the ones still on my phone. It wasn't the pictures of us as a big, happy (or so I had thought) family that stung—primarily because I avoided those at all costs. The impossible photos were the ones from the two horrible years: the year that my husband had disappeared inside the house, and the year that he left it.

Separate, we were still connected. I would drop off the car in the morning for him at work—we still shared a car, evidence of not just a mostly co-operative situation but more to the point, a mutual financial desperation, also caused by the split—and park it at the meter next to a billboard featuring a large picture of his face, advertising his radio show.

We shared more than a car, of course.

Years into this, the first Christmas that our son would spend with his dad, and not me, I volunteered to work at the newspaper. I would write about fires or some other yuletide tragedy while my son opened presents and ate turkey and stuffing with my former stepchildren, my former husband and his new (although by this point, she was hardly new) girlfriend.

I know, I'm Jewish; I don't celebrate Christmas—so what's the big deal? But this happy-families-in-matching-robes-around-the-fireplace holiday felt particularly hard to face alone. Even after all this time.

But then, I started to get mad. At myself. Enough already. And then I thought: if time wasn't doing its job, some perspective might help. I thought this was bad? A billboard ad? A missed turkey dinner? This was nothing. Think about what my parents had gone through.

This go-to self-scold, which may have messed me up in my formative years, brought me some hope during this mid-life misery—misery that I knew was itself a luxury. If I immersed myself in some real tragedy, perhaps I would, as my ex-husband suggested during some of our more heated exchanges, get a grip.

My big idea on how to get a grip was to start reading about the Holocaust again.

I was so desperate to think about something else, to find answers that might help me figure out what had gone wrong with me—and also to recognize the real tragedies that had befallen my family—that I forced myself to return to it.

Maybe in my desperation to deny what was right in front of me—the dissolution of my life as I knew it—I needed to go back to something in my past, or past my past. Something much worse, and undeniable. It was a punishing way to seek perspective.

I returned to my Holocaust reading with a vengeance, as the saying goes. But it wasn't vengeance I was after. It was that perspective. Information. Comfort. Comfort? I don't know. I wanted my parents; I had never needed my mother's love or my father's strength and protection more. This was the closest I could come, I figured, to accessing it.

It may have also been the increasing awareness of my mortality that drew me back to the dark world of my pre-past, a need to figure things out before I departed—a departure that would be much calmer and more civilized, I imagined, than the terror-soaked exits my grandparents had to endure. I was in my fifties and started to think of my life as beginning to wrap up; everything was heading toward that end, far too soon. I went on my first post-separation date and told the guy I figured I had maybe twenty Christmases left. There was no second date.

Piles of these books sprouted all over my bedroom. Where there had once been love, there were now little stacks of destruction. Annihilation, everywhere. Whatever I needed to remind myself of the real tragedy of my life and rustle up some perspective. I read history books; memoirs written by survivors, including friends of my parents; books by descendants of survivors, who, like me, were trying to piece together the horror that had come before them. I read about intergenerational trauma. In so many of these books, I found little bits of myself, passages that jumped off the page like a mirror and a warning.

I was alone, but I wasn't alone.

My Sundays were spent with these books, with horrifying descriptions of things that could have happened to me. Jacob would come home at the end of his day with his dad and I would hug him extra hard, haunted by what I had read while he was off with the family that used to be mine too. I would present as elaborate a dinner as I could manage; I was teaching myself to cook.

I was also thinking about trying something else: writing. Writing this all down. To have a record of what my family survived—or didn't—might bring me closer to them, I thought. It could help me in other ways, too, to organize all of these thoughts. Maybe, I was starting to think, it could one day help someone else. I can't be the only one. Alone, but not alone.

In the midst of my personal crisis, I sought connection by reading about other separations—not comfortable modern-day divorces with lawyers and custody arrangements, but separations of the truly devastating sort: children ripped from mothers' arms kind of separations, men and women sent separately to the gas chambers kind of separations, like what my family had experienced, or may have experienced. So I spent the years after my husband moved out reading World War II memoirs and history books, spending long sleepless nights watching Holocaust documentaries.

I understand how bizarre this sounds—that to try to soothe my broken heart, I made the decision to read about these most grisly of events. But the truth is, I was trying to find some way to connect to the family I had lost. The ones I hadn't known, sure—but mostly my parents, whom I missed desperately.

The piles of Holocaust books in my bedroom grew, and so did the list of horrors I read about. They defied belief. I don't know what I was thinking. I wasn't really thinking. I was too busy feeling sorry for myself.

I read about horrors that were on par with the babies and the bayonets. An Austrian man fighting for the Germans described for his wife infants flying in great arcs through the air, the soldiers shooting them to pieces in flight, their bodies falling into a watery pit.

A group of soldiers at Auschwitz tying a thirteen-year-old boy to a tree, using him as target practice. They shot his arms, leg, foot, an ear. Also at Auschwitz, a woman in labour had her legs tied together by a group of soldiers. They would not untie them. She screamed in agony.

Naked Jews in the middle of countless forests, forced to lie facedown in slave-dug pits or at the edges and shot in the head or neck point-blank; dogs used to tear at Jewish throats. One perpetrator described executions where victims' brains would splatter onto his face.

Hundreds of Jews forced into a Catholic community centre in Bolechow, in what is now Ukraine, where for a day and a half they were tortured, humiliated. The guards forced the Jews to stand on each other's shoulders, like a human pyramid, with an old rabbi on top, then knocked him down. The Jews were forced to sit on hot stoves. People were shot. A rabbi had his eyes gouged out and a cross carved into his chest. He was forced to dance with a young girl, a teenager, both naked, while another person was forced to play jaunty music on the church piano.

Again in Bolechow—and also from Daniel Mendelsohn's book *The Lost*—German and Ukrainian soldiers throwing children out the windows of a building where they would land on the pavement, or taking children by their legs and bashing their heads on the edge of the sidewalks. Laughing, they made a game of it: trying to see if they could kill the kids with one blow.

Ivan the Terrible—a guard at Treblinka—would carry a sword and torture the Jews, naked and going to their gas chamber deaths, by stabbing at them, or cutting off pieces of their bodies: ears, breasts. He would stab pregnant women in the belly. One girl, about twelve years old, ran from the gas chamber crying "I want my mommy," and Ivan—there has to be a better word than Terrible for him—shot her, sending her body into a pit.

A woman from a town near Minsk saw a German soldier walking with a one-year-old baby impaled on his bayonet. She recalled that the baby was still crying weakly. And the German was singing.

At times, reading these details, I had to force myself to look up from my computer screen and out the window, to remind myself that I was free in Vancouver. Where in the winter, the maple tree in front of my house—the one that was planted when my husband still lived here—had lost its leaves, allowing me to catch a glimpse, on a clear day, of the mountains.

It had been years since the bayonet practice scene had sent me, then a new mother, running from my Holocaust obsession. I was now the mother of an almost-adolescent. He had survived this long without having his baby brain bashed against a sidewalk or his little chest pierced by a bayonet. An ordinary story. A miracle.

And didn't that miracle deserve to be written about? After all, my generation's story could be examined as "a strong case study in the deep and long-lasting impact of atrocity," as Eva Hoffman put it in one of the books I consumed, *After Such Knowledge: Memory, History and the Legacy of the Holocaust*. Not just the Holocaust, but every other mass trauma I had been thinking about. And so many others to come, or happening right now—Syrians, women under Taliban rule in Afghanistan, Uighurs in China, climate refugees.

From Hoffman's book I found a new way to consider those revenge fantasies I had when I was younger, where I imagined being left alone in a cell with a concentration camp guard. To torture him slowly to near-death. To leave him debilitated and alone in that cell for the rest of his life, his family shamed by his actions. I wanted him to be very, very thirsty.

I am embarrassed about these thoughts now and no longer think about doing such a thing. But I admit my desire for revenge was deeply satisfied by a story Hoffman shared in her book about the death of a former Gestapo official at a British nursing home. The death was terrible, a nurse had told her. Because the old SS guy realized there was either no afterlife—a terrifying thought—or that there *was* an afterlife: an even more terrifying thought for an old Nazi. I felt some gratification reading this, contemplating that sort of terrorizing end for those war criminals who got away with murder in this lifetime. Who got to die comfortably in an old folks' home.

But there was something else. In her book, Hoffman has a message for anyone who wants to write about the Holocaust—something I was thinking very seriously about doing. "One had better approach this theme with utmost intelligence and a sense of imaginative responsibility," she wrote. My ambitions, developing this whole time, to write this all down became quiet at that moment—my plans intimidated not only by this justified warning, but also by Hoffman's own beautiful writing. What else was there to say?

...

Something that felt like a bit of a relief: the trauma I grew up with was normal under the circumstances. I read repeatedly that being adversely affected by the Holocaust should be considered the standard. How could it be otherwise?

Auschwitz survivor, psychiatrist and author Viktor Frankl wrote that an "abnormal reaction to an abnormal situation is normal behaviour."

Elie Wiesel, in that speech he gave to that 1984 conference of children of survivors, noted that the great majority of the second generation remained healthy and generous, with a sense of humour, culture and humanity. "That you are so well-adjusted seems almost abnormal."

Too bad he didn't meet me, I thought to myself when I read this.

Auschwitz survivor, psychologist and author Edith Eva Eger objects to the use of the term "disorder" in relation to post-traumatic stress. "It's not a disordered reaction to trauma," she wrote in her book *The Choice: Embrace the Possible*. "It's a common and natural one." She recognized, years after her own trauma, that she wasn't a damaged person, but was suffering the fallout of an interrupted life.

As her sister said to her during a post-liberation conversation Eger recounts in her book: "One thing's true: Hitler fucked us up for sure."

So how much did Hitler fuck me up, one generation later?

I didn't put it exactly that way when I reached out to some of the experts in this field, but I did have many questions for them. About transmission of Holocaust trauma, about epigenetics, about scientific findings related to intergenerational trauma, about intergenerational trauma and me.

"I feel like I have no resilience, that I want to crumble. I think if it were me in the war, I would not have survived; no way," I told Robert Krell, the Vancouver psychiatrist and child survivor, during one of our conversations.

"Perhaps if they"—the survivors—"heard such stories, they might have felt like giving up. But once exposed to it, they somehow found a reservoir of resilience," he answered, after a thoughtful pause. "We actually don't know what we have in our reserves. I agree with you. If that were me, I don't think I would last another day."

He told me that one of the most common things he heard from survivors with deep depression was: *Doctor, can you take away the memories? I don't want to think about this; it's a torment.* And he would respond by telling them: *No, I'm going to help you keep your memories.*

"The reason I took that approach," he explained to me, "was whatever memories lingered in a survivor, probably the most important one was the parting from a family member, a mother or father, and that would have been the last time that they saw them." It was the worst moment, he said, but still a crucial moment that leaves an image of the parents, to be treasured.

At this point in the conversation, I was immediately transported to the Toronto airport, saying good-bye to my father on July 11, 1984, as he headed to Sweden. Then I was in that same airport, more than twenty years later, walking with my mother, trying to find the right check-in counter for her flight to Miami.

When I spoke to Eva Fogelman, she told me that any kind of separation can be excruciating for some survivors. "Because separation in the family very often meant death," she said. "Someone would go to the store to get bread for the family and they would come back and the family was deported. Or someone went to get bread and never returned. Separations have triggers that evoke post-traumatic stress disorder."

All this time I have been so focused on what my parents' unexpected deaths, while on separate trips, had done to me. And now I wondered, belatedly: What had those good-byes felt like for them? Did they have a flash of a thought, in their final moments—my father in a Swedish hospital, my mother in a Florida condo—*I knew it; I knew I would never see Marsha again.*

I asked Natan Kellermann whether my father's death—so unexpected while on an overseas trip four days after my eighteenth birthday—could have triggered some sort of episode of Holocaust trauma transmission.

That was its own trauma, he told me.

The death of anyone's parent, unexpected like that, at a young age—was a trauma, period. It didn't matter that my parents had survived the Holocaust and the fallout from that lives on in me in some way. My father's death on its own was traumatic for me. I don't know why, but hearing that from an expert was somehow comforting. Anyone would have been messed up after this event. Gone on to date the wrong kind of men, to not achieve her potential, at least for a little while, because she was just so devastated.

Not all of what I read and heard in my quest was comforting. A lot of it—like what those good-byes must have felt like for my parents—was difficult to contemplate. Or any kind of pain my parents might have experienced—as if they needed more suffering.

"You heard your mother make light of Auschwitz and the death march," Robert Krell said to me, remembering what I had told him about my mother's Shoah Foundation interview: her lack of details, her little jokes. "But you cannot think for one moment that it was not uppermost in her mind every day of her post-war life. It was there every day of her post-war life. Because we hear trains and hear whistles and hear dogs barking in the neighbourhood and we watch the news. And there was no survivor who could get through a half-hour of news and not think of where he or she was."

Listening to this man, talking to him, reading his work, I have thought so many times: if only I had had a Robert Krell to help me when I really needed it. It never takes me long to leap to my next thought: I think I still really need it.

...

I asked my experts about common psychological problems or personality traits in the second generation. I heard a lot about problems with separation-individuation, which I had to look up. There is a normal developmental stage early in life where a child achieves independence while also feeling securely attached to the caregiver—especially the mother. When a traumatized parent clings to their child for fear of that child's safety, this is problematic. Because the child needs to form a separate and positive self-image from the parent. And some parents have trouble understanding the child's needs as a separate human being. Difficult emotions feel catastrophic for the survivor parent. This can lead to separation anxiety, especially in female children of survivors. Hello.

I heard about difficulties dealing with any sort of violence, feeling easily guilty (the parents suffered guilt and used it in the upbringing of children), an abundance of ambition, anxiety, hypervigilance—after growing up with parents who constantly warned them about danger. One characteristic listed by Zahava Solomon, who had found impacts of the Holocaust in Israeli soldier-children of survivors, really hit home: "A narcissistic vulnerability—the fact that life is very fragile."

I asked Solomon about separations—the sudden deaths of my parents on trips, the end of my marriage. Could these events have awakened my silent inheritance, the intergenerational trauma?

"Every trauma can actually cause reactivation of previous traumas, even if they're second-hand," she told me. "But if the current trauma bears a lot of resemblance, is reminiscent of the original trauma, then its capacity to ignite or reactivate the previous trauma clearly increases." So war, or a life-threatening disease.

Or separation from a loved one.

"The Holocaust is related to a lot of losses and separation, and many of the stories that Holocaust survivor parents were telling their children is how they separated from their loved ones. So obviously that's related," she said.

And with parents who are overprotective because they fear losing their loved ones once again, separation anxiety can be easily reawakened, she told me.

But a divorce? Or separation?

"Definitely, definitely," she said. "Because there is separation anxiety. You feel that if you separate from loved ones, your whole world collapses.

"Because what actually kept people going [in the Holocaust], a lot of them, was their loved ones," she continued. "And once this is gone, there isn't any hope for anything else." My mother and Auntie Ella.

"Divorce or the death of a loved one, any separation, it is seen as a major tragedy, and people feel that they are unable to survive at times. So they're actually flooded with anxiety. Definitely divorce and death of a loved one is seen as sort of the end of the world. Whereas other people say it's a very tragic experience, some people might even say it's for the best, where for us, it's inconceivable to say that."

Losing a loved one is a universal, devastating experience. But it can somehow be even more difficult and triggering for a Holocaust survivor, for their children.

...

I had never considered not having children because I was worried I might pass on this terrible legacy to them. I guess I didn't understand that I could be passing it on until it was too late. Not that that would have changed a thing. My biggest fear was not being able to have a child at all. Jacob was my miracle.

Rachel and Doris each have three children, and at the moment I'm writing this they have nine grandchildren between them—and likely more to come.

They are our greatest gifts to the ancestors who could never meet them, who maybe in their last moments ached with the knowledge that there would be no more Lindzens, no more Ledermans.

Both of my sisters married in the 1970s, before it was common for women to keep their last names. Rachel became a Brass; Doris, a Schulman. That made me the last person with my father's last name in the family tree that stretched far back into the 1800s, and of course, beyond that. This had been a source of huge disappointment for my father. When I became pregnant, my husband and I instinctively agreed—I think it was his idea, in fact—that our child take my last name, so it could live on. I would not be the last Lederman.

...

My family continues to grow. Rachel and Jack's children, Howard, Laura and Eric, are all married and have kids. When Doris's daughter Melissa married Joe in 2013, Jacob was a ring-bearer. They live in Vancouver now and one of the most important people in his world is their daughter, Adelaide.

In 2019, there were two more big weddings: Jacqueline, Doris's daughter—who was named after our father—married Jesse. Earlier that year, Doris's son Rafael—named for our mother's father—married Michelle.

I guess I could have looked at all these happy couples and felt sorry for my sad, divorced self, but I didn't. I was ecstatic. I felt excited for them, for our family, for possibility. Theirs, even mine. Miracles happen. In each of the crazy horas at those two Toronto weddings, I felt like I was in the middle of one. A miracle.

Jacqueline and Jesse—doctors who met at medical school in Israel—got married on a very hot August day. Nobody would know it then, but it would be the last time in, well, who knows how long, as I write this in the middle of a pandemic, that we would all be together.

Jacob and I had made a summer vacation of it, staying at Rachel and Jack's large home, swimming in their pool, visiting Canada's Wonderland one too many times.

Rachel and I also used the time to catch up on the family research she had been doing. One morning, sitting in the library of her house—photos of Moshe Rafael and Rachel Lindzen, Devorah Lederman and Moshe Aron Lederman on the walls around us—we were going through a file folder of documents and notes Rachel had taken.

We came to a sheet of paper on which Rachel had typed up notes about my mother's aunt Raisel—Doda Rushka, as we had called her. This is the woman who survived Auschwitz with my mother and Ella, who was liberated with them on April 1, 1945, in Kaunitz, Germany. The youngest sibling of my mother's mother, the Zweigenberg (however you might spell it) clan in Radom. The only person on either side of my family of that generation to survive the war. The closest thing

I had to a grandmother. My grandmother's sister—short, stooped, extremely loving.

She had moved to Israel after the war, so I rarely saw her. But when I did, I experienced the kind of love I think I would have received from a grandmother, even when I was a snotty teenager and didn't show her the respect she deserved.

She had two children of her own—Miriam and Yakov, who among them have six children—and a growing brood of grandchildren. And because of Doda Rushka and her husband, Tzvee, Doris had met her husband, Sam.

So many children and grandchildren and beyond because that woman survived.

Miriam happened to be in the house while Rachel and I were reading this material; she and her husband, Haim, had travelled to Toronto for the wedding and were also staying with Rachel. It was great fun, this summer family reunion. I hadn't seen them in close to a decade, and yet they felt like they always did, family. The descendants of the survivors.

Miriam's mother, Raisel, we learned from that piece of paper, had suffered another tragedy in her life.

This note we found—it had come from a story our mother's friend Fela, also a survivor from Radom, told Rachel—revealed a huge family drama. Raisel's first boyfriend, name unknown, had left her the night before their wedding. "Doda was very, very upset," Fela recounted.

This was a shock; I knew nothing about this story. Even Rachel, who had written it down, didn't remember it.

Outside the library in the hallway, we could hear the beep of the front door opening—Miriam and Haim were leaving for a day of Toronto sight-seeing. Rachel and I bolted out to them, holding the piece of paper.

Miriam, did you know about this? We read the passage to her.

No, no. She was shocked.

I thought: *It must have seemed like the worst thing in the world for Raisel to be left at the altar.* Hard to imagine the heartbreak, the shame, the bleak prospects for someone in that era after such an experience. But that personal tragedy had set her on some other path, one that allowed her, miraculously, to survive the war. The only sibling among six—maybe it was even more—to live. If that guy had married her, she likely would have had children, she would have lived elsewhere, who knows what would have happened to her. They might have all ended up in the gas chamber. *Sometimes the worst thing can turn out to be the best thing*, I told myself. *Even if you can't recognize it at the time.*

...

With so many vanished family members, we were always on the lookout for possible relatives. At various points, we had hired private detectives to try to find my mother's older brother, Yankel Yosef, the one who had sought a more progressive life outside of his Orthodox family, away from Poland, in Palestine. The one who had sent post-cards from Yugoslavia and maybe Palestine too. The one who might still be alive.

The detectives we hired found nothing. But with no definitive result, we were allowed to hold on to a crumb of hope. We did not know for sure that he was dead. We knew almost nothing for sure about him, period. Imagine: there could be a whole other set of our family—an uncle and cousins, living who knows where. Israel, probably. But anything was possible. Maybe they lived down the street.

Yankel Yosef—separated from his family of origin by his own deci-sion, on his own terms—was our greatest hope. But there were so many other missing people—aunts, uncles, cousins—dozens of them, probably, who had gone up in smoke. We didn't know how many there had been. We did not know for sure what had happened to them. Had some cousin escaped? Or somehow, like our mother, survived the whole long hell of imprisonment? In the post-war chaos, with barriers of language, geography—and trauma—maybe they were never able to connect. We would get very excited when we came across anyone with the last name Lederman or Lindzen.

The more we knew about what had happened to our parents, the more ammunition we had for our search. The odds were long, but the stakes felt high. Imagine.

...

In the period after my mother died, in January 2006, we all reached out as often as we could to Auntie Ella. Before she moved to assisted living, she and her husband, Uncle Kuba, lived in a condo in North Toronto, across the street from our mother's condo, where my sisters and I spent weekends going through her things, dividing treasures up. When I made my first choice, it was a *Mona Lisa* print—made to look like a painting, complete with golden frame—that my parents had bought on their first trip to Paris in 1976.

(Back when we were shitty teenagers, a friend of mine, poking fun at my parents, asked them if it was the original *Mona Lisa*. My father deadpanned in his accented English: "It's an original reproduction." That story is part of why I love that *Mona Lisa* so much. If you come over, you'll see it hanging in my home.)

One evening, Rachel made a routine phone call to Auntie Ella to check in. Ella said she was very busy watching *Larry King Live*. She told Rachel to turn it on, that it was extremely important, and that they should talk afterward.

Rachel clicked on CNN and saw that Larry King was having a panel discussion about climate change. What the heck, Rachel thought. Had Auntie Ella become passionate about global warming? It didn't track.

Until one particular panelist started speaking, and Rachel understood what Ella had been on about. This man was identified onscreen as a professor named Richard Lindzen.

Rachel called Ella right after the show. CNN still blaring in the background, Ella was agitated and excited. "He looks just like my father," she told Rachel. "This has to be my nephew."

Richard Lindzen was the Alfred P. Sloan Professor of Meteorology at the Massachusetts Institute of Technology, a Harvard graduate with a PhD in physics. He was also, at the time, one of the world's most renowned climate change skeptics.

Rachel and Jack, on a trip to Boston a few years later, met Richard Lindzen for dinner. All sorts of commonalities emerged. And clues.

Richard Lindzen had been born in 1940 in the U.S.; his parents had come to America before the war. He was their only surviving child.

They had come—boom!—from Radom, the same city as my mother. Even more of a boom, his father had been born in Jedlinsk, where my mother's father, Moshe Rafael Lindzen, had been born. Jedlinsk was a shtetl—a small village—near Radom. According to Auntie Ella, all the Lindzens from Jedlinsk were related. "It's one big family," she used to say.

There was also the fact that Richard's Hebrew name was Rachmiel, the same name as Gitla and Ella's little brother, who had used his Gentile looks to escape from the ghetto on the regular and trade family treasures for bread. The one who would not go live with the violin-playing neighbour. The boy who died in the gas chamber at Treblinka, when he was eleven or thirteen.

In Jewish tradition, we name people after dead family members. Was Richard Lindzen named after the same dead ancestor as this uncle we had never met? Some previous Rachmiel who had been born in and perhaps died in Jedlinsk?

There was also his appearance—what Ella was sure was a family resemblance.

We never hit the we're-related jackpot with Richard Lindzen, an absolute certain connection. But he became part of our extended family nonetheless, invited to family celebrations, with both Doris and Rachel keeping in touch with him.

I met him for the first time when he travelled from Boston to Toronto for Jacqueline's wedding. Richard was lovely. (I was careful not to bring up the topic of climate change.) It was nice to have another member of the family, even if our world views differed so greatly, even if our connection was only a maybe.

Around that same time, after the two weddings were in the books, Doris unearthed that long letter from Roza—we called her our aunt, but she was actually my father's first cousin; when you have so little family, everyone becomes an aunt or uncle. This was the emotional letter where she answered Doris's questions about our father's family. In that letter, Roza revealed how she, by accident, met up with "your so dear Father!!!" after the war. These were difficult details to read—all these sad experiences, all of these beautiful people, gone. But the way she ended it hurt me in a different way. "Thank God you have a good nice husband and beautiful children."

I did not have a good, nice husband anymore, I thought. It still, always, came down to that. I was getting so sick of myself.

All of this—the research, the stories I had never heard (my great-aunt, ditched at the altar!) and the ones I had (the Italian man calling my mother *bella*, my father and the gold watch)—made me feel something nothing else did. And they served as a reminder of all I had. And the reason I had wanted to get into the business of telling stories to begin with. My obligation, the one that had been denied to my grand-parents and parents. There are horrors all around us and yet descendants of survivors like myself with our "never agains" and "never forgets" were standing by, allowing other atrocities to occur.

Those who cannot remember the past are condemned to repeat it.

It was so hard writing these things down, but it was also fulfilling in a way. It was fulfilling the obligation I was born with.

The obligation to remember. In Hebrew, *Zahor*. I have the obligation to remember and to tell.

...

You have probably heard that soldiers dying on the battlefields often cry out for their mothers. Still wounded years after the death of my marriage, I was enacting a version of that. I missed my mom.

Pearl—of the normal childhood down the street—recommended a book to me, written by someone she said reminded her of my mother: *The Choice: Embrace the Possible*, by Edith Eva Eger.

I was half a page in when I knew this was going to be an important book for me. Not because the woman who wrote it reminded me of my mother, but because of the point she was making.

Eger, an Auschwitz survivor whose parents were murdered by the Nazis, became a psychologist after immigrating to the U.S. If anyone knew trauma, it was her.

In 1944, when she arrived at the concentration camp with her mother and one of her sisters, Magda, a guard asked Edith, pointing to her mother: is this your sister or your mother? Edith, sixteen, answered truthfully. Her mother was then separated from her daughters, sent to the line that went straight to the gas chambers. Edith would have had no way of knowing the consequences of answering this basic question honestly. But the moment haunted her. She blamed herself.

And yet, in spite of everything she has suffered, Eger preaches and maintains a remarkably positive outlook on life. "Freedom lies in learning to embrace what happened," she writes.

Her hard-earned beliefs come out of her own experiences, but I understood that they applied to my experiences now too. That was the intention of her project—her book, her life.

Eger would have been in Auschwitz at the same time as my mother, so reading the details of her story, just as I was finally trying to map out my mother's, was particularly excruciating. Like when she wrote of something my mother had also spoken of: the six women to a bunk, how if one woman needed to move it became a domino negotiation with the entire group. What it was like to wait for hours upon arrival, not knowing what was happening. The ill-fitting clothing.

It was also agonizing when Eger wrote of something I had not known about that my mother may also have experienced, something she had never told me. During that long wait after arriving at Auschwitz and being sent in the direction of life—they were naked, Eger wrote. I don't recall my mother ever telling me that. Had she still, all those years later, felt the humiliation; did the shame silence her?

At Auschwitz, Eger wrote, prisoners were forced to donate their blood for transfusions for wounded German soldiers. Did my mother have to do that as well? I think for a moment about how I always feel faint (and have actually fainted) when I have a blood test. Under the best of circumstances—in a comfortable medical lab, after having eaten well, slept well. Not dragging boulders around.

When I have my blood taken these days, I feel vulnerable and sad. Who will pick me up if something goes wrong? And if they find something wrong in my blood, who will take care of me, now that I'm alone in the world?

In *The Choice*, Eger also wrote about her sister and her having their heads shaved. My mother and Ella had laughed. Edith and Magda had had a different sort of exchange. Magda asked Edith how she looked; she asked her to tell the truth. Magda looked like "a mangy dog," Edith recounts thinking, but the answer she gave out loud focused on Magda's beautiful eyes—so much more noticeable now that they were no longer covered up by all that hair. "It's the first time I see that we have a choice: to pay attention to what we've lost or to pay attention to what we still have," Eger wrote.

My mother was long gone, but Eger's words were coming to my rescue. "Suffering is universal," she wrote. "But victimhood is optional."

I recognized myself in her description of a victim's mind—"a way of thinking and being that is rigid, blaming, pessimistic, stuck in the past, unforgiving, punitive, and without healthy limits or boundaries. We become our own jailors when we choose the confines of the victim's mind."

This is a woman who had survived Auschwitz. And yet I was reading this stuff thinking about my silly little divorce. I hated myself for this.

But Eger would not have hated me for it. That in fact was the point of the book. Eger emphasized that there is no hierarchy of suffering—that just because I wasn't imprisoned in Auschwitz didn't mean that the pain of my heartbreak wasn't legitimate.

"I would love to help you discover how to escape the concentration camp of your own mind and become the person you were meant to be," she wrote.

Okay, even if my suffering was justified, her wisdom taught me that I was not justified in how I had shaped my life around it.

"We cannot choose to have a life free of hurt," she wrote. "But we can choose to be free, to escape the past, no matter what befalls us, and to embrace the possible. I invite you to make the choice to be free."

Remembering is important. But we can't live there.

PART THREE

Home

TWELVE

Going Home

IT IS ONE OF the many burdens of losing a parent early that we are too young to appreciate them as a human being until it is too late to express those feelings—to even realize them. And to ask the right questions.

I did not think of my father as a courageous, cunning survivor who had outwitted the Nazis and disguised himself from the world, even the people with whom he lived so intimately, and managed to start again in a new country and a new language—starting again being an astonishing feat of courage in and of itself.

I thought of him as a too-old dad with a thick accent, driving an embarrassing car, who didn't like me very much. (He really didn't. I wouldn't have then, either.)

I did not think of the courage it took, I wouldn't have understood it then, for him to travel back to Poland and Germany on his own, in 1979—his first trip back to the country of his birth and enslavement and the country of his escape and rebirth. I understand the compulsion to return, but I'm not sure what exactly he was looking for. He had no reason to suspect any family members were alive and living quiet lives in Poland—although maybe he dreamed of this. In Germany, however, there was the farm and the farmer, my father's second family.

My father hadn't returned to Lodz after the war; he felt there was no point, I guess. Or maybe it was too difficult to try. Or perhaps, like Freda, he had heard about the pogroms elsewhere in Poland, where Jews who had miraculously survived the war were then murdered by their former neighbours—not Germans, but Poles.

But in 1979, he felt he was ready to go back. Poland was behind the Iron Curtain then. The war was still in living memory—closer in years then than my father's trip back there is to me now, as I write this.

And Poland was still the place my parents referred to as home. When they talked about something happening "at home" I understood this home to be Radom or Lodz, not our suburban Toronto bungalow. How they could still call it home after what they had been through, after the people they had lived among had turned on them, was astonishing to me. No, "astonishing" is the wrong word, because that would suggest I gave it a lot of thought. I guess it just seemed a little weird.

This—1979—was before the March of the Living educational program began taking students to Poland, before packaged roots tours to Eastern Europe tailored for survivors and their descendants became ubiquitous. This was before international travel in general was common, affordable, almost taken for granted. This was before it would have been an easy trip to take, even if you discounted the difficult subject matter.

"My trip to the past ..." my father titled the journal he kept in a little green notebook. We found it among his things after my mother died.

According to the journal, he arrived in Frankfurt on Monday, September 3 at 5 p.m. He reports details such as the cost of a burger ($2), a hotel room ($120–$180 a day, which seems astronomical for the time) and a pair of decent pants on display in the window ($70–$80—again, astronomical). Could he have been confusing Deutschmarks for dollars?

Among the many things that stood out for me as an adult reading this document were sentences like "Making plans for tomorrow and thinking of the fine home I have far away ..."

That little bungalow, the one I had disdained and wished to be rescued from—that house was an impossibility for my father, a surprising and regal outcome, that little patch of suburban land where we got to live. Imagine how it would have compared to what he had had in Poland—even before the ghetto. Our modern washrooms, the kitchen with its many cabinets, the large veranda where we sat in the summer on little chairs, munching fresh fruit. This was a happy twist of an ending for him, inconceivable when he was growing up in Lodz.

In his journal, he records his efforts to find pieces of familiarity. He is thwarted at every stop. "The same story all over, everything is different, the stores I used to deal disappeared, owners dead," he writes about Gutersloh, Germany. "I walk the streets with familiar names," he continues, "but very strange." There's no longer a train to Kaunitz, he notes. Only buses.

"Nobody remembers in Kaunitz anymore about 1945, no trace of anything of those exciting years is left, disgusted with that peace and beauty. I went and found the place among those trees where all the Jewish women were sitting on April 1, 1945. This is still here!"

I kept stumbling over that word "disgusted." Was he disgusted that everything just went on, that people were simply living their lives, when this country had wrought such devastation—in general and to his own family? That with the peace and beauty, this history was erased, replaced with a pretty little village?

On September 6, 1979, my father got a ride to Verlar and walked two kilometres to the farm where he worked during the war.

He approached on foot from the nearby village. Hubert, one of the farmer's sons, threw down his pitchfork and yelled "Tadek?!" They ran to each other and were in each other's arms, crying.

The farmer who had employed my father in 1942, Bernhard, had died in 1968 (my father referred to him as "my farmer" in his diary). Bernhard's wife, Katharina, was still alive. "My coming created an official holiday," my father wrote, with the whole family gathering. They ate, drank, took photos. "Walked around familiar corners, been in my room, seen the ultra modern addition for the young farmer Hubert," he wrote. Hubert now owned the farm.

Hubert's sister Mia drove my father around the area. He wrote in his diary that he saw the church "where I prayed to the Gods for my life." He also visited Bernhard's grave.

He ended that day's journal entry with this: "I had a wonderful exciting day and my motto stands again forever: I will never forget you Germany for the peace and security I found here among these fields, meadows and trees in those murderous inhuman times of the year 1942."

The next day, my father went back to Kaunitz and visited the house where he had lived with my mother, his new wife. "Everything changed a lot, but it is still a very touchy feeling to go back to those memorable, most happy times!" (He repeatedly used the word "touchy" in his entries instead of "touching," the word I think he meant.) Of all the ways I thought about my parents—as Holocaust survivors, victims, orphans, immigrants, financial failures—I hadn't really considered what they were in this time of their lives: newlyweds.

"Tired as a dog but very happy with this day!" he wrote. Even all these years later, I am moved—not just by his joy, but by the hurt I still feel that he had never expressed his emotions to me in any way. I am sure he never said "I love you" to me. Maybe it was his way of protecting me. Or himself.

On Sunday, September 9, he spent another day wandering around Bielefeld. "The Germans lead again a real 'gemutlich' happy and comfortable life again," he wrote, "like nothing would ever happened. . . . The streets extremely safe and full of life and chatter. . . ."

I looked up *gemutlich*: pleasant and cheerful. Exactly what my father was not. Because of those Germans in their cafés, or at least what their parents and grandparents had done.

It was his descriptions of his days wandering Germany—shopping, using his German again, writing postcards to Canada and Sweden—and his little lines summing up his days that touched me

the most. "Another stormy and busy day is over!" "Reading, writing &
relaxing! Easy day. . . ." "Did a lot of reading in German today, doing
very well!" This journal is the closest I have gotten to knowing my
father. And I see from it that we are alike in so many ways: he was an
observer, he was a writer, he loved to wander, he loved to wonder.

And he was funny. He writes of arriving in Warsaw and of an im-
promptu party with friends, where they complimented his "unspoiled"
Polish: ". . . excellent foods and plenty of drinks, many times to my
health (will for sure be very healthy after so many toasts)."

And, like me, he could hold a grudge. "The German graves in the
nearby cemetery are wiped out," he writes while visiting Lublin. "I am
having a bit of satisfaction!"

Though it began joyfully, my father's visit to Poland was devastating.

After a good time meeting old friends in Warsaw, he took the train
and then a taxi to Treblinka. "It was a very tragic and shattering experience," he wrote. "I walked around the death-camp for a few hours, tried
to figure out the layout and operation there. The ramp is intact, so are
some roads built by Jewish slaves. The monument and other symbols
are all very impressive, so quiet and green everywhere—so different
from those horrible times!"

This is the place where his entire family was murdered. His mother
and father, his older sister, his little brother. What was it like to take a
taxi there, and then walk the grounds, alone, on a September day?

Then he went to Lodz, to the area and house where he was born
and raised. "I am very shocked to meet some women whom I knew
before the war. Walking back and forth in very familiar places, finally
being let in by some very friendly family in the room where I was born.
I am looking around at every tiny detail, remembering where every
piece of furniture used to be, then I showed them where my sister's bed
used to stay. I am breaking together and can't talk anymore. Extremely
heartbroken I am leaving."

It was his imperfect English, but I was so moved by the way he
described how he was feeling: "breaking together."

His next stop was Piotrkow Trybunalski, where he and his family had been confined to the ghetto. "Walked for hours the familiar streets, went into the house and room where I left my family never to see them again. It was a shattering experience again."

He wrote that he learned some heartbreaking facts from the woman who lived there at the time. He provided no details.

What I know of this—and the term "heartbreaking" certainly applies—is that my father found out that his parents had left a letter for him before they were evacuated from the ghetto, expelled from the city and then, not long after, the human race. A Polish woman who lived there at the time, or moved in after the liquidation—I'm not sure which—had come into possession of that letter. There were photos in this packet, and some other family keepsakes.

The woman said she had held on to these items for a long time, but after so many years without word, she lost all hope that my father had survived; she figured nobody from the family had. She threw the packet away.

What was that like for him—to learn that his parents had left him something: a declaration of their love, a wish for his future, some unknown secret, an explanation of what was happening to them? And to learn that those things once touched and left for him by his parents—a written document, photographs, who knows what else—proof that his parents had existed, evidence of their love—had survived, only to be discarded?

That particular journal entry is one of the very few that did not end with an exclamation mark.

How on earth did that woman come to the decision to dispose of those things? To Marie Kondo this packet like it was some knick-knack that gave her no joy? How did she not at least donate that letter and those photos to a museum or send them to the Red Cross or, I don't know, ask someone with a brain for their advice about what to do with those most personal of documents, that excruciating piece of history? Exclamation mark.

My father visited the Lodz cemetery and found the grave of his grandfather, who had died in 1934. "I am the first and only one who came near this grave since 40 years," he wrote in his journal. "The grass and weeds are taller than me. The monument in perfect condition. I am realizing again the great obligation attached to me, the last one of all the family."

He wasn't the last of the family, I wish I could tell him. I am the last Lederman. Or I was. Now, it's my son, Jacob.

In the first Jacob Lederman's return to Piotrkow I read what is, to me, the most heartbreaking entry in the entire journal. "Found all mass graves, took some pictures of that tragic scene, looked with horror at that huge grave which my dear, gentle brother with sweat and blood over His face helped to dig under the inhuman rigor of the S.S." As is the practice in German—he must have been that immersed in the language while writing the diary—my father capitalized the word "His" to refer to his long-dead brother, a boy who never left Poland, who never got to become a parent, who never got to become my uncle.

"Walked from one grave to the other and said a prayer for them, because I knew very many of those young, fine men and girls, women and little kids who are buried there in those big piles," my father continued. "My trip through Poland is one big shattering experience and there is no letup."

Had my father witnessed his little brother digging this mass grave? Or had he heard about it afterward? How was it that Isaac had not ended up inside that pit with an SS bullet in his back? Did he manage to run away in the chaos? If so, his efforts were for naught; he would have made that heroic escape only to be sent to a different horrifying death, at Treblinka. At least, I tell myself, he had been with his parents and his sister in the end.

And then, it was Rosh Hashanah, 1979—or 5740 on the Hebrew calendar. The Jewish New Year. My father attended services at a synagogue in Lodz, where people looked at him, he wrote, like he would be from another planet. He couldn't stay too long, he wrote; I don't know if it was the emotion of the experience or something else that sent him from the shul. Afterward, he went to a friend's house for Rosh Hashanah dinner. They served ham.

Here's what I do remember from that trip of my father's when I was thirteen years old, back in Toronto: he came home early; it was too difficult, being there. I didn't understand at the time that the difficulty had been emotional; I pictured it being physically difficult: long empty roads, no cars to drive him, trails full of obstacles. As a souvenir, he brought me a mechanical pencil set in a black leather case that opened and closed with a mechanism made of nails. It was beautiful to look at, but I don't think I ever used it. I don't think I could figure out how. Somewhere along the line, in one of my many moves—probably the one to Vancouver, to get married—I lost it. Or Marie Kondo'd it.

Whatever happened to him in Poland must have been so emotionally harrowing that when he cut his trip short, he also gave up a chance to see Doris, who by then was living in Sweden and was planning to meet him in Poland; she had booked a ticket for a boat over to Gdansk. He called her and told her not to come; he was leaving early. Doris hardly recognized his voice. He sounded like a broken man.

This cancelled trip is why my father mentioned Doris by name in his journal. But I hadn't known that when I scoured it years after his death, hunting for any reference to me. But no, there was no mention of his youngest daughter. Just Doris.

He did refer often to our mother, with great love, which makes me so happy. Guta was waiting for him at the airport on her own, "happiness on Her face" he wrote. "We pick a 'Lincoln' for the ride home, why not the best after the hardships and dramatic sights of our former motherland."

I wanted my father to miss me too. He never did name me, but I did take heart in this: "A long and story adventure to Poland is coming to an end. I am very happy and excited about the thought that I will see Canada very soon again and all my dear ones over there," he wrote.

I like to think that I was one of his dear ones.

His journal ends with these words: "Good-bye horrible and so dear holy places of Poland. I won't forget you my dear restless souls gliding over the greenery over Treblinka. I will come back to face you again— I promise not to forget you in this Land of Peace and Plenty!"

...

Almost twenty years after my father's trip, my family and I returned to Poland. "Returned" is probably not the right word; only my mother was returning. The rest of us were going there for the first time.

Every spring since 1988, Jews from all over the world descend on Poland for the March of the Living. On Yom HaShoah, Holocaust Remembrance Day, thousands of people march the three kilometres from Auschwitz to Auschwitz II—Birkenau. In the days leading up to this, they tour Poland, taking in all the horrific sights: concentration camps, memorials to the dead, old ransacked Jewish cemeteries.

After this immersion in devastation, the participants board a plane for Israel, where a few days later they mark Israel Independence Day, the anniversary of the birth of the country that rose from the ashes of the Holocaust. After touring death site after death site, it is a powerful thing, no matter your politics.

It's an education program, aimed at high school and university students, but there are concurrent adult trips as well. In 1998, my family decided to go. I was thirty-one, still working at the radio station where I had made that documentary series.

My mother, Rachel and I, and our first cousin Roshelle, Ella's younger daughter, travelled from Toronto. Doris would meet us in Warsaw, flying in from Stockholm. My niece Laura, Rachel's daughter, was on one of the school trips.

We eased into the horror, with a posh-for-1998-Warsaw hotel, and our first stop: the vast Jewish cemetery in Warsaw. Among its countless tombstones—crooked, mossy and wayward with utter neglect and trees bursting everywhere, life among the death—we found a couple of dead Ledermans: Hersz and Franciszka. Probably not relatives, but still exciting enough to pause for a photograph.

This cemetery is one of the happier remnants of Jewish Poland; most of these people died a non-Holocaust death. They got a proper burial, with a stone, with their name on it, engraved, forever. Yes, some of these stones ended up paving roads under the German occupation. Yes, the cemetery was partly demolished during Nazi rule—and also used as a site for mass executions. Yes, the cemetery has been vandalized over the years. "Jews for slaughter" someone painted on the cemetery gate in 2015—seventy years after the end of the Second World War.

But Hersz and Franciszka Lederman and the thousands of others buried here had, for the most part (one can only imagine), experienced a better death than their descendants would. They at least got a grave all to themselves. Even if the tombstone has since tumbled down, now lies flat or leans at a forty-five-degree angle, the names and dates obscured with some detritus of nature; even if it has become part of a domino formation of forced abandonment. It is a stone, a permanent mark in a cemetery in a land that they—thank God, for them—did not live to see become one gigantic cemetery.

Fortunate was the Jewish Pole who died before the Second World War and was buried this way, with space and dignity and a stone to remember them by. There would have been no visitors for years because of the events that followed their deaths. But now here we were.

Later that day, still hazy with the overnight LOT flight, we made a pilgrimage to one of the few remaining walls of the Warsaw Ghetto and to the notorious *Umschlagplatz*, the deportation square, where more than three hundred thousand Jews were forced onto trains to the death camp Treblinka. There's a memorial there; the four hundred most common Jewish-Polish names of the time are inscribed into a wall. I saw names that both my parents went by.

What added to the shock of this place was the geography. "Right in the centre of Warsaw!" Doris recorded in her diary. She tried to picture the Jews being rounded up there to be taken to Treblinka.

It happened so very publicly. What could other people see? Did they just walk by and avert their gaze, the way we might when we encounter anything unpleasant—a couple fighting on the sidewalk? A road rage incident?

A brighter spot, if you can call it that, was the memorial to the great Janusz Korczak, the Polish-Jewish pediatrician, educator and author who continued to care for the Jewish orphans under his watch after they were moved to the ghetto. Despite having been offered asylum and possible escape himself, he chose to stay with the children until the end, accompanying them ultimately to Treblinka, never letting on what they were in for. Witnesses in Warsaw reported seeing them marching in rows of four, with Korczak (whose real name was Henryk Goldszmit) leading the group of about two hundred boys and girls, looking straight ahead, holding hands.

They were all murdered in the gas chambers of Treblinka.

Abandoned by the world, they were not abandoned by their teacher.

Everywhere we went in Poland, I looked for signs of the life before. I would get as close as I could to the front doors, in search of any door-post with an outline indicating that a mezuzah would have once stood guard. When we drove past the forests with their tall green trees, I wondered about people hiding in the thickets, behind the giant branches. I imagined myself doing it. It was impossible for me to think of this place as anything other than a blood-soaked historical record of unconscionable barbarism dressed up as a pretty country.

By day two, we were deep into our doom tour. And this time, it really was personal.

Treblinka was the camp with the name that sounded so much like terrible that I always associated it with terrors as a child, even before I knew what "concentration camp" meant, or that so many of my family members had been murdered there.

It wasn't, by strict definition, a concentration camp. This was an extermination camp. If you were sent there, that was it. There was no temporary reprieve from death, like pointless boulder duty for a couple of months. Your number was up. It was straight to the gas chambers. More than nine hundred thousand people, mostly Jews, were murdered here this way. Then their bodies were tossed into mass graves. Later, the remains were dug up and cremated, with old rails being used in the operation.

The bodies were placed on those rails, splashed with gas, and burned. According to an escaped prisoner who wrote a book about his experience there, this burning of the bodies was horrific—going on for hours, with the pyres operating around the clock. He wrote that the bellies of pregnant women would explode from boiling amniotic fluid.

Overseeing the operation were German and Austrian commanders, with the assistance of mostly Ukrainian guards.

This is how the lives of my grandparents Moshe Aron and Sara, and Moshe Rafael and Rachel, and their children Devorah and Isaac and Rachmiel, came to their end.

This was a visit to a family graveyard.

The terror of the place had been erased, bombed to bits by the Nazis, trying, in retreat, to cover up evidence of their evil as the Allies approached. What we found was a dramatic memorial—giant jagged stones jutting out of the green land, more than two hundred of them—representing the hometowns of the people who were murdered at Treblinka, and thousands more monument stones beyond.

We said *kaddish*, the memorial prayer, at the Radom stone. My mother, a little stooped, didn't bother with her unopened umbrella or the hood on her blue March of the Living windbreaker. "My whole family, my entire family," she muttered. We placed a little rock on the monument, as is the Jewish custom, to mark that we had been there. This stone was from Eilat, the beautiful Red Sea town in Israel, retrieved by Doris and brought to Poland for this purpose. It had travelled from the hot desert in the land where the Lindzens might have found refuge, to this place, their cold and rainy burial ground.

"I just can't believe that this happened here in this quiet peaceful place," Rachel said, blinking rapidly and looking off in the distance as Doris videotaped her. "All of my grandparents were murdered, and my aunts and uncles. And it's just too hard for me to believe. Too shocking."

The whole operation took a couple of hours, our guide told us as we gathered in a circle. The victims would be brought in and forced to wait in the wagons.

"In the snow. In the cold air," my mother said, standing just a little outside the circle behind him, her damp hair coming up to his shoulder. She was nodding, the voice of experience—a woman who had survived a similar kind of gruesome operation. *Yes*, she told us all, *naked*.

There were logjams due to heavy volume, our guide explained. Only twenty rail cars could fit onto the platform at a time. Up to forty cars, packed with prisoners, would be paused outside the camp.

"People waited to die," I'm overheard saying on my sister's shaky video.

My overwhelming memory of the place is green. The grass, the trees—green everywhere. The silence of the landscape interrupted only by the birds.

This manmade hell had transformed back to a haven for nature. And the birds were letting us know who was in charge now. Had their ancestors been here then? Had my ancestors looked up and envied the freedom of their flight? Or had the birds stayed away, scared off by the unnatural stench of mass murder?

Later, when I reread my father's diary from 1979, I was struck by how similar our reactions were to this place. He too remarked on the quiet, and all the green.

These blossoming fields, I thought, were concealing a massive cemetery. New life from so much death.

More than twenty years later, locked down in my house during a pandemic, I looked up which birds would be active in that region at the time of year we had been there. I consulted a calendar I found on

a website for a Polish nature tour company. Woodpeckers are plenti-
ful. Also, owls. In addition to this sort of information, the calendar
served up a quote from Albert Einstein, who—coincidence, I'm sure—
happens to be one of the more famous and accomplished Jewish
escapees from Nazi Germany. "The only reason for time is so that
everything doesn't happen at once."

All this searching about the birds of Poland and I realized, sometime later, that it would in no way bring me closer to understanding
this aspect of what the Jews experienced there in the 1940s. To begin
with, terror can be very loud; would the birdsong have been audible
over the wailing in those railcars and in the passage to the gas chamber? If there even was birdsong. In *Mes Sept Mères*, the French documentary about the young women from Radom who helped each other
survive, my mother is talking in one scene with her friend Freda about
Auschwitz. They're in a lush Toronto ravine and Freda remembers
how they would wonder at any little thing that moved in the air at
Auschwitz, any natural thing above them at all, like a bird. My mother
corrects her: "There was no birds," she says.

"We hardly saw any, that's true," Freda replies. "There were no birds.
There was nothing. You couldn't see a thing. All you could smell is the
ashes. From the ovens."

I have no reason to believe this would have been any different at
Treblinka. No woodpeckers drumming on trees, no owls. Just ash.

On the way back from Treblinka (*a sentence my grandparents never
got to say*, I think as I type this), we visited a former *shtetl* called Tykocin,
a village I had not heard of prior to our trip. Tykocin had been an
important Jewish centre in Poland, home to Jews since the early 1500s.
By the time we got there, there were none left.

The focus of our visit was not the little town—where old women
stared at us with what felt like animosity (but maybe I'm projecting).
It was the Lopuchowo forest nearby. This is where almost all of the
1,400 Jews of Tykocin, after being rounded up with help from the local
Polish police, were thrown into five-metre-deep pits and shot—or

buried alive—on August 25 and 26, 1941. Jews made up nearly half of the town's population before the war. Only a handful—we're talking about thirty people—survived.

Imagine, the guide told the students at that site, imagine every single person in your life killed in one day.

I think about this: your family, your friends, your teachers, the rabbis, the butcher, the boy you have a crush on, everyone. It's unimaginable, actually. And yet we must continue to try to imagine it. To conjure up that vision of the killing squad that came to the centuries-old community and put an end to it over a couple of late-summer days. Dogs barking, children crying, everyone clinging, guards yelling, pits dug, shots fired, bodies falling. The teacher who taught you how to add and subtract. The rabbi who officiated at your brother's bar mitzvah. The boy you had a private dream about. Your baby sister.

It has been more than twenty years since I visited that forest and town I had never heard of, learned of a massacre I had never heard of. And the memory still invades when I seek peace and solace in the forests of anywhere. It has followed me all the way here, to beautiful British Columbia, where the trees are so tall they can block out the sun, and the soil so rich that the ground feels like a carpet. Thoughts of that forest execution always manage to pierce through. The evil nature of man haunting the nature I seek for respite. Stanley Park, Cathedral Grove, Mount Seymour. One moment I am breathing in the conifer air, the next I am imagining a pit filled with naked bodies, some still a little bit alive, a pile of chaos and trauma.

In Tykocin, we visited the old village synagogue, a grand shell of a shul. Turned into a stable by the Nazis during their occupation, it is now a museum. Next door, we saw some graffiti scrawled on a red house: "*Yude Raus*"—Jews out.

"You got your wish," someone in our group said.

The next day, we visited the last synagogue standing from pre-war Warsaw. The Nozyk Synagogue, which opened in 1902, was used by the occupying Nazis during the war for storage and, again, possibly a stable. When we visited, we had to enter through the back door; the front door had recently been firebombed in some sort of attack.

The interior had been beautifully restored. But rather than finding myself impressed with its grand beauty, I felt consumed by the vast space, this crushing absence. All the people who had once prayed here, all the people who should be praying here, denied of their lives, wiped from history. It felt too large, too cold. Its emptiness dominated. Here, we met one of the last surviving Jews still living there. He chatted with members of the group in Polish and Yiddish. I could not understand why he stayed. I quietly thanked the stars that my parents had had no desire to return to Poland after the war and restart their lives where they had begun.

The restoration of this synagogue felt to me like little more than a bow to international tourism. Because how many people were left to pray here? To offer up their thanks to God?

That day we also visited Majdanek, a concentration camp on the outskirts—barely—of Lublin, and a place I did not realize I had any personal history with. I later learned that both my aunt Ella and my brother-in-law Sam's mother, Anita, had been prisoners there. And that the factory labour camp in Radom where my mother had been a slave labourer had become a subcamp of Majdanek after the ghetto's liquidation. So my mother had been, in effect, a prisoner of Majdanek. I don't think even she knew that when we visited. It's not like she, as a slave labourer, would have had access to the organizational flow charts of the Nazi bureaucracy.

But none of my family members, at least none that I know of, were killed there.

I was less anxious about this stop than I had been about Treblinka. After visiting the site where most of my family had been suffocated in gas chambers and then buried in pits or burned to ashes on rails in an hours-long operation, I figured anything else would be, if not exactly a walk in the park, maybe less of an ordeal.

Really, I should have known better.

If Treblinka is a vast green memorial, Majdanek is a whole other kind of eerie experience, with the feel of a fully equipped, ready-to-roll concentration camp. It was so well-preserved, it gave the impression that you could flip a switch and the electrified fence would power up and the gas chambers come whirring back to life.

The camp had been hastily abandoned by the Nazis in July 1944 as the Soviets approached—no time to dismantle the infrastructure and cover their tracks. It's a museum now; the barracks are filled with artifacts. And I do mean filled. In one barrack, hair. Hair shaved from the heads of victims. Then, in the next barracks, shoes. Caged shoes pretty much floor to ceiling, on both sides of these wooden buildings, one barrack after the other. The shoes were a torment. Every pair represented a person who had selected that particular footwear for this journey to places unknown, never suspecting, one hopes, that the journey would end like this. Did they choose them for comfort? For style? Or was there no choice? Perhaps they only owned that single pair. These were people who once thought their lives were going somewhere, who bought those oxfords or loafers or boots with dreams and plans: for dates with a special person, for a new job, for school. For Rosh Hashanah. Or Passover.

Some of the shoes were very little.

There were about eight hundred thousand pairs of shoes found at Majdanek at liberation in 1944. Thousands of these were displayed in 1998, when we visited, in those barbed wire cages. These were just the rejects, though. "Shoes representing direct utility value had earlier been sent to Germany," a sign informed us.

Years later, I was looking online, trying to find out more about these shoes, when I came across a report about a memo that had been sent to concentration camp commandants, dated July 11, 1942. It seems there had been some problems with parcels of clothing that had been sent from the camps, addressed mainly to the Gestapo administration in what was then called Bruenn (or Brünn, now Brno in the Czech Republic). There were complaints about damage to these items: "in some cases this clothing was perforated with bullet holes and blood stained . . . and strangers were thus able to ascertain the nature of their contents."

The hair, cut from the Nazis' victims, was also sent to Germany and processed. "It was a business," our guide said, as we entered the bathing area of Majdanek.

"Occasionally the prisoner had an opportunity of a hasty bath lasting a few minutes," the sign at the museum read. "For washing the prisoners were not given soap or towels. Prisoners were also given baths here before extermination in gas chambers in order to quite [*sic*] them down."

And then, as the tour continued, another sign: "Experimental gas chamber for exterminating prisoners with Cyclone [*sic*] B thrown into the chamber through holes in the ceiling." I approved of this typo: Cyclone B.

Carbon oxide was also used. Extermination with Zyklon B took about ten minutes; with carbon oxide, about forty, the sign said.

When we visited the crematorium, the sign told us that it was heated with coke, the bodies burned at a temperature of about seven hundred degrees Celsius. "The daily yield was about 1,000 bodies."

There was a concrete tub in the crematorium. The SS guy on duty would take a bath in water warmed by the fire from the ovens.

At the end of the tour, after we walked through these barracks, still stunned from the hair and the shoes and the tub and the unnerving authenticity of the place, we ascended to an enormous dome. This is a monument and a mausoleum. Inside: ashes. With bits of bone. Endless pieces of people, massive and impossible to process. Who were these people? Children who dreamed of growing up to be doctors. Women pregnant with their first child. Boys yet to be bar mitzvah'd. Rabbis. Midwives. Tailors. Professors. Farmers. People. My people. I was wrong about this not being personal. Everything here was personal.

There was another element of Majdanek that I found particularly creepy. From the camp, you could see right into people's backyards. People lived there, abutting this death factory. Even separated with trees planted to create some kind of border, some kind of shield—the people who live in these houses must be aware of what is on the other side of their yard. Did they have any sort of view of the old camp as they gathered for family barbecues and other al fresco get-togethers? Would a photo taken to capture the joy of the event—kids jumping through sprinklers, dad at the grill, a group of friends laughing over some chilled white wine—also capture a slice of what was just beyond the trees? A former prisoners' barrack, a gas chamber? That historic barbed wire fence: a thornier border, easier to see through, harder to permeate.

There is an excellent reason for Majdanek to remain as it is: a warning in architecture that leaves little to the imagination. But I can't think of a single reason why anyone would want to live adjacent to this well-preserved former mass-murder operation.

One of Majdanek's liberators was a Polish Jew named Bernhard Storch. He was serving in a Polish Army division of the Russian military (after having been sent by the Soviet Secret Police to a work camp in Siberia). In an interview published in *GIs Remember: Liberating the Concentration Camps*, Storch—who emigrated to the U.S. after the war—recalled encountering a mountain of human ash with human bones scattered in between. Just as I had experienced, but he would have come upon it fresh—and without having had any idea beforehand what he was about to walk into. Warehouses with hundreds and thousands of shoes—men's, women's, children's, "all sorted out." The gas chambers and crematoria. "The irony of the whole thing is that the Polish people were living outside the camp, farming, as if nothing were happening," he said.

Irony is one way to put it, I guess.

Alfred Hitchcock was also struck by this proximity—not specifically in Lublin, but to the west, in Germany proper. After the war, Hitchcock was hired by film producer Sidney Bernstein, then with the British Ministry of Information, to make a feature-length documentary to be called *German Concentration Camps Factual Survey*. The plan had been to use film footage of the camps shot by liberating Allied armies—the images are absolutely horrifying—to provide undeniable evidence of the atrocities, for the German public in particular to see. Hitchcock wanted to demonstrate just how close the bucolic German farms and towns were to the death factories nearby, using maps. He would juxtapose the deeply disturbing concentration camp images with footage of happy, well-fed Germans, living their lives, nearby.

One segment was to feature beauty shots of the holiday resort Ebensee, Austria, where Germans or Austrians are seen smiling, relaxing—even romancing—in the mountains. "Everything is charming and picturesque," the script says. Hitchcock's plan was to then cut to a photo of emaciated concentration camp inmates behind barbed wire, the scenic mountains of Ebensee in the distance. "But what use are mountains without food?"

(Googling Ebensee, I land on a tourist website aimed at potential visitors. "Go on long hikes through the mountains, ice skate on a frozen lake and visit the site of a former Nazi concentration camp.")

The movie project was shelved, but a team at London's Imperial War Museum completed the film nearly seventy years later using the original shot sheets, script and rushes. Director André Singer made a documentary about the project, *Night Will Fall*.

"[Hitchcock] wanted to know whether the Germans surrounding the concentration camp knew about it," said Bernstein in a 1984 interview used in the 2014 documentary. Hitchcock drew concentric circles around each of these sites on a map. "His idea was: show the area surrounding each camp and show how people had lived a normal life outside."

This was in Germany, but in Poland too—where the Germans had built giant extermination factories like Auschwitz and Treblinka— some locals said, afterward, that they had no idea this was happening. Really? All the Jews disappeared, their friends and neighbours, while other friends and neighbours were employed to guard them, they watched and smelled the rank stench of body ash chugging up through a chimney with alarming regularity, and they had no idea? They bought up the disappeared Jews' kitchen tables and children's toys for a song, while their apartments were still warm with their presence—and they didn't have even a teeny tiny inkling that something nefarious was going on? Were they that stupid? Am I that stupid that I should believe this?

Even before Germany invaded Poland, the Polish government had enacted restrictions on Jewish businesses and encouraged non-Jews to boycott them. Jewish stalls in marketplaces were targeted and Gentiles were warned not to do business with them. I thought of my grandmother, Rachel, selling her textiles at her little stand in the Radom market. Did anti-Semites taunt her? Yell at her customers, telling them to take their business elsewhere?

The pre-war Polish government was right-wing and its leadership railed against Jewish economic influence. Prime Minister Slawoj Skladkowski called for "economic struggle" against the Jews, "by all means—but without force."

Well, there was force. Between 1935 and 1937, nearly 1,300 Polish Jews were injured and hundreds were killed by their countrymen. And the Polish government largely looked the other way—or worse. When I read these facts in one of my many books, I felt so sad. I thought: even before the Nazis marched into Poland, changing everything, my parents would not have felt completely at home, at home.

My father—who might have lived with these Polish-enforced restrictions on his family business—had visited Majdanek on that trip in 1979. I was reminded of this when I reread his journal many years after my own visit. It was toward the end of his trip and he too found this place very hard to take.

"Many barracks intact, walking through them like in a daze, horrible extremely touchy exhibits all over, very original and different, a lot of material, gassing rooms, 'bath' installations, clothing, hair, belongings and big piles of shoes from our dear ones killed all over this blood soaked country. I am very tough by nature but it gets to me more and more, a human can only take so much!"

When Auschwitz was liberated by the Russians in January 1945, they found large bales of hair—seven thousand kilos of it. Can you picture that much hair? Can you calculate how many people would have had to have been robbed of their hair in order for it to amount to seven thousand kilos? And that's just the hair that hadn't yet been shipped back to Germany to be used by companies in the manufacture of everything from socks to carpets to mattress stuffing.

"I have been told that some of those products manufactured in those plants may still be in use in German homes today," I read in a 1993 piece in *The New Yorker* by Timothy W. Ryback, then director of the Institute for Historical Justice and Reconciliation at EuroClio, the European Association of History Educators, in the Hague.

Had I walked along one of those carpets when I had backpacked through Germany in my twenties? Or slept, in one of my low-rent hostels, on one of those mattresses?

The shoes had seized me at Majdanek. At Auschwitz, it was the hair. There are heaps of it in the museum there. Endless hair, much of it dry and discoloured with age. In one of those piles, my sisters and I spotted a braid—long, blond, perfectly intact. My mother had had long, blond braids when she was a girl. The loss of her hair when she arrived at Auschwitz, Auntie Ella, and the laughter, was one of the few stories from that horrible time that she talked about for the rest of her life.

And now she was back, with her daughters and one of Ella's daughters—as a visitor in 1998, one of the Living.

It is as harrowing an experience as you can imagine to visit Auschwitz with your mother, knowing that she had been a prisoner at this very place—that she, as a teenager, had been enslaved, humiliated, starved, abused and tortured in countless ways right where we were. It is unlike anything I have ever experienced before or since, the sick dread of walking through that place with her. The desire to go back in time and protect Gucia when she was a teenager—to shield her from the blows when she could not stand properly at roll call, to hold her as she mourned her parents, to sneak her a crust of bread. She was nineteen then.

All I could do was walk with her on that day in 1998, and watch over her, like I fantasized about doing as a time traveller. That braid in the museum display, I kept thinking, could have been hers. (Not possible, in fact, because her braids were long gone at that point, but this was the gut narrative I could not shake. That braid belonged to some other girl, her name lost to history.)

Auschwitz is now a state-run museum. My friend Eileen—she of the damaging classroom exercise—recalls that when she visited on her own back in 1989, she encountered a kiosk where she was asked to pay an admission fee. Eileen refused. Her grandparents were Holocaust survivors; family members had been murdered at Treblinka; and she did not feel she should have to pay to get in to see where her people had been slaughtered and forced into slave labour.

This was not the matter of a few zlotys; this was the principle— my friend's grief and helpless rage, being channelled toward this clerk who she saw as simply following inane rules while not factoring in all of the pain. Her grandmother and grandfather had been enslaved in a concentration camp. Did their years of suffering not warrant free admission, at the very least?

So perhaps there was something worse than going there with your loved one who had survived. Maybe it was even more difficult going back as the descendant of a survivor without that person, not being able to hold their hand or watch over them as horrific scenes played back in their memory machine. I could not imagine walking through this place alone, as Eileen did, after she reluctantly paid the entrance fee. (A spokesperson for the Auschwitz Museum insisted when I asked him about this that there has never been an admission fee to simply enter the grounds or the museum. Eileen remembers otherwise and says she is certain about this.)

Auschwitz is enormous, and parts of it are well preserved. It was impossible not to look around and imagine what it was like when

Gucia and Ella were there. "Were you in this area?" my cousin Roshelle, Ella's daughter, asked my mother at one point. "Is this where my mother was?"

We were inside one of the rooms at the museum, one on the second floor, and my mother moved over to the window. One of our guides, a woman named Carla, approached her.

"What I remember about your mother is vivid," Carla told me years later. "I had lost my mother only 3 years earlier, and it was wonderful to see you and your sisters with her, the way you supported each other, and honoured and loved her. I've never forgotten.

"During the visit to the museum, you were all engrossed in the exhibit and she had moved to stand alone at a window. . . . I approached her quietly, not wanting to intrude on a private moment, but also wanting her to know I was there if she didn't feel like being alone. She looked at me so intensely, shook her head and gestured out the window. 'We never thought we would walk out of here alive,' she said, 'and now, look at this, all these Jewish kids, it's a miracle.'

"I am totally sincere," Carla continued, "when I say that every time I'm there (and it's been about 30 times) I find myself stopped for a minute and reliving that."

The actual March of the Living took place later that day—the Living being thousands of Jews, mostly high school students who had travelled to Poland from all over the world; the March being the walk from Auschwitz I to Auschwitz II, more commonly known as Birkenau. Auschwitz I is where the museum is housed, with its brick buildings originally built for the Polish military, dating back to the First World War. Birkenau is thirty times the size, an endless barren landscape of crude wooden barracks, each once housing hundreds of emaciated prisoners. This was the main death camp, a factory chugging away at all hours. Whose product was the extermination of human beings— more than a million of them—about 90 per cent of whom were Jewish. Birkenau—the Germanized name of the Polish village there, Brzezinka—was where the gas chambers and crematoriums were built, before they were dismantled and bombed to bits by the retreating Germans and, in the case of one crematorium, by an inmate uprising. Their foundations remain. (Over in Auschwitz I, a gas chamber and crematorium have been reconstructed using original elements.)

Please understand how enormous this place is: in 1944, it held over ninety thousand prisoners. One of them was my mother.

We marchers were all supplied with blue jackets and a blue backpack, so we were a sea of blue, our uniform nylon bombers declaring our continuing existence, our insistence on survival, in spite of everything.

"I never thought I'd be here surrounded by thousands and thousands of other strong, young, thriving Jews," I am heard saying off-camera, on Doris's film, as we began to assemble.

We stood in groups behind signs that identified us—"Canada Adults," "Polish Friends of Israel." "Never Again!!!" a large banner read. We stood, waiting to walk.

There were boisterous cheers from one group—these were teenagers after all, and this was a collective triumph, thumbing our noses at those who wished us eliminated from the earth. Then sombre violin music, the blowing of the shofar, and we began to march, in silence. Out the gate, looking at *Arbeit Macht Frei* backwards. And then three kilometres along a stretch of roadway to Birkenau. We marched silently, each of us with our private thoughts, surrounded by thousands of people.

If every other stop on this trip through Poland had been devastating, this was a surprising something else: empowering. It was triumphant, glorious, an assertion of our existence, a silent parade of *fuck you, we are still here*. I felt an almost joy. I felt strength—my own, that of the family and strangers I was surrounded by, and my mother's—even though she wasn't with us at that moment. Unable to walk the whole distance, she was driven over to the destination point with other elderly survivors.

There were things I'm glad she missed: the long walk, to begin with. It felt especially poignant to me that here she should be able to rest those feet that were ruined by the Nazis and their ill-fitting blocks of wood that passed for shoes. The damage plagued her always—at the mall, on vacation, back at Auschwitz. For once, at this place where she had been worked to the bone, where her feet and God knows what else were wrecked forever, she was able to rest.

But also, thank God she did not have to witness the hostility we encountered along the way. This was another surprise. Young Poles were watching us. Many were supporting our walk, which was appreciated; I have a photograph of some Polish soldiers, presumably, in full camo gear, one of whom appears to be in mid-clap. They were applauding us.

But others were openly hostile. "One swore at me," Doris wrote in her diary, indicating that he had given her the finger, "another put out his fist. These were Young Poles—why do they hate us so? I felt proud to be a Jew."

I also felt proud, and strong and protected as I marched with my sisters, and with Roshelle and Laura. None of us would have existed had Gucia and Ella not survived this place.

My mother joined us at the end of the march. After the formal ceremony, we had some time to look around. We tried to find my mother's barrack. (What a weird way to put it, using the possessive, as if it belonged to her in any way.) She said it was barrack #8. We were having trouble locating it in the sea of giant, cookie-cutter wooden sheds.

This exercise was unbearable for me. When we couldn't find barrack #8, we went into another one. They would have been identical, or at least nearly so. Walking through that prisoners' quarters, I looked at my mother and pictured her sleeping on one of those wooden platforms, wasting away and nearly dead with typhus. How could this have happened to my sweet, gentle mom? It was overwhelming to even contemplate.

During this visit, my mother withstood it all, never breaking down, not saying a whole lot. She was almost cheerful—what I recognize now as detachment. I wish I had asked her more about what she was thinking and feeling, but I couldn't stand it. I couldn't stand to think of her there in 1944. I also had to detach. And I just went quiet. Then I walked outside the substitute barrack; I had to leave.

Looking at my little mother among those wooden planks that stood for beds, I felt too angry and sad to even stay in that room with her and protect her. I had to run away. An option that had not been available to her. Once again, I failed her.

Doris wrote in her diary that finally, as we were about to get on the bus, my mother spotted barrack #8 through the barbed wire fence. It was too late for us to be able to see it. "Perhaps it was for the better that she didn't go in," Doris wrote.

We left Auschwitz-Birkenau not in a cattle car but riding high in our fancy tour bus. As we rolled away back to our comfortable hotel, I conducted some interviews with members of our group for a radio documentary I was making about the trip. This, I have learned over the years, is a very good way to suppress pain: ask other people questions, lose myself in their answers.

These were questions I should have been asking my mother.

There were two more stops on our Poland itinerary, two private trips that our family alone was going to take on the scheduled free days. The two places that were really home to my parents: Lodz and Radom.

In Lodz we visited the huge Jewish cemetery—the largest Jewish cemetery still in Europe, we were told—but we were unable to locate our great-grandfather's stone, the one my father had found on his trip in 1979. It was impossible; that place was so vast and overgrown.

Anyway, that was not the main point of the journey to Lodz. We were there to see, as my father had nineteen years earlier, the home where he grew up.

We drove to Chojny, the suburb where the Ledermans had lived, and using the research we had conducted, our taxi driver's knowledge, and the intel my father had scrawled in handwritten notes all those years ago, we arrived at the address. It was impossible to know if the building matched the description my father had provided. Because there was no building. It was gone.

We had arrived at a vacant lot on a corner, surrounded by a chain-link fence. Inside stood a porta-potty and some scraps—old pipe and other construction materials. Next door was a sign for an import business. And on a little trailer, unoccupied, on the lot, there was some graffiti, in red spray paint: two Jewish stars bracketing the words "*Idze Jude.*"

I knew what *Jude* meant. *Idze* I wasn't sure about. What a weird coincidence, though. Was this a posthumous message to my father and his murdered family members who had once lived here?

It took me a few years, but I finally figured out the meaning of this graffiti, thanks to a couple of acquaintances who know their Polish culture.

Idze was actually a reference to a soccer club in Lodz called Widzew. *Jude* was an insult in this context, aimed at the soccer club. Ranking of Polish insults, my friend informed me: "1. Faggot. 2. Jew."

I did not know this at the time. And, in any case, the graffiti bothered us far less than the absence of the home we had travelled so far to see.

We asked around, queried some passersby. Did they remember a building being here? Yes, one woman told us—it had been torn down about ten years earlier.

"It's very upsetting," I said in my commentary on Doris's film. "Our father got to see it. He wrote in his diary that it was incredible to see the rooms he grew up in, his sister's, his bed, and now there's nothing left."

We decided to make the best of it. To envision what had been there, to imagine it. "It was on this corner where my father grew up," I said.

"It was on a main street and it must have been a good location for their store, which was right here on the corner, and they lived upstairs."

Doris aimed the camera at the street, panning around to show our surroundings. They were a good match for our disappointment.

"Who knows? Maybe this fence stood when Daddy was alive, when he was a boy and played. Maybe these trees were planted when he was a boy," I said. Maybe the garden was there when he was a child, maybe that field was a place he played.

"This is the view my father would have had when he looked out his window, across the street," one of my sisters said off-camera—Rachel, I think (we all sound alike). It was a busy road with streetcar tracks. "Buses, cars, trams. Lots of activity."

There was nothing else to see. After lunch—at McDonald's of all places; comfort food, I guess—we drove back to our hotel, bereft. This country just couldn't stop letting us down.

The next day, we would try again. This time our destination was Radom, where my mother had lived as a girl. Where her family had been forced to leave their home for cramped quarters in the ghetto; where her little brother Rachmiel had snuck out of the ghetto to try to sell their possessions for a bit of food; where my mother had been forced into slave labour for the Germans; where she had repeatedly witnessed her friend being called a spy and threatened with having her eyes gouged out by a drunk Nazi; where Rachmiel and Rachel and Moshe Rafael had been taken away to Treblinka and murdered.

After Friday's letdown, I kept my expectations in check.

But Saturday was different. We drove up in our taxi and there it was. The facade had changed, the outhouses my mother grew up using were now storage sheds, what used to be grass was now asphalt—but it was definitely the apartment house where my mother had lived as a girl.

She recognized it right away. We walked into the courtyard and there was her building, number four.

She pointed up to the top-floor windows where her family's apartment had been. "We were very happy kids here," she said.

Then she was off in wonder, remembering. "I had a friend here, a very close friend." I had known about that friend; the two of them had bonded in part because they had the same first name—one was blond, the other had dark hair. She would tell me about that often, because when I was a teenager, I landed a new best friend, Marsha. She had dark hair, I was blond. This parallel delighted my mother—and me.

When she told me that story as a child, I always pictured these two girls being named Jean. But of course, that was not my mother's name yet. She, as Jean, did not yet exist. And that dark-haired girl—her name must have been Gitla or Gittel or Guta—no longer existed once my mother became Jean. She did not exist after the war. This girl was only a memory for my mother.

We would try to go inside—who knows? Maybe the occupant would be home and let us in.

"This was the entrance that Mummy took when she was a little girl," I say to Doris's video camera. I bounce up the exterior stairs, past indistinct graffiti etched into the concrete walls, pretending to be little-girl Gitla—my elbows out and swinging, a make-believe smile on my face. "I'm going up the stairs with the long hair, going upstairs to play."

Inside the building, Doris filmed me ascending the staircase. "Going into the building where Mummy lived. And she would go up these stairs, these wooden stairs, with the wooden banister," I say, walking deliberately and slowly up the steps in my very heavy, very white Nikes—bought for that trip, probably—sweeping my hand up along the banister. At the landing I look up to the next floor, the sun stream-ing down from an unseen window, shedding all kinds of light. Then I disappear behind the next flight of stairs.

And then, on the film, we're inside, my mother jabbering away in her perfect Polish to the current occupant, telling him where things used to be, when she was a girl. Sometimes, when we would ask what they were saying, she would say, "Oh, that's nothing," as if every word exchanged in that impossible place was not of utter importance.

I feel such gratitude that the man who lived there was home and welcomed us, let us in. That he was not at all suspicious of us, not wor-ried that we were there to reclaim our property. He seemed to under-stand that it was a different kind of reclamation we were after.

We toured through the apartment. I was worried about my mother, but no—she was excited, even euphoric. I caught a glimpse of that happy kid she once was.

It is quite a thing to see the house where a parent was raised when you are in your thirties and have been denied the experience your whole life. Growing up, there were no visits to grandparents, where we might have seen our mother's or father's childhood bedrooms—maybe even spent the night in their old beds at sleepovers. There were no drives by the place where either of them had grown up, the way I often do now when I visit Toronto with Jacob. The way we took the kids to see where their dad grew up in Ottawa.

I had never expected to be able to walk through these rooms in Radom. We had put it on the itinerary, sure, and planned the journey, hired the driver. But I don't think I had actually thought through the possibility of being let inside. I don't think my mother had either; she seemed ill-prepared for this extraordinary access to her past.

Doris remembers that outside the building, our mother had started to run away before we went inside; she was afraid, initially. That while I was bouncing up the stairs, pretending to be her, my mother was having a moment. She was flustered, muttering that she couldn't do it. She looked nervous, fearful. Doris and Rachel comforted her, encouraged her. And I apparently—I don't remember this; this is from Doris's memory—came back outside and, all excited and unaware of my mother's emotional state, told them cheerfully, *Come on, let's go*. And in we went, the group of us, Doris with her video camera recording it all.

The man's wife was sleeping in my grandparents' former bedroom, so we weren't able to go into that room. In the main room, a couch stood where, in my mother's day, there had been two beds: one for her and Ella, one for the boys. My mother was holding her arms around her middle, hugging herself, as if to say, *Can you believe this?*

Later, telling Joseph Morder about this experience for his film *Mes Sept Mères*, my mother described herself as being very sad that day. "I hardly could talk, I was so choked up," my mother told him about that visit to her childhood home. "Everything reminds me," she said. I hadn't realized.

Over the double doors into the bedroom where Moshe Rafael and Rachel had slept and conceived my mother (I assume), there was a crucifix nailed to the wall. And next to it, a calendar with a photograph of the pope—Pope John Paul II, the Polish pope. The pope who had been involved in anti-Nazi resistance through his cultural activities and had, people have said, helped Jews escape. The pope who, my mother once told me, had had a *Jewish girlfriend* when he was involved in the Resistance. (This seems unlikely, and I have no way to confirm it, but that's what Gucia said, with a nod of the head, as if to say "trust me, I know about these things.")

Nothing in the apartment was the same, my mother said during the visit. The gap in the kitchen between the washing machine and the counter—this was where her mother had done the laundry, by hand, of course. A red folding chair stood in that spot, the kind of chairs my father used to drag up from the basement when their friends—all Holocaust survivors, also from Poland—would come over to play poker on a Saturday night.

The floors in the apartment were different. But the windows—they were the same. And the door to the attic, where the laundry would dry. And the hallway. And the stairs, with the peeling paint and the wooden bannisters. Yes, those were the same. My mother stopped on the landing on the way down, and held her hand up to her face. It was elation, it was disbelief, memories flooding back. A Jewish professor had lived in that apartment, she said, pointing to another door. At apartment number 13, with double red doors, she paused again, to remember. "There were one, two, three, four boys. And two girls. Six kids." Six children, all murdered by the Nazis, no doubt.

At times that morning, my mother's face was lit up with an almost girlish delight, the kind of innocent joy that must have preceded that darkest time. A time I had rarely considered, as her whole history seemed to be bound up in this horrific event.

That trip back to my mother's pre–World War II childhood home brought with it a revelation: her story was not only about the

Holocaust, and it was essential that this other element of her early life be recognized.

Helen Epstein, author of *Children of the Holocaust*, has said that when writing the book back in the 1970s, she found that the story of the war had displaced the story of the family.

(After her mother's death, Epstein wanted to write a book that would bridge the pre-war, Holocaust, and post-war history of her family. She did extensive research in what was then Czechoslovakia and produced *Where She Came From: A Daughter's Search for her Mother's History*. This was a search I was familiar with. Why do we wait until after they're gone to try to dig up this history?)

This displacement of childhood stories by tragic tales of war was my family's experience precisely. But before my mother became a victim, she was a girl, and an adolescent, and a young teenager. This was where she lived when she was that person. When she was just a kid without a real care in the world, other than the odd pint-sized drama, like a misguided crack by a kind uncle about a pair of shiny new shoes.

There was a park where my mother used to play when she was a girl, where families would mingle, especially on Shabbat. Until Jews were banned from the parks. In 1998, she wanted to visit. I expected a rinky-dink patch of grass. But instead, we were presented with a grand park, with wide promenades and tall trees. Imagine starting off life playing in places like this, and then ending up at Auschwitz. I pictured my little mother from another time playing in this park, saying something in a sweet innocent voice—before it was roughened by the Nazis, by age, by cigarettes.

My mother had not lived in the Jewish area—not before the ghettos were later established and the Lindzens were forced to relocate. There was no trace of the little ghetto, where her family had been imprisoned, that we could find. We walked through the area of the larger ghetto, on streets where Hela Morder and other friends of the Lindzens had lived crammed together. Now, the area had been completely rebuilt and was dotted with some lovely homes—villas, is how Doris described them. It was hard to imagine the place as a ghetto. Doris's father-in-law, Jim Schulman, had drawn her a map of where he had lived as a child with his family, but we couldn't find that either. We did find the house where Hela had lived.

Thinking about how the Jews' possessions had been sold or given away to locals, I wondered if, behind the walls of any of the homes we passed, lived heirlooms that once belonged to my family. Candlesticks? Dishes? Furniture? And the one thing that has haunted me—my grandfather's violin. Where did that end up? Maybe with the neighbour. Or did some Polish musician learn how to play on a dead man's violin? I wouldn't mind that, somehow. I would rather my Zaidie's violin was alive making music in someone else's hands. Better that than the instrument falling victim to the Nazis in a crazed bonfire of Jewish things, like the man who had once played it.

Our last stop was the site of the former synagogue. Built in the 1840s, it was destroyed during the Nazi occupation. There is now a memorial there to the Radom victims of the Holocaust. It was in a desolate square, surrounded by a low fence, and beyond that, there were some apartment buildings, at least one of them derelict and boarded up with a large green dumpster in front of it. Even the trees in that square were barren. This did not appear to be a well-visited memorial. But the locals knew what it was, of that we became sure.

Because as we, five women, stood and looked at this memorial, a group of boys standing in a nearby doorway started chanting something at us in Polish. It sounded menacing, like it might be a taunt. I couldn't understand what they were yelling, until they got to one term I did recognize: "Auschwitz-Birkenau." It didn't sound like they were expressing their condolences. This time, I did not ask my mother to translate.

Thank goodness, she had not heard it. But the rest of us had and we were shaken. Our cab driver, waiting for us nearby, felt like we might be in danger. We quickly piled into the car and explained to Gucia what had happened while en route out of there.

This left me rattled. How could we be so unwelcome, all these years later? How dare those boys? I was full of rage. The video camera captured my muttered, immature reaction. "Enjoy your life here in your hovel. We're going back to our luxury hotel."

Later, watching a documentary, I saw a scene featuring a gathering of Polish and Jewish youth as part of the March of the Living program. A Polish teenager explained to the visiting Jewish kids that some Poles were not so happy about the event. "Old people, they're not glad. I mean most of old people are thinking something like they're coming back to take Poland again.

"In my generation it's like it's trendy to be Jewish, I mean it's very different. Some people would like to throw stones at you. But some are really very glad that it's happening."

I understand now—my stupid luxury hotel comment aside—that those boys probably had no idea what they were talking about. Poland doesn't have a stellar record on Holocaust education—nor, for that matter, on owning up to the participation, tacit approval or silence of some of its people, and the anti-Semitism that preceded and followed the war. Non-Jewish Poles suffered massive losses, millions of deaths, during the war as well. I wonder if there is some resentment about the Jews hogging the tragedy spotlight.

This question of competitive traumas, of a hierarchy of suffering, is not what I was thinking about at the time. After that joyful morning, when my mother got to go home, to have that taunt levelled at us hurt deeply. Maybe it was a good metaphor for what my mother experienced early in her life. Kindness from some people—the open door to her old apartment, the fine man who lived there. And then ridicule from bullies around the corner, when our guard was down.

THIRTEEN

Pushing East

IN MY TRAGIC FAMILY HISTORY—and, about twenty years after that trip to Poland, a decision to write about it—I found something that had eluded me ever since the marital trouble had begun at my Vancouver home: a refuge and a raison d'être. Beyond, of course, my central raison d'être—not unrelated—of raising my son. This writing was more than a make-work project, more than a distraction. Immersed in all of this horror, I felt . . . happy. Purpose, like hope, is a potent fuel. I was finding new things to hope for.

I had so many questions—questions that once upon a time could have been easily answered in an afternoon around my mother's kitchen table, over tea and her famous apple cake. Time travel was not an option, so I booked myself a more traditional sort of trip.

I had sent a request for information about my family to the United States Holocaust Memorial Museum in Washington, D.C. The person on the other end of my email was helpful, but it became clear that I would have to be there in person to get what I really needed. There was a reading room and vast archives. As a child of survivors—and a researcher—I would be able to access whatever I needed.

It felt crazy—to spend the time and expense with no guarantee of anything—but I booked a trip. Going to Washington, staying at a nice hotel, by myself! Not for my job, but for me. My own solitary project. And, even crazier, there happened to be an exhibition about Auschwitz at the Museum of Jewish Heritage in New York. I decided to fly to New York so I could see that first, then travel to D.C. by train.

It would be my first trip to New York since the divorce, since we had travelled there as a family, all five of us, in 2014, our last happy summer. I was worried about what that was going to do to my soul, to be back in New York alone, immersed in Auschwitz.

It would also be my first trip to Washington since I had travelled there with Pat, back when we were happy, in love. And he was alive.

I braced myself for utter pain. But I arrived at JFK, after the red-eye from Vancouver, to a feeling that had become unfamiliar in my mid-life grief: anticipation. There was an adventure ahead.

For my two days and one night in New York, I would avoid any place I had been with my family on that previous trip. This meant no smoked meat on rye at Katz's Deli, no visit to the Metropolitan Museum of Art. No High Line. No Central Park, where we had spent many hours that steaming July. I allowed myself a ramble through MoMA, only because it had been completely redone in the interim.

On Saturday night, I would get to see a show. Staying on theme, I booked a ticket for as Jewy an experience as I could imagine, a performance of *Fiddler on the Roof*—in Yiddish.

The burly security guard searching my purse as if I were about to board a flight to Israel from some hostile country was a little disconcerting, but there you have it. A Yiddish play in New York is going to be a prospective target; this is a fact of life.

The lineup outside the theatre seemed to be made up entirely of Jews—and it felt . . . easy. I could blend right in and just be one of the crowd. I don't know if it was being outside my usual experience—my country, my time zone—or if it was my emotional fighting stance, on guard against any vulnerability I was feeling about being back in New York, all alone, in every way. But as I entered Stage 42 surrounded by what felt like an almost entirely Jewish audience, I did not, for once, think about us all being shoved into a gas chamber or a synagogue to be burned alive. I just thought: *This is nice. This feels like home.* I was alone, but not. I felt like I was among my people. And I was. It's a thing that can annoy me easily, being immersed in any sort of Judaic homogeneity, but here on this night, on my own and about to descend into a difficult itinerary, it was comforting. *We are all family*, I thought. Maybe literally: there was a chance I was related very distantly, or maybe not even that distantly, to someone in that auditorium. Or maybe someone on the stage.

It had been so long since I had heard Yiddish, the language of my childhood, my daily soundtrack up until the point when it wasn't. I had longed for English-speaking parents and made no effort to learn my parents' language. What irritated me as a child—*speak English!*—was now like a balm on the rare occasions I could find it. There is something very comforting about hearing the language you grew up with when that language is spoken so rarely now, at least in your own world. I am exposed to Yiddish almost never, these days.

From the opening moment of that show, the sound of the fiddler playing the violin, I was transported—to early-twentieth-century Russia; to later-twentieth-century suburban Toronto. The music, the language. While I certainly made good use of the surtitles, I was surprised by how many words I actually recognized—some of them sounding very funny in the context of this off-Broadway theatre. Like *bobbe meinses*—"tall tales," but better, with an air of dismissiveness. A great expression. It was something that would have come out of my mother's irritated mouth when she would catch me in a lie: "Don't tell me such *bobbe meinses*," I could hear her scold.

It was hard sometimes not to laugh at the surprise of these words. But mostly that night, I had a lump in my throat, remembering my family, where I had come from, and how far it was taking me. Where it was going to take me in the days to come.

The songs, so familiar. The language, so familiar but now distant. The senseless anti-Semitism, the violence, the pogroms. So familiar. Not as distant as I had once thought.

At the weekend's main event, a trip to Auschwitz on the southern tip of Manhattan, it was the women I had the most trouble with.

I have often wondered about the women of Auschwitz—not the prisoners, but the women in charge of them. Women participated in this operation, enforcing the rules, often cruelly, according to my mother and other accounts I have read and heard. But could women—even the worst women—have dreamed up the concentration camp concept and then brought the idea of killing factories to life? Planned out the details of an extermination assembly line? This is where we'll force the prisoners to strip, this is the lie we'll tell them about showers, this is how we'll get them into that killing room, this is where we'll drop the gas, this is approximately how long it will take for them to die, this is how we'll remove the bodies, this is how we'll remove their gold teeth, this is where we'll turn their bodies to ashes; we'll need chimneys this large and they should go here and here. The children? Oh yeah, we'll gas them along with their mothers. They won't take up much extra room.

Could women have come up with the idea and ironed out the logistics of industrial-scale murder with genocide as the objective?

In New York, the exhibition "Auschwitz. Not Long Ago. Not Far Away" at the Museum of Jewish Heritage put the extermination camp in context. Auschwitz didn't pop up overnight; an entire society had to be groomed first, the women included. Maybe especially.

There were photos of cheering women welcoming Hitler—nearly orgasmic throngs, their delight, their fervour, as the fascist dictator motored by in his open-air car. The women reaching out with a *pick-me! notice me!* kind of enthusiasm and an excitement bordering on sexual as he rolled into Vienna or Nuremberg or wherever. Women

offering up flowers and seeming to want to offer up more. As if it were
The Beatles they were there to see.

There was another part of this exhibition that enraged me beyond
measure, that made me wish I was not alone so that I could turn to
my companion and say, *Can you fucking believe this?* It was a selection
of photos of Auschwitz guards, on their days off work, at a resort about
thirty kilometres—and a world—away from the main camp. Time off
to relax and unwind at Solahutte was rewarded to those who had performed exceptionally on the job.

I hated the men—the actual SS guards—in these photos. But even
more, I despised these women. The young women were SS-Helferin-
nen—female auxiliaries—who worked as communications specialists.
They knew exactly what was going on there. They contributed to it.

But in these photos of the Nazis at rest on the Sola River, they were
laughing and giggling and flirting as these repulsive men told them a
joke or, in a couple of shots, played the accordion. In one photo, the
women were wearing matching leisure-wear skirts and blouses—they
had discarded the blazers they were wearing in other photos; perhaps it
had become too warm. These women had been eating blueberries and,
the berries all gone into their ample mouths, they turned over the empty
containers, and one woman for whom I developed a particular hate-on
was pretending to cry for the camera. *Wah, the blueberries are all gone!*

These pictures had been discovered in an album once belonging
to Karl Höcker (or Hoecker), the adjutant to the commandant at
Auschwitz. He had been stationed there from May 1944 until the camp
was evacuated in January 1945.

In the exhibition, these images were juxtaposed, kitty-corner, to a wall
of photographs that prisoners had brought with them to Auschwitz,
which had been confiscated upon arrival. Most of the deportees carried
one or more family photographs with them; the photos were taken
from them and destroyed—they were of no use to the Nazis. But some
brave imprisoned workers, as an act of resistance, had clandestinely

buried hundreds of these pictures. Unlike most of the people in them, the buried photos survived.

On the wall in New York were a few examples of these family photos: a group of women, dressed up for some sort of occasion; a toddler, smiling at himself in the mirror. Who brought that photo of the toddler? Was it his mother? Was she still with him when the photo was taken from her? Were they sent to the gas chamber together? Maybe by one of those guards on the other wall singing to the accordion?

These photos—heartbreaking on one wall and infuriating on the other—to me represent the heart of the matter. Who were these normal people who agreed to participate in these abnormal things, to murder the women in their finery and the smiling toddler—or whoever was clutching these photos as they arrived at Auschwitz?

What kind of person do you have to be to not only do this but to gleefully participate? The kind of person who, if they perhaps felt the tiniest bit of guilt, was able to deal with that work stress by blowing off some steam, partying a few miles down the road at a camp built by their slaves for this purpose? Slaves who were, in most likelihood, dead by the time these overstuffed Nazis were living the life, joshing around with the accordion and the blueberries. The guy playing the instrument has his SS military cap a little askew—enough that it looks deliberate, as if he were adding to the fun of the moment with his jaunty headwear. The women are shrugging their shoulders and making cutesy faces at the camera; one woman is doing some form of down-turned Nazi jazz hands, bending her left knee, her left foot with her toes pointed to the ground, heel in the air, as if she's mid-dance, just full of joy, and life. In another, Jazz Hands is still dance-laugh-posing next to Jaunty Accordion Guy, while some of the women come running at the camera, seeming to be in hysterics. The smiles on those women's faces! They were having a blast. The time of their lives.

What did these women tell their children, their grandchildren, about what they did during the war?

Do descendants of Germans look at old photos like I do, scouring them for a glimpse of a possible relative? Could that emaciated woman with the shaved head possibly be my mother, or my aunt? Or that child in the ghetto, wearing a blanket over his shoulders in a futile effort to stay warm—could that have been my mother's little brother? Do Germans my age inspect these same photos for any sort of family resemblance, but look instead at the guards?

These photos at the resort were taken in the spring and summer of 1944. The day trip for the female guards with the blueberries was on July 22. Where was my mother then? She was in the final days of her stint as a slave labourer in what had been her hometown, Radom, building ammunition for her jailors. Shortly before being forced to walk for days on foot, on that transit march, then locked in that jail as she awaited transfer.

Soon she would be in an enclosed cattle car on her way to Auschwitz, sharing the airless space with the dead and dying—and people who didn't know that these would be their last hours. Then forced out onto the infamous ramp, being selected to live, not die. Getting the tattoo that would mark her left arm forever.

She would have still had her own family photos; they would be confiscated when she arrived. Were they burned by the Nazis, or buried by the resisters? Soon she would be fully integrated, hauling stones around in a pointless work assignment. I wonder: what does an accordion weigh, compared to a boulder?

At the same time, the women around me in the exhibition, the real ones, alive right now, were also making me crazy—in a more benign way. I guess it was just my bad luck, the women who happened to be close by. One complained bitterly about her companion having gone on ahead through the exhibition without her and why wasn't her audio guide working properly? Another made a comment upon encountering a display case filled with objects from a Jewish-owned liquor factory, the first factory established in Oswiecim, Poland—the city renamed Auschwitz by the occupying Germans. The woman, seeing these old empty bottles, joked to her friend, "I would be an alcoholic too." Her joke echoed through the solemn space filled with artifacts from the dead.

Deeper down, beyond my outrage at the inappropriate wisecrack, maybe I was just sad that I had nobody by my side to joke with, to commiserate with, to anything with.

On the train to Washington a few hours later, I dulled my senses by checking social media. What had I been missing on Twitter, Facebook, Instagram? Trump was about to be impeached, for the first time. I successfully avoided "Facebook memories" that might have included wedding/honeymoon/anniversary shots. November was still a hard month for me.

On Instagram, I saw that a work acquaintance—a woman I really like and respect—was visiting Germany. "Another fun day exploring #berlin," she wrote, under a photo of her in between the giant concrete blocks that I instantly recognized as that city's Holocaust memorial. And from the smile on her face (I zoomed in), you could see that yes, it was fun! (If a bit chilly, the hands in her pockets suggested.) The post included several hashtags, including #memorialtothemurderedjewsofeurope." A friend commented "Haha I forgot what Europe cold feels like!"

I put my phone away and closed my eyes.

I arrived at the U.S. Holocaust Memorial Museum first thing on Monday morning. My plan was to spend a week there, using their reading room and vast archives. The museum had assigned me a researcher who had taken on my case. It was a service available to anyone who needs it, but there is a waiting list. Survivors are given top priority; children of survivors are next. Because I travelled to the museum, my case got bumped up the list.

It was a godsend.

When I arrived that morning, my researcher had a pile of documents printed out and ready for me—information about my family, right there, in a file folder. My researcher asked me: What was my dream accomplishment for the week? What did I really want to find out? What was the one thing?

My dream, I told her, was to find the unit, the battalion, the regiment—whatever I can narrow it down to—that liberated my mother. To track down one of the men who had been there that day, who helped rescue her. Or, knowing the chances of those men still being alive were getting slimmer every day, a descendant of one of those men, who had heard the story from her dad or his grandpa.

Of how they had come upon a group of women in a meadow, emaciated, with large yellow crosses painted on their backs, and given them chocolate and cigarettes, and told them to go into the houses of those Germans and take their food and their clothes and their beds. I wanted to know what the soldiers' impressions were of these women, whether they were able to speak with them, understand what had happened to them. Did the women laugh? Cry? I needed to better imagine that scene. What I wanted most was to say thank you.

So that was my dream, I told my researcher, to find some clues so I could find one of my mother's liberators.

My best bet for an answer, she told me, would be found not at the Holocaust Museum but over in the next state, at the National Archives at College Park, Maryland. Accessible by shuttle bus, no problem. She wrote the information down on a slip of paper.

I wouldn't be able to find her rescuers at the U.S. Holocaust Memorial Museum. But on that Monday in Washington, I did find my mother.

After my meeting with my researcher, she directed me to the library. I took an elevator up to the floor where the museum's offices and reading room are located, walked through the glass doors and approached one of the people behind the big research desk. I was nervous. But, I told myself, it's just like using the library. It is a library.

Again, kindness. I could take any seat in the room, use any computer, look up what I wanted to see. The person helping me mentioned that the video testimonies filmed by the Shoah Foundation were all accessible on these computers.

This I hadn't considered. My mother, her video, in the database of this great place, part of it. Accessible to anyone researching the Holocaust. Accessible to me. I hadn't seen the video at that point in years, not since we had first received it back in the 1990s.

It felt like a risky thing to do from an emotional standpoint. Day one in Washington, less than twenty-four hours after that Auschwitz exhibition, all on my own for nearly another week. Did I really want to do this to myself?

Of course I did. That's why I was here. I searched the database, I found her name, I clicked on the video. And I braced myself.

My mother was dressed up in one of her best blazers, a white grid on navy, with a cream-coloured silk blouse underneath. At her neckline was her diamond pendant; gold hoops weighed down her ears. She was in the living room of her condo, sitting there like it wasn't the biggest deal in the world that she was alive. Behind her you can see a plant and—deep breath here—the sideboard that was part of the dining room set she had cherished so much, the one piece of furniture I paid a fortune to transport to Vancouver, where it does not match my taste or anything else in my house (except for, maybe, the *Mona Lisa*) but has the most prominent spot in the place, right next to my front door. I sat there in the silence of that Washington library, her voice in my headphones, bursting at the reunion.

The beautiful surprise of that video was the comfort it brought me to hear my mother's raspy-from-years-of-smoking voice, her little expressions ("Och, don't ask") and her immigrant grammar. "They didn't give us to eat. Forget about."

And her little jokes. When the interviewer asks what the women talked about in the camps, my mother tells her "normal things"—food above all, also their families. "Not about romance, that's for sure." The way she said "romance" was the kicker, with an emphasis on the second syllable: "Not about ro-*mance*, that's for sure."

I was also struck by her many references to being an optimist. "Did you think you were going to survive when you were at Auschwitz?" the interviewer asks her.

"A lot of times I didn't think. And sometimes I was optimistic. My sister was very much despaired. 'We won't do it.' And I said we will, we will."

I had always identified with that pessimistic sister, Ella, while my mother was the optimist among us. I felt like Gucia was sending me some guidance from the beyond: *Change your attitude. Things are going to be okay. After all, it's not like you're in Auschwitz, what you're going through.*

But then she talked about the comfort of being with her sister in Auschwitz, and how they never parted after that reunion.

"It's always better to be together with somebody than alone. You can help each other," she said. "So we tried to help each other."

And I thought: *But Mummy, I'm all alone now.*

A few weeks later, going through the notes I had taken in Washington as I continued my writing, I read that the Talmud teaches that when we quote someone who has died, their lips whisper from the grave.

Maybe I wasn't really all alone, after all. Maybe I had never been, never will be.

The next morning, I boarded a shuttle bus outside the National Archives in D.C., a building with the directive "Study the Past" etched onto its exterior. I arrived at College Park, got my little I.D. card, and became immersed in the very specific microworld of people who scour through military records on the regular.

I received more help from very kind librarians. As I returned time after time with questions and queries, I felt like they were silently cheering for me. My quest became theirs.

First things first, I needed some very basic education—about how to use that library, but also about the military. One of the librarians helpfully printed off a Basic Military organizational chart, from group of armies at the top right down to squad. All of this was brand new information for me.

There is a field army—with tens of thousands of soldiers—and then a corps, also tens of thousands. In each corps, there are divisions—still thousands—and then a brigade. Brigades are made up of companies and now we're into the hundreds. Companies are made up of platoons, which are made up of squads of a handful of soldiers.

The squad was my dream. But if I could identify a platoon, it would help narrow things down. I would be satisfied with a company or brigade. Even a division would help. I could find some names and start making inquiries—find someone who could refer me to one of his old buddies who might remember that momentous Easter Sunday in Germany.

I got to work, with help from the library people. I learned the system—looking up information in various books, putting in a request at the main desk, waiting for my files to be fetched. Grabbing many coffees in the soulless ground-floor cafeteria as I waited.

The librarians helped me determine what to look for: after-action reports, intelligence reports, engineer journals. In these documents, I might find the details of my mother's rescue, from the U.S. military perspective.

I had a date and a location: I knew my mother had been liberated on April 1, 1945, in Kaunitz, Germany. I looked for reports from that part of Germany from that date, and the days previous and after. Would there be a note about finding hundreds of emaciated women in a field, about making a U-turn and liberating them?

The librarians would pack boxes of files onto a cart. I would wheel the boxes of files that the U.S. government had entrusted me with over to a table. And inside—oh my gosh—were the originals: typed up notes of what those soldiers had experienced that day, as they moved east through Germany, conquering the Nazis. Detailed maps with handwriting on them. All of their observations—what they had seen, what they had wrought, as they pushed from France toward Berlin. I have never felt closer to the men who saved my mother.

I had Google Maps working on overdrive on my laptop; I was plugging in the names of places on these maps and in these reports, using the directions function to check their proximity to Kaunitz.

"By March 30 the 2nd Armored under XIX Corps was across [the Rhine] and attacking east," I read. This was two days before my mother was rescued. The penultimate night of her imprisoned life. She would be liberated about two hundred kilometres east of the Rhine.

On March 31, the XXX, XIX and XIII Corps were all near Kaunitz. The weather forecast was overcast with drizzle in the morning, breaking in the afternoon.

The 17 A and B Divisions of the XIX Corps advanced three miles that day from Buldern to Appelhulsen, securing the road from Appelhulsen to Nottuln. The Second Armoured Division was just east of Ascheberg—I was particularly interested in armoured divisions because I recall that there may have been tanks involved in my mother's story. The 83rd Division was assembling west of Haltern. I was Google mapping everything; these places were so close to where my mother would have been.

From April 1, this note: "The 2nd Armored by-passed the great city of Hamm, leaving it to be cleaned up by the 95th Division, and angled southeast to Lippstadt where they met the 3rd Armored Division on the afternoon of the 1st of April to close the Ruhr Pocket." Lippstadt, where my mother had been a slave labourer! Where she had started her death march four days earlier. This was so exciting to read. "Here the Ninth and First US Armies cut off and captured over 300,000 German troops, and the last remaining industrial area of Germany. Germany's doom was sealed!"

And then this: "Great numbers of depots, airfields, factories, stores, rolling stock and dumps fell into our hands in this area; the roads began to fill with hundreds of thousands of Russians, French, Jugoslavs [sic], Poles, French, Dutch, Belgian, Hungarian and Italians."

There was no mention of Jews. But my mother was Polish, and she was with mostly Hungarian women. Italians too. *Bella*. On the road. I was shaking, reading this.

And this, written on a map: "Tens of thousands of slave workers and liberated prisoners thronged the roads."

My mother was one of them.

I was getting close.

From an Infantry Regimental Journal on March 31, the final day of my mother's imprisonment, the soldiers moved from Ascheberg at 0500 to Liesborn at 1830.

"Seems likely the rescuers were a component of the 30th Infantry Division," I typed into my laptop in excited all-caps. This infantry division kept coming up!

I checked my military crib sheet. A division is generally ten thousand to sixteen thousand soldiers. Oy.

Then I found that the 30th Infantry Division had moved to Drensteinfurt on April 1. Close—but still about sixty kilometres west of Kaunitz. They were in Kaunitz on April 3. It wasn't them.

"PULL," my notes said: 41st Infantry; 113th Division; 83rd Division; 204th tank. I requested, I waited, I drank the bad coffee, I picked up my boxes, I read file after file.

One note I found in an After-Action Report dated April 30, 1945, for the 113th Cavalry Group and M11 Team 420-G: "While in combat every member of this team helped quite a few Krauts to die for the Fuehrer and Vaterland."

The 8th Armored Division moved from Lippstadt to Paderborn on April 1. But the route, Google Maps cruelly informed me, would have been to the south of Kaunitz.

The 119th Infantry moved by motor overnight from Drensteinfurt to assembly areas in the vicinity of Neuenkirchen to Kaunitz closing at 0930 on April 2. But this was too late to have liberated the women in Kaunitz early on the morning of April 1.

From the 120th Infantry report of April 1, 1945, the overlay showed an assembly area encompassing Verl, where Kaunitz is located. They were behind the 2nd Armored Division. "Combat efficiency and morale— excellent," the report said. I was thrilled to read this, imagining these happy soldiers. Liberating slave labourers—in addition to capturing Germans—would have been quite a morale boost. A great day on the job.

To read these descriptions, knowing that they were about my mother, in essence, and to read the words of these men, to read about their experiences, made me feel closer to them. The weather reports, a call from an 83rd Infantry Division captain to let the guys know that they had found a brewery in town. It felt like I was stepping back and witnessing a little bit of their world—their world that had allowed mine to be created—on these typewritten sheets of paper.

"Liberated Displaced Persons have been fed exclusively from German civilian stocks and captured Wehrmacht food," a military government report said.

It felt like a major discovery, reading about these liberated displaced persons, knowing my mother had been among them.

"Displaced Persons have been employed on a voluntary basis through Mil Gov to work for military."

My mother was employed by the army, though I'm not sure if it was the U.S. or British Army. She worked as a cleaner for a regiment of the 71st Division, she had written in a note that Doris found in her papers. It was probably the British; they had taken over from the Americans, as Kaunitz was in the British Zone. But still, this felt close. Exciting.

At the same time, some of what I read in these boxes of files about the Displaced Persons, the just-liberated slaves of the Nazis, was deeply upsetting.

"The health of DP's, especially that of political prisoners, has been very bad in many instances." Most of the cases of illness, the report said, were the result of malnutrition. DPs were dusted with DDT powder to control the spread of typhus. Was my mother dusted with this powder? She had never mentioned it.

The 330th Infantry's report for April noted: "The most difficult phase of the operation was the controlling, feeding and administering to the thousands of displaced persons as well as establishing military government in the areas overrun, and guarding installations, warehouses, etc., to prevent looting by German civilians and displaced personnel."

An account from April 8 described a "Concentration Camp Train"—2,500 people crammed into a forty-five-car prison train. "No food had been received for three days, and those who still had the strength were almost dangerously ravenous, some swarming into the local bakery to lick up raw flour."

Imagine what it was like for these soldiers, encountering these scenes of extreme deprivation, these stories of unimaginable cruelty. Today, we are well versed in the horrors that took place, and yet it is still shocking to read details of what these people had been put through. Imagine seeing it with your own eyes, having no knowledge about what had gone on, until you witness a bunch of emaciated people licking flour off a bakery floor.

The Americans spoke with twenty passengers, learning that they were Jews and other political prisoners who had been at Bergen-Belsen. They heard about the clearing out of Jews from Poland, the burning of bodies at Belsen. They encountered a German officer who abandoned his post and hid his identity by wearing civilian clothing. "His own attitude was one of hand-washing apathy. He was not responsible for what went on, was just a pawn," the officers recorded.

The worst account I read that week came from observations by military government officers.

The prisoners had been fed and deloused; beds and clean sheets and blankets had been set up for them in barns and other buildings, they reported. "The setup looked beautiful, but only for a short time. The personal standards of cleanliness of many members of the group were bad, and some even went so far as to defecate on the floor of their living quarters."

It noted that rehabilitation for "the victims of Hitler's Europe" would need to be about more than relocation, more than providing a place to live and food to eat. "True rehabilitation must provide for even so fundamental a thing as a sense of physical decency for a large number of those who have been treated and have lived for years as animals."

I felt shame reading this. Embarrassed for those poor people, the ones who had lived for years as animals and then defecated on the floor. I wondered if it was not in fact an issue of behaviour, but urgency, illness. Dysentery. These prisoners had had their first real food in years.

For some of them, it was chocolate. What would that do to your digestive system? There was probably no time, I thought, to locate a toilet.

I found information in these reports about the area that encompassed not only Kaunitz but also the place where I believed my father's farm was located. One description gifted me with some peace, thinking about how my father was able to live—even if in a constant state of terror—for nearly three years.

"Past the main cities of resistance, past the broken roads and shattered farmhouses and torn-up fields, we suddenly come upon towns that stand intact and fields that are green and farmers who are at their job working. There was no fighting in these areas and the people have profited. HALTERN is peaceful and quiet. Then in the open country behind MUENSTER and south to PADERBORN, you see the thousands and thousands of liberated foreign workers and prisoners of war from every army in Europe. Mingling with them are German workers walking back home from the RUHR."

I pictured my father on one of those still intact farms, in a green field, working at his job. Peaceful and quiet.

The Germans, the reports described, were complaining about their former slaves stealing their chickens. The U.S. Army was having none of that. "The truth is that the eastern workers are astonishingly well-behaved. For years they had been kept in semi-starvation and treated as indentured labor without any basic human rights. Now they are free and they are still hungry. They are still as comparatively docile as they were in German factories and fields. They neither take revenge on the Germans nor mistreat them. We have heard of no case of violence. Since they cannot buy food or clothing, they take it where they can. German complaints are a mixture of hypocrisy, impudence and subtle propaganda."

The freed prisoners in rags were described elsewhere as "surprisingly cheerful, surprisingly orderly." Reading this made me feel what we call in Yiddish "*naches*"—a proud, pleasurable satisfaction as a result of the achievement, even good behaviour, of a loved one. Almost like a proud parent. A proud future daughter.

I came across a description of an unfinished letter, still in its typewriter, at an abandoned German military post, translated from German: "Dear Mother: This will probably be the last letter which I will write to you during the war. The enemy is in the immediate vicinity and here all hell has broken loose. I believe we all must . . ." The letter ended there.

I felt for this boy, this German son, who must have been so terrified. Who had to run from his letter to his *Mutter*.

Some of the most lyrical and upsetting military writing I found in those old file folders about that time came from the division histories, written after the war. Almost like a yearbook, they describe what the division had been through and accomplished. Losses, too.

From the history of the 331st Infantry Regiment, describing the events of late March and early April: "Here and there we met streams of the newly liberated. Down the road they came singly, in couples, in dozens, and in great clusters of 50 and 100. These were the slave laborers of the Germans and we had helped liberate them."

From the History of the 83rd United States Infantry Division, also known as the Thunderbolt Division: "Now, during Easter Week, we swept him [the enemy] across Germany . . ." it read. I loved that young men in a division known as the Thunderbolts had been there for my mom, or people like her. Go, Thunderbolts!

"The press acclaimed the fact that we had established and held the only American bridgehead over the Elbe. But we will remember other things. The beauty of the country—and the horror hidden beneath that beauty! For years we had read of the barbarisms practiced by the children of Hitler. For years we had tried not to believe. But now we saw with our own eyes. We were nauseated. There, beyond the stench and vermin of the concentration camp wire, was the gentle countryside, blossoming into spring. And there were the huge white flags, the docile, guiltless people. It made a fellow wonder.

"When our drive was finished and the world had proclaimed our accomplishment for a moment, we could only remember the hate that had risen within us as we passed through those camps, saw those thousands of helpless people. If we had not known hatred of the German before, we knew it now. Its proportions frightened us. We saw the thing that had been done to mankind. We will never forget it."

I had three days at the library in Maryland. I needed to be back at the U.S. Holocaust Museum on the Friday, to spend a final day in the reading room and also tour the museum itself, which I hadn't yet done. It would be closed on Saturday, and I would be flying out that afternoon.

By Thursday, this adventure had developed some routine. Board the early shuttle bus in Washington, look at the benign scenery along the way, check in at the archives, put my stuff in a locker, request the files, drink the coffee.

In the batch of files I requested that morning, I found a note from April 3, 1945.

"Mil Gov Detachment I3E3 investigated 600 female Displaced Persons in Kaunitz and found them located in private homes and being cared for locally. Two female doctors were reported in the group but having little or no medicine."

The number of prisoners was approximately right. The location was right. The women had been sent to private homes for shelter. And I knew from reading the testimony of another woman who had been on that death march that there had been two female doctors in the group.

There was my mother, part of history, here in the National Archives of the United States.

I had never doubted her story, but there was something very powerful about seeing those details there in black and white. My mother's story, the one she had told all of her life, told here from the perspective of the great army that had liberated her. This was my story too—and it was part of a much larger story, in the history of the world.

She had been part of, as the Action Report of the Second Armored

Division put it, the "spectacular RHINE-ELBE thrust to accelerate the collapse of the German Wehrmacht," where large factories were seized—like the one in which she had been a slave labourer. Where she had been a slave.

"Countless thousands of Allied prisoners of war and forced laborers were liberated in overrunning important industrial and agricultural areas. Systematic tabulation, movement and evacuation of most of the liberated prisoners and displaced persons was accomplished during the period."

Amazing. But this report was made two days after liberation. I still wanted to find the group that had done the deed, set my mother and Auntie Ella and Doda Rushka free.

In another batch of files I requested, I noticed that the information was becoming familiar. Not because I had become so well versed in these events. But because, I realized, I was requesting boxes of files that I had already read through.

I tried again, with other files on the list I was making as I went. It happened again. Files I had already scoured. I was researching in circles.

It appeared that I had satisfied, to the best of my limited abilities, all of my leads.

Rereading the familiar words, I read the writing on the wall. I knew how the search was going to end. It was ending.

I was not going to find the platoon or squad or any man who helped liberate my mother. I was not going to find the description I dreamed of reading: "Found hundreds of women in a meadow in a town called Kaunitz. Made a U-turn. Provided food from our supplies. Instructed the Germans in town to let the women stay in their homes. The women told us they had been prisoners. They were very thankful; some of them kissed our shoes."

I would not find that.

I came so close that week, digging up reports from all around that part of Germany around April 1, 1945. Those incredible days came to life for me, rising out of those dusty old file folders. But I wasn't able to put a pin in it. I did not have a brigade, a name, a description of what happened that day.

I could not connect any particular group of soldiers to the liberation of the women of the LEM Factory in Kaunitz, Germany, on the first of April, 1945. Easter Sunday. Passover.

I was going to have to leave it. I packed up the files and rolled them back to the desk, slowly. *Any more requests?* they asked. *No, thank you, none.*

This revelation would remain in the dark, maybe in a box I failed to request.

But if I had learned anything posthumously from my mother that week—and I had learned a lot—it was to look on the bright side. Okay, so I didn't find the squad or platoon. But I learned all kinds of things from those old files. What the guys who saved her were like. The horrors they saw. The satisfaction they felt, the pride, the disgust. I had come close. I had come close to finding my mother's liberators. And, in my search, closer to her.

That week I also managed a quick visit to the National Museum of American Jewish Military History in Washington. That's where I bought the book in which U.S. soldiers described their experiences of liberating different concentration camps. I scoured it, hoping for a mention of seven hundred women, mostly Hungarian, by the side of a road near a village called Kaunitz. There was no such mention.

Still, reading the stories in *GIs Remember: Liberating the Concentration Camps* about what these soldiers had experienced, I got a picture of what these men may have seen, a version of it anyway. Death everywhere. This was not a battlefield. This was a whole other hell.

A college student who had enlisted in 1943 recalled liberating a camp, hearing cries for "wasser"—water, in Yiddish (or German, I suppose). Reading this, I was transported back to my childhood kitchen. I could hear my father asking my mother for a glass of *wasser*. Was it always, I wondered, a luxury, for them to be able to walk into the kitchen, open a cupboard, grab a glass, turn the tap and fill it with water? To be able to drink whenever they were thirsty?

All these years, I had been imagining fully grown men liberating my mother, men with experience and well-earned swagger. In fact, some of these men were boys, teenagers, just a few years older than my own son. It would have been one thing to liberate a group of young women; yes, that would have been thrilling. But for the boys who walked through the gates of Buchenwald proper or Bergen-Belsen or Dachau, imagine the horrors they saw. Hundreds—thousands—of bodies everywhere. Emaciated. Dead. Or alive, barely. Walking skeletons. Torture victims. Something they would have been absolutely unprepared for. What would it make a fellow wonder?

...

It seems impossible to immerse yourself in racially motivated persecution and genocide in the capital of the United States without considering the devastation of that country's history of slavery. After six straight days of Holocaust-related activities, I spent my final day in D.C. a few blocks away at the Smithsonian National Museum of African American History and Culture. This is a place that every American needs to visit.

I learned—and realized—some difficult lessons during this visit: in particular, how tied up the U.S. economy was in the slave trade. This was not an invader's horrors coming to the shore. It was the people who were or would become Americans: the government, the residents. It was systemic.

Still the victims of deadly prejudice, Black people in the U.S. are surrounded by descendants of enslavers, living on a land where it was allowed. No, not merely allowed. Encouraged. Celebrated. Rewarded. Part of the fabric. Where there had to be a fight to dismantle it. Where states—where people—went to war rather than agree to abolish the horrific practice.

I felt a kinship—my parents had been slaves too, albeit for a much shorter period of time and always with the hope of the end of war and liberation, unlike the generations of Black people who had been slaves in an endless state of tyranny. I also felt a supreme weariness. Would it ever end? This story continues to play out, for Black Americans, for European Jews, for Chinese Uighurs, for Indigenous Canadians. Different stories of horrors and inequalities. All of them preventable. None of them acceptable. And yet.

At the African American History museum, I was confronted with so many parallels. Black slaves, for instance, were forced to wear badges, as Jews would later be forced to wear a yellow star. I read about Owadu Equinew, eleven years old when he was forced onto a slave ship. The same age, maybe, that Rachmiel Lindzen, the boy who would never grow up to be my uncle, was when he was sent to the gas chamber at Treblinka. The same age as my son, back home, who could barely manage to take his dishes to the sink after a meal.

Because of the way you move through the museum, the direction of flow, I kept seeing the same people. There was one woman I began talking with. She had come from slaves, she told me. She was a beautiful older Black woman, with a purple rose on her lapel. I felt a special connection to her that Saturday morning. Both of us wandering through, learning, sad. Both of us free.

We hugged good-bye. In a few short months, we would not be able to do even that anymore, hug.

FOURTEEN

Reunion

BACK FROM D.C., HOME with Jacob, I was fuelled with new inspiration for my project: those young men, the ones who were excited about finding the brewery, astonished at the survivors licking the flour. My mother's rescuers. Mine. My son's. I was learning so much—about the Holocaust, about my parents, about myself.

There was more to this than just ("just") writing about the Holocaust. It is a story that needs to be repeated, not only so we will never forget, but for the never again. And not just never again for the Jews. But for Muslims and Black people and Indigenous People and . . . I could go on. The list of the persecuted is never-ending. And this was not just about never again, projecting into some amorphous future of persecution. Again was happening now, all around.

I wrote. And wrote and wrote. I would sit at the little IKEA desk in my bedroom, a candle burning next to me. Or at the kitchen table downstairs, where I began my writing ritual by turning on two little lamps: one was a battery-operated string of twinkly lights in a bottle that my friend Mel had brought over for me as a Chanukah gift during a dark post-separation holiday season. It had become a little symbol of friendship, resilience and hope. The other was a silver table lamp with tree-shaped cut-outs that I had bought with my sisters when they came to Vancouver to see me on a post-separation rescue mission—a gift from them. It threw light on the wall and warmed up the lonely room. The lamps sat on either side of a photo of my parents, Gucia and Tadek dressed up for some event back in the days of black-and-white photography. My mother is glamorous in a satin gown, a huge smile on her face. My father is wearing a suit with a boutonniere, and he's got an almost-smile on his face, as he leans into my mom. Survivors. Back in the light.

The barrel of negative emotions I had felt at the pathetically common turn of events in my own personal life did not dissipate, but at least I had a new outlet for it—the rage, in particular. Those vacationing Nazis at the museum in New York. The adoring German women with their heaving breasts, reaching out to Hitler with their bouquets.

My emotions could fill my house, my city, the world. My anger could bolt like lightning from Vancouver to Poland. It was that power-ful, this rage. So powerful it could displace my other worries, my other sorrows. This rage, another step through the stages of grief, felt right. Healthy, even.

Over these hours, I would not be in my bedroom where my heart-break had been most acute, or at the kitchen table that once bustled with family dinners and breakfasts. I was somewhere else: the freez-ing or boiling barren lands of Poland and Germany, learning about my parents' fate, writing about it, digesting it. Google, along with the stacks of books in my bedroom, gifted me with many more horrors.

But also some gifts. I felt closer to my parents. Immersed in the details of their lives, I could feel them—inside me, around me. A weird reunion. A beautiful one.

...

The same month I was in Washington, the Holocaust came to my doorstep. The World Federation of Child Survivors of the Holocaust happened to hold its annual conference in Vancouver that year.

I am obviously not a child survivor and neither were my parents, but there was a lot of relevance here for all survivors and 2Gs. The majority of the more than four hundred people who attended were second generation types like myself.

My cousin Mia—Ella's granddaughter—was the only person I knew there, and on Friday afternoon she introduced me to a few friends of hers, an extended 2G family that adopted me for the weekend. I spent a lot of time with them, talking about very intimate things, because that's what happens when you get together to focus on Holocaust trauma.

"You are sharing a miracle," Robert Krell told the crowd, in an inspirational keynote on the Saturday morning. Krell, the Vancouver psychiatrist who had been studying the impact on the second generation for decades, is a wonder to listen to. And as a child survivor of the Holocaust and also a child of survivors, he is a miracle indeed.

"We were not meant to be," he said, meaning all of us.

"The genocidal objective was annihilation."

I let the wisdom of his words wash over me. So much of my project had been about going as dark as I could. But that morning, I found some light. Some understanding, some common ground. "It was not normal to be normal," he said, of Holocaust survivors. And for us, their children, we learned not to ask.

"Silence served us at one point," he said. But now we must speak out, he urged us. "We cannot afford to grow complacent."

I attended a few workshops that weekend, where some of the other 2Gs talked about their intergenerational issues or, as one person put it, "our inherited schticks." They described a heightened anxiety and increased neuroses as they age, a tendency to hide their Jewishness to protect themselves, feelings of dread that the Nazis are coming for them. That when they are in an unfamiliar place, like the conference room we were occupying in that fancy Vancouver hotel, they have a tendency to keep an eye on the door, and figure out an escape plan in advance. The Nazis—or a contemporary equivalent—could show up at any time.

"Any decision," someone said, "could be a life and death decision."

Others shared that they think about what, if the Nazis did show, they would take from their homes—which photos, family heirlooms, possibly an expensive piece of jewellery that could be used in future for bartering purposes. "We are on guard," the man leading that workshop said. "Many of us are on guard."

I would take that signed Art Spiegelman book, I thought. The one with the picture for Jacob. Not because it could be valuable to sell. But to remind me—of what was, what could be.

Later that afternoon, in a different session, a 2G described how, after her parents had died, she found money hidden in the freezer. And at another workshop, one of the speakers told us that she always backs into a parking spot, always chooses an aisle seat at the theatre. The need to flee could come at any moment.

I was on the verge of feeling smugly normal when others spoke up with concerns that much more closely mirrored mine: a feeling that the other shoe is always about to drop and that the world is not safe. Being plagued with obsessive doubt. A heightened ability—one might call it a curse—to observe and gauge others. The desperate need to have people like you. A constant expectation that someone is going to get you. The difficulty in being able to trust anyone.

I drifted out of that room for a moment, recalled how difficult it had been for me to trust a man, ever. And that when I finally did, when I finally learned to quell the obsessive doubt and enjoy the love and security and the healing embrace of certainty, the other shoe dropped. Trust had been a mistake. It had been awarded in error.

People talked about their inability to throw out food—that, as children, they didn't think there were any grandparents in the world. And, about the next generation. "What scares me is that I'm passing it on to my child," one woman said.

I tried to signal her with my eyes from across the room. Me too.

"It's so great to know," someone said, "that you're all just as crazy as I am."

I had found my people.

At the conference, there was a philosophical discussion about bringing light to our unlikely lives. How do we learn to love life? It can't all be doom and gloom. The world is a beautiful place. We shouldn't let go of the dream of optimism and the joy of living. Don't we also have an obligation to lead fulfilled lives? "You can be vigilant and still live a good life," someone said.

Vigilance, though, was exhausting. I wanted some of that joy and optimism people were talking about. I wanted pleasure to be easy.

They did talk about being very sensitive to persecution—seeing it everywhere, and seeing it broadly, beyond just us, the Jews. *These powers*, I thought, *should be used for good.*

This was my heightened sense of justice, or my heightened anger at injustice. We were empaths who, through our suffering, had learned to feel for others. We know the pain; maybe one of the ways to lessen it— or at least to harness it—is to fight for others who are in the anguish of persecution. Whether it lessens our pain or not, isn't that our obligation?

"We should be like a light to the world," someone suggested.

The conference centre crowd had become a mirror of me—people with the same issues, the same fears, and people with the words I needed to hear. "We all have two lives," one man said. "And our second one begins when we realize we only have one."

On the Saturday afternoon, at a session about dealing with the death of survivor parents, we sat around a conference room in a semi-circle, telling stories, things some of us had never said out loud, to anyone.

We shared the guilt of not knowing our parents' full stories, of not learning the details when they were still alive, when we could still ask. Of trying, too late, to fill in all those gaps. Of being embarrassed, when we were young, by their accents. Of telling them to speak English.

I was one of the youngest in the room, but I fit right in. It wasn't so unusual to feel ashamed by immigrant parents, to not know all the details of their heroic and tragic lives, to not have asked enough questions. And to be plagued with all the unknowns.

Someone suggested that we learn to be okay with not knowing it all, to accept the mystery in our lives. Our parents were survivors, victims, forever mourning, always plagued with trauma, unable, in some cases, to be the best parents they could be. So we were victims too.

"Our parents are very complex," someone said. "And maybe we should honour that."

That night, there was a live band and dancing. It sounds a little strange, I know—Holocaust conference dance party. But everyone needs to cut loose, I guess, and nobody more than us that weekend.

I did not make it over to the dance floor. I remained at my table having a long conversation with one of my new friends, Sheryl Kahn, a beautiful blond woman originally from South Africa. As happens at these things, we hadn't really delved into aspects of our lives beyond Holocaust-related subject matter—Auschwitz first, "So what do you do for a living?" way later. We were at the so-what-do-you-do-for-a-living part of the weekend when she told me she worked as a counsellor at BC Women's Hospital, in the clinic for women who have postpartum depression.

Wow. I told her: *That clinic saved my life! It was a godsend when I needed it. I always say if I win the lottery, that clinic is getting a chunk of the winnings.*

Sheryl asked me which counsellor I had seen. I honestly couldn't remember the counsellor's name, but I could picture her: long, dark hair, a foreign accent, a name that was Arabic, perhaps?

Then we moved on to my job: *I am a journalist*, I explained, telling her what I write about.

Wait, she asked. *Is your husband a journalist too?*

Ex-husband, yes.

And did he have children from another marriage?

Yes.

I could see where this was going.

I didn't always look like this, she explained; *I wasn't blond.* She found an old photo of herself on her phone and there she was: Sheryl Kahn, long dark hair, with the exotic accent and the Arabic-sounding last name. Here she was, the woman who saved my life, sitting next to me at a conference for children of Holocaust survivors.

I remember, she told me, *that you weren't being supported. You weren't getting the support you needed. Your husband was busy at work and with his other children, you were new to Vancouver, you didn't have family here.*

Yes, yes, all of this.

She had been there for me when I had been suffering from postpartum depression. And eleven years later, with the dance music blaring and the children of Holocaust survivors busting a move on the parquet dance floor, here she was, again.

And here you are, she said.

Here I am.

We were both crying now, and hugging. It was the most unexpected reunion. The Holocaust had brought me back to this woman who had brought me back to life. Rescued me.

Sheryl asked me to show her a photo of myself with my baby from that time. I didn't have one on my phone, but I said I would look through my photos when I got home and bring one in the next day.

On Sunday morning before heading back downtown to the conference centre, I braced myself and went through the old photos. Old photos of your life as a happy family are hard to look at when you are heartbroken (being in the middle of a conference about the Holocaust didn't help). But I forced myself and looked. First in physical albums, then on the computer. Turning pages, scrolling, scrolling. So many photos that were so hard to look at, still. When I had been part of a beautiful family, married to the love of my life. Stepmother to his exceptional son and daughter.

There were countless photos of infant Jacob and his dad, infant Jacob and his brother and sister. But I couldn't find any photos of infant Jacob and his mom, me, other than the goopy ones from the hospital. Where were those photos? Where were all the photos an adoring husband would take of his wife and their baby?

I did eventually find one—a shot that my sister Rachel had taken on a visit to Vancouver: Jacob and me outside, bundled up. But by then I had stared down the truth of this excruciating exercise: my husband had taken virtually no photos of me and our newborn. No ten million photos of breastfeeding, baby sleeping in my arms, first walk with him nestled in the BabyBjörn. Not even six million. Not even one that I could find that morning. It became so clear on that Sunday, on the day before what would have been our twelfth wedding anniversary.

There was no evidence of any inclination on his part to take photographs of his wife with our new baby. He, like me, must have been miserable even then, less than a year into our marriage. But his misery had not been hormonal; it was not a postpartum depression, temporary and biological. His was something else, and it had stuck.

FIFTEEN

The Red Stairs

IN THE JEWISH TRADITION, the number eighteen is considered lucky. The word for eighteen is *chai*—which translates literally to "life." Cheques for charitable donations or gifts for celebratory events—weddings, Bar Mitzvahs—are often given in multiples of eighteen.

It was eighteen years after that trip to Poland with my mother, sisters and cousin that I experienced a sort of death, the end of my marriage.

And when my sisters travelled to Vancouver for their long-weekend rescue mission, Rachel said she had a story to tell me.

That weekend, my sisters took me out for meals; we went for walks, went shopping. We drove to a furniture store to check out a blue chair I was thinking of buying, each of us sitting in it and evaluating its merits. At a shop nearby, I found that silver lamp, the one that throws tree-shaped light onto my walls. At another store, we debated whether Doris should buy a necklace or a pair of earrings. God, it felt good to discuss something that unimportant. My little neighbourhood felt even cooler, seeing it through my sisters' eyes. And my cluttered duplex felt even smaller, compared to their pristine, gigantic houses.

We crammed into my compact kitchen, the three of us, so they could teach me a few recipes—chicken and more. We reorganized my cabinets so that the kitchen, once the domain of my excellent-cook husband, could become mine. Really mine.

The tiny space became a junk shop as we emptied every cupboard and sorted through the detritus, laughing at the very-expired tins, or the so-scratched-they-were-going-to-give-me-cancer pots and pans.

It is an amazing thing that after all these years, my biggest laughs are still with my sisters. They took the pain of that kitchenware—some of it once belonging to my husband, or purchased together, or received as wedding gifts—and gave it a new association. The hilarity, the new memories, became empowerment.

And then they were packing to go back home. I felt a little bit stronger. Would it last without my sisters nearby? And then we were leaving for the airport. But something was wrong; I had to pull over. The car felt weird, was making a strange noise—out of nowhere. Doris had to catch her flight, so we called a cab for her. Rachel's flight was later in the afternoon, so we waited at home for my almost ex-husband to come and have a look at the Honda we still shared.

We had some time to talk, Rachel and I, just the two of us, while he examined the car. Time for her to tell me more about the trip to Poland she had taken a few weeks earlier. We had talked briefly about it on the phone, but my life was blowing up and there wasn't much room in our conversations for subject matter other than what was happening to me and how was I going to survive it. Suddenly, because my car sounded like it was also about to blow up (it was a punctured tire, by the way), we had an unexpected morning together.

Rachel had returned to Lodz in search of more information about our father. She hired Jacek, the researcher who had found that photograph of our grandfather. Jacek had found more than that photo: he found the apartment house where our father once lived. It wasn't a vacant lot after all. We had somehow gone to the wrong address in 1998.

Rachel, back in Poland in 2016, initially visited the correct address on her own, but could not find the building. She went into local grocery stores, bought an apple as a reminder of the harmless pranks

Isaac's friend Stanley had told us about in New York. "I walked the streets," she wrote in her journal, "sadly a depressed area with a few leafy green surprises."

She continued: "Daddy, I'm here with you, I wish I could hug and kiss you, but I can't. Instead I'm walking in your youth with you. This togetherness is something I have been dreaming about for years. We are now together again."

The next day, Rachel connected with Jacek. And this time they found the building, and went inside. It was dilapidated, there was graffiti—Jewish stars, even the name "Jakub" scrawled on one wall.

They returned the following day and knocked on doors. After visiting with several tenants who knew nothing of our family, Rachel and Jacek were about to leave. On their way out, they encountered a woman, arms weighed down with shopping bags; she was just back from the market. When she heard about their plight, she invited them into the garden for a chat.

This woman, amazingly, was the granddaughter of the wartime owner of the building. She was too young to have remembered our father's family; she had not yet even been born. Had her parents or grandparents said anything about the Lederman family? No, she couldn't remember.

They kept chatting. And at some point, suddenly, something dawned on this woman.

She recalled hearing about a Jewish man who had visited the building when she was away at university. Home for a break from school, she heard a heartbreaking story from her parents—about a man who had returned to the building where he had grown up. This had happened, the woman figured out based on when she went to university, in 1979.

Rachel froze. That was my father, she told them.

They were astonished, all of them.

The woman then shared with Rachel what her parents had told her about that visit. What she remembered, in particular, was how it had ended.

After touring through what had been his childhood home—seeing the room where he was born, where his sister's bed used to stay—this man—our father!—left the apartment and walked outside to the building's communal staircase. These were the stairs that every person who lives and lived in the apartment house must climb to enter and descend to exit. These were stairs where his parents, sister and brother had once walked. Where he had once walked with them.

The man, our father, was crying. He knelt down, tears falling, and kissed them—the stairs.

Rachel showed me photographs—the woman, the building, the wooden stairs leading inside, once a shiny red, now in disrepair, shedding flecks of paint.

This story, of our father's grief when I was so deep in my own, was both sorrow and solace. It was also a summons. It was time to change the focus of my anguish.

I needed my parents at this moment; I felt a particular yearning for my father, who I had never really been able to properly know. Maybe this was a way to feel close to him, to gain strength from him.

I started thinking about going back. I wanted to dine at the Grand Hotel on Piotrkowska, as my father had when he visited in 1979: "My first time in life that I been to this very elegant place for V.I.P.s," he wrote in his diary. I wanted to visit that pit my uncle Isaac was forced to dig out near Piotrkow Trybunalski, and say *kaddish* for all the people whose lives had been brought to an end there so brutally, who had no one left to remember them.

But most of all, I wanted to see the home where my father lived—not a vacant lot, after all. I wanted to see those red stairs, to plant my own footsteps on the staircase where the family I had never met had walked—up to their home countless times, then out one last time to the ghetto and later, their deaths. What footwear had they selected for that final descent? Where did those shoes wind up?

I had this idea that returning to the scene like my father had when I was thirteen years old and a world away, and bending down to kiss these steps, could be a kind of healing pilgrimage. Some sort of posthumous attempt at a connection to this man who had died too young, whose family had died too young. I channelled my whirling emotions—there were so many of them at the time—into those wooden planks that had once played a minor role in everyday life for my father and his parents and his sister and brother. Their lives—and way of life—had been extinguished. The stairs were still there, some sort of peeling, red relic.

"My dear Daddy, I felt your presence with me as I walked your walk," Rachel wrote in her diary from that trip. "You have been firmly in my heart every pounding moment of this journey!"

I made a decision. I was going back to Poland.

I have no homeland to return to. I am not from Israel. My immediate ancestors were from Eastern Europe—not sure where before that. There is no home to go home to. I am in a state of perpetual exile, at home in a diaspora. To perform any sort of pilgrimage, I would have to go back to the places my parents had meant when they said "home."

There is so much we don't know for sure. I don't know the exact chronology of what happened to my parents. I don't know what happened to my mother's older brother. I don't know, will never know, what happened to all of those aunts and uncles, cousins and other relatives. I don't know if my aunt Devorah had her breasts sliced off by a madman before she was gassed to death. If it was my grandmother's wig on the stairs, or her mother's wig. This is a common thing, this not knowing. So many of us, wandering around North America, not knowing, not finding each other.

I often think, if it hadn't been for the war, I would be a kid living in Poland. But it's more than that, of course: if it hadn't been for the war, I would not exist. My mother would not have been death-marched to Kaunitz and my father would not have been living under a false identity nearby and would not have visited the Jewish women hoping to find his sister who in fact had been gassed to death with his parents and little brother. My parents would have married other people, I would never have been born. Jacob would not exist.

How do you think about the most horrific thing when it has given you the best thing, the only thing—life?

...

Three years after my marriage ended, I was in a better place. I had gone to D.C., learned so much more about my parents. I'd found Sheryl, and so many other connections at the Holocaust conference. I was not completely healed from the split with my husband—would I ever be?—but I was able to function again. Able to dream and plan, and mean it. To plan that pilgrimage to Poland, to my father's childhood home. It was a building, still standing, still a container for life, people travelling up and down those red stairs on their way to school and work, shopping and church. People going about their lives, like I was.

And if I was going to see the place where his family had lived before the war, I also wanted to go to the part of Germany where his war had ended in the spring of 1945. To Kaunitz, where my mother's death march had been terminated in a meadow. Where my father had gone to look for his sister but had met my mother instead. To the village that marked the end of the road for both of their Holocaust nightmares.

Kaunitz had been this magical place in my childhood stories, where my mother had been liberated, where my parents had met—because of a motorcycle accident. And destiny. Where they had fallen in love and been married and lived as newlyweds and new parents. I wanted to see that place. A place where my family had experienced this unlikely joy.

I talked to Doris and Rachel about coming with me. They were as excited about the idea as I was. The three of us, together, travelling back to our parents' first home together. We decided we would go the next year, in 2020. We settled on March—another hard month for me, the month my husband had moved out. This trip with Doris and Rachel would be a good way, I thought, to mark four years of being on my own.

This would be a different kind of pilgrimage than the concentration camp tour we had taken with our mother more than twenty years earlier. This trip would follow a less tragic itinerary. We could try to find the road my mother had been on when the U.S. soldiers came to her aid, maybe find our parents' home—my father had drawn a map for my sister Rachel decades ago. I'll rent a car, I told them, and we can drive around to nearby farms, maybe find the place he had lived—he hadn't left the location with any of us. Even just to be in that area would feel special, even if we couldn't find the exact farm.

Doris dug up our father's diary from his 1979 trip—something none of us had read for many years. She combed through the little green notebook for clues. A short time later, she texted us a big one: Our father had written that, on that trip in 1979, he had travelled from Paderborn to Geseke and then to Verlar. From there, he walked two kilometres to the farm. Wow—how many farms could be two kilometres from Verlar? The out-there idea of actually finding the property suddenly seemed like a possibility.

And then, another text from Doris. She discovered a name in the diary. Flottmeyr. Or Flottmeyer. Our farmer!

Non-German speaker though I am, I tried to find our Flottmeyers, concentrating on that part of Germany. The Flottmeyers were not on Facebook. They were not on Twitter. I found a few on a peculiar "Locate Family" website that required me to tweet publicly to find them—which I did, repeatedly. No response.

This is when we started working with Andrea Tebart, the researcher in Köln.

"We are trying to find out some information ahead of our trip to the Bielefeld area in March. In particular, we are trying to find the farm where our father worked, under false papers, in the area," I wrote in my first email to Andrea in February 2020, just a little over a month before I was due to leave for Poland.

"We are hoping to have someone help us find the descendants of the farming family and, ideally, the farm where my father lived. And the church where he prayed. And, we hope, organize a meeting when we are in town."

Andrea responded quickly and asked for details about our parents' lives and war experiences.

One thing that was so beautiful about my correspondence with Andrea, with all of our Germans, was the way they approached the project—with a gentle, sensitive respect. Andrea would send us a difficult email—about another Jewish prisoner's journey from Auschwitz to Lippstadt for example, and try to soften the blow of the facts. "The next text is probably the most brutal and absolutely terrible that I've emailed you so far," she wrote. She offered apologies about the difficult content. She wrote subject lines like "puzzle pieces" and "please look." Or poetic musings about information she was sending us—about ornithological facts about that area of Germany, for instance, after I told her I had had a dream about birds.

After some time, she wrote "as a person, as a historian and journalist (of course also as a German), I have never done something meaningful like working through the history of your parents and making it understandable."

This was more than a job for her. And she was more than a hired researcher. In those days, as we were in constant touch, she began to feel like part of the family.

A few days after I sent her details about the farm, as well as what had happened to my mother in Kaunitz, she responded that she had found two Hubert Flottmeyers in the phone book. "I'll call them on Monday," she said.

And then this: "Yes, there is still this meadow where the women have been liberated by the US military. There is also a plaque above it. And of course you will see them."

Ten days after I sent her the first email, Andrea wrote to me again. "I think I found the farm!!!" The family name, as it turned out, was Flottmeier.

"It's just one letter that made the difference."

Andrea wrote the Flottmeiers a long letter—she didn't want to leave a message on their answering machine—telling them about my sisters and me and our wish to visit. "It is of great concern to all of them to meet the descendants of the farmer Flottmeier in order to thank them personally," she wrote.

A few days later, she received a call from Katja Flottmeier, the daughter-in-law of Hubert, the original farmer's son. Hubert remembered my father. That's how we learned about that scene as my father first approached the farm on his visit back. "[They] are the right family!" Andrea wrote to Doris, Rachel and me.

The family couldn't wait to meet us, Katja told Andrea. "Hubert is quite old at eighty-seven," Andrea wrote to us. "So his children told him very gently and carefully that the daughters of 'Tadek' are visiting. And? He had tears in his eyes."

The whole family was excited about this meeting, even Hubert's little granddaughter, she wrote, who was ten years old. One year younger than Jacob.

They were going to help us with the church too, the one where my father prayed for his life. The church was called St. Philipus Neri. The Flottmeiers would get the key so we could visit.

Andrea sent us all kinds of information, including a scan of a typed list of the women who had been transferred from Auschwitz to the Eisen- und Metallwerke slave labour camp in Lippstadt on November 23, 1944. The list was organized not alphabetically but by prisoner numbers. Prisoner number 25535 Linsen Estera—Auntie Ella. Prisoner number 25536 Linsen Gitta—my mother. They were both identified as "*Naherin*"—seamstress. The fact that their names were next to each other softened the blow of the document. I imagined that they were together throughout the ordeal of the transfer, and that's why they were listed one after the other.

Andrea drew up an itinerary for our visit. On our first day there, we would see Rachel's birth certificate in Gutersloh. We would also be able to view our parents' marriage certificate—which would include their address at the time. And though the street names and numbers had changed, we would be able to use that information to find the actual house in Kaunitz where our parents had lived as newlyweds and new parents, if it was still standing.

Later in the week, we would visit Lippstadt. Andrea found a tour guide for us, who knew about the history there. "What was new to me," Andrea wrote, "there are still tracks on which your mother arrived in Lippstadt in 1944." Train tracks.

On the Wednesday afternoon we would visit the Flottmeiers, the whole family. First, we would walk to the church, taking the same route as our father had every Sunday during his wartime life in Germany. "Just you three," Andrea wrote in an email, ten days before I would leave Vancouver. Katja would unlock the door and let the three of us have time in there on our own, privately.

A journalist wanted to write about us, document our trip for a chain of German newspapers. Plans were made for a celebratory dinner on our last night in Bielefeld with the group of German helpers we had cobbled together. Andrea would travel from Köln to meet us in person.

It was going to be the trip of a lifetime.

…

In early March, Germany started reporting a cluster of coronavirus cases. Berlin, I figured. But when I looked it up, I discovered that the main cluster was in fact in the German province of North Rhine–Westphalia. That would have meant nothing to me a few weeks earlier. But North Rhine–Westphalia, I now knew, was where my mother had been a slave for Germany, where my father had worked on his farm under false papers, the province we were about to visit.

My flight was booked for Thursday, March 12, arriving in Warsaw on Friday the 13th. I would meet my sisters in Bielefeld on the following Tuesday morning, March 17. They would arrive the day before.

Or would they? With the North Rhine–Westphalia cluster, we began a daily three-way debate: do we postpone the trip?

I'm going, no matter what, I told my sisters. I needed to see that farm, meet the Flottmeiers. Visit that meadow. The cluster was in another part of the province, Andrea told us. An outbreak connected to an amusement park.

March 8: there were now 850 cases in Germany. I was still going, I assured everyone.

But as the number of cases rose, my sisters, both older than me—and Rachel immunocompromised—became more nervous. And rightly so. In the days before our departures, they did the reasonable thing and pulled out. First Doris, then Rachel.

It's okay, I told them. I knew it was the right decision for them. But not for me.

The night before my departure, my bags all packed and waiting by the door for the morning drive to the airport, the U.S. president held a live television address and announced that he was closing the American borders to European travellers.

This was a stunning development and felt like a sharp turning point—the coronavirus denier was closing the border. Suddenly the danger seemed more real. I felt sure I wouldn't get sick. But what if I got stuck in Germany? Or Poland? In the little hotel in Lodz? I had responsibilities back home; I was a single mother. What would happen if I was stranded in Europe and then had to quarantine in Canada? What would happen if I couldn't get back?

But the meadow, the farm, the Flottmeiers. The church.

At 3 a.m. on March 12 I rose from the couch where I had been doom-scrolling Twitter all night, logged onto my computer and started cancelling everything. I couldn't go. As much as I felt I needed to see where my father had lived as a child, and the farm where Jacob Lederman became Tadek Rudnicki, I had a bigger responsibility to someone else: my son, Jacob Lederman.

Andrea—who, like the rest of the world, was sheltering in place—had time to continue her research. She did this on her own initiative; it remained personal for her. "Since the beginning of your assignment,

I knew that it was an important topic. And I really wanted to do it well because it's so important," she wrote. She kept asking: should she continue?—worried that it might be too upsetting for us to read the results of her research. But the upsetting part had already happened, long ago. We just wanted to know as much as we could about it.

"You won together: over Hitler, the Nazis and their terror regime," she wrote in that same email. "And I was allowed to participate a little. Thanks for that."

She sent us an old map of the Kaunitz area, one with a red square showing that meadow and a few handwritten words: "Ubernachtungs-platz der Frauen am 1.4.1945." Non-German speaker though I am, I understood: it was the place the women had been liberated on April 1, 1945.

She sent photos of that field and the path the women walked on their death march to liberation. "There are people from farms who saw the train of women," she wrote. "It was probably very lonely there as in the photo."

She dug up some information from the LEM factory. The number of hours worked by the forced labourers in February 1945: 200,596 hours (up from 146,751 in October 1944). There was hardly anything to eat, but break times (!) were observed—"completely cynical and terribly German," she wrote. 9:00–9:15 a.m. and 12:30–1 p.m. for the day shift. For the night shift: 9-9:15 p.m. and 12:30–1 a.m.

She found the name of the LEM commander: SS Hauptscharführer Bienek, the man who had been riding the bike during the death march to Kaunitz. I couldn't help myself; I went on Facebook and searched "Bienek." The world's Bieneks are like the world's everyone else on social media—they post photos of children, boyfriends, scenic mountain vistas. There are a lot of them. They have families, they're in relationships. A doula, a fly-fisherman, a financial planner, real estate agents. Photos of cute animals—including a black cat, like mine.

For a brief moment I considered contacting some of them. Asking about their father, grandfather, great-grandfather. What did he do during the war? Was he in the Resistance? Or did he ever happen to mention doing some kind of work at a factory? Was he just following orders?

Or had the Hauptscharführer Bienek long ago changed his name to avoid detection and prosecution? Did my mother's oppressor shed his actual name and become a Mr. Brown or Mr. Blank or Mr. Bean?

Andrea later told me that no, as far as she knows, he did not change his name. After the war, many people responsible explained that they had only been obeying orders, she wrote. "Many got away with it."

Anyway, it was the children of the liberators I had hoped to find, not the descendants of the SS guards. I sent no Facebook messages to these guiltless people.

Andrea sent us a scan of our parents' marriage certificate—normally verboten to do by email, but the local officials made an exception given our circumstances. There were names of two groomsmen—witnesses—we did not recognize. Probably men who worked at the town hall, Andrea figured.

We had so many questions about our father's life on the farm, things we had planned to ask Hubert in Holsen on a Wednesday afternoon in March, surrounded by this family. But with no idea when we'd next be able to travel, we decided to try to ask our questions from afar. We wrote up a list and sent it to Andrea and Katja, who also calls herself Katie, hoping that Hubert's daughter-in-law could have the conversation we had hoped to have with him.

The answers, when they eventually came, were brief and short on actual information, but they were something.

Hubert couldn't remember when my father arrived at the farm in wartime—maybe during the summer? He couldn't remember when he left either. Sometime after the war, he said. Tadek ate with the family, ate everything they did, and lived in a room accessible from the *Deele*—a wide three-leaf door that you could drive horses into, or today, a tractor—via a staircase. In his room there were two beds and a cabinet. It still looks the same today.

It still looked the same. But I couldn't see it, I couldn't be in that room.

The farm in wartime had about twenty dairy cows, as well as chickens and geese. In the fields they grew rye, barley and oats. "I think Tadek's job was to look after the animals and work in the fields, but I can't say that exactly," Hubert said. "I was a child!"

Still the description of the farm—dairy cows and chickens, barley and oats and my father's beloved rye—conjured a bucolic scene, especially given what my father had been through, what his people were going through all around him. That farm was a refuge. An island of pastoral normalcy in the cataclysm. No wonder, I thought, he had always loved to putter in our garden. No wonder he harboured such nostalgia for Germany.

Hubert shared a memory of my father sitting at the kitchen table with Hubert's parents, telling Bernhard and Katharina that he was Jewish. "That's how I found out. It couldn't be known that he was here as a Jew. If anyone had known, Tadek would have been killed. You knew what happened to the Jews, but you never talked about it," Hubert told his daughter-in-law.

This was not the story as we had known it. We understood that our father had hidden this fact from the family until after the war, knowing how crucial it was that his real identity be kept secret. It had, however, seemed entirely possible that the family had suspected. Which was why we asked the question: Had they had any inkling during the war that Tadek was Jewish?

"No, nobody suspected that he was a Jew. But dad knew it. It was not talked about, it was kept secret. My father always said that nobody has to know that he is here," Hubert answered, very thoughtfully, according to Katja.

Had Hubert misremembered? Or had the story evolved in the Flottmeier family lore over the years, to suggest that the farmer had known our father was Jewish, thus making Bernhard's employment of Tadek the actions of a hero? Or had the information indeed been shared by my father at the kitchen table, but after the war, and Hubert had the timeline wrong? Even then, perhaps, there would have been a need to keep it quiet—Bernhard might not have wanted his neighbours to know they had been sheltering a Jew all that time. Or had Bernhard known all along, or at least, before the war ended? It really does not seem beyond belief that he would have had this suspicion. That he would have done the heroic thing by keeping quiet and keeping my father employed, safe, alive.

Andrea says it is plausible that Bernhard knew and warned the family to keep it an absolute secret.

It is impossible, now, to know. And it doesn't really matter to me. This family had saved my father, either way. This family is the reason I exist.

I was so moved by some of Hubert's beautiful little remarks about my dad, there in Andrea's translation of Katja's interview transcript: "He was (Hubert laughs) a very nice guy !! ;)"—the winky emoji!

And his final remarks—probably in response to my question "Is there anything else you remember about Tadek that you can share with us?"—were "Tadek was always happy, was nice and helpful! He was just a good guy! (grins)"

Something Hubert remembered well—even his son Michael remembered—was the day my father came to visit in 1979.

Michael, then six, was playing soccer in the yard. From a distance he saw a man approaching the farm from the main street to the courtyard. When he was only a few metres away, Hubert came out of the *Deele* door and looked at the man. "I didn't recognize him right away, but I somehow sensed that it was Tadek!" Hubert recalled.

"And then when I recognized him, I'm headed for him! We were in each other's arms! I called 'Man Tadek!' We both had tears in our eyes."

Michael described his father pronouncing the name "Tadek" with what I perceived as a thrilled surprise and a bit of disbelief. "Shortly afterwards the two ran towards each other and hugged each other," he recalled. "It was very emotional . . . they cried for joy."

Andrea was later able to speak with Mia (actual name Maria). Mia was the fourth of Bernhard's five children, now living in a nursing home in Paderborn. Born in 1935, she had no recollection of driving my father around in 1979—she was a bit forgetful—but she said she remembered Tadek from her childhood.

"She says he was a very, very dear and a good person. She literally sees him in front of her," Andrea wrote.

She recalled that "with Tadek, life would have come into the farm." As children, they would run through his room often. They played soccer in the *Deele*, and he would join them.

Tadek the Himmel Kicker, I thought.

Mia had some good information: she recalled that there had been three labourers on the farm. She (or Andrea) used the term "forced" labourers—although we had had no indication that my father was a forced labourer. At the noon meal, the labourers always sat at a separate table from the family. Mia had found that strange as a child. Andrea says that would have been a state regulation. The other two labourers were a Russian named Nikolai and a Polish woman that Mia identified as Maric. That name was probably actually Maria, Andrea said, or something like that. Marie?

Rachel and I had the same thought: was Maria the woman who had been Tadek's girlfriend on the farm?

The Russian would have spent the night in a camp, worked and eaten at the farm in Holsen, and then returned to the camp at night. If he was picked up by guards, Andrea wrote, "it was of course a critical situation for your father, at least I imagine it was."

My God, did my father have to face German guards on a daily basis, if they came to pick up Nikolai? What would that do to a person?

Not to be able to hear Hubert's answers in person, or Mia's, not being able to visit the room where my father had slept, to walk the fields where he had worked, felt like a crushing loss. Not to be able to see the landscape, which Andrea had described as being full of birds.

And that church. I kept thinking about Andrea's description of the itinerary for that day: *We will meet in Holsen and you will walk along the road to the church, it is about one kilometre, just the three sisters. Katja will meet you there with the key and then you can have private time in there, as much time as you need.*

We asked Katja if she wouldn't mind sending some photos of the church. She emailed a couple of the exterior, and also sent photos of the farm. The farm was not at all as I had pictured it. Less falling down, less rickety. It was lovely. It felt nice that my father had lived in this beautiful place at such a horrible time.

Then, one morning, I woke to a video on my phone via WhatsApp. Katja had asked the church sexton, a friend of hers, to make a recording for us.

This was not the simple house of worship I had imagined. I had pictured something primitive—a favourite word of my father's—a wooden building, perhaps, dark, dusky.

But this was something else. St. Philipus Neri shone with a compact, ornate magnificence. It seemed incongruous to the austere, *Little House on the Prairie* kind of structure I had always imagined.

The wood-and-glass doors opened into a sanctuary of marble, gleaming wood and exquisite works of Catholic iconography.

There were shiny wooden pews, large stained-glass windows, an illuminated Bible turned to a colourful page. There were candles burning on the altar, fresh flowers, a container for the holy water.

The sexton had added a soundtrack—church bells and organ music—to the video she edited together.

Outside was a high bell tower that would have been visible, I guessed, from the farm, or at least on the road to the church, while walking there on a Sunday morning.

I tried to picture my father in there, imposter Catholic with his little Polish prayer book, straining to follow rituals he did not understand. Looking at the Pietà, did he long for the arms of his own mother? How foreign it all must have felt—and how beautiful. This would have been nothing like his own experience of religion, maybe in a synagogue but more likely in a cramped, colourless *shtiebel*—a makeshift house of prayer in an apartment or house. The colours, the candles, the icons, the bells. It was all so pretty, such a refuge from everything ugly he had witnessed and experienced. I wondered if my father was ever tempted to convert for real.

To have been there with my sisters in person, to have been able to light a candle for my father in that place where he prayed, would have felt like an actual religious experience. A true pilgrimage. I wish we could have done this. *Maybe I will, one day,* I thought. *When this other gloomy chapter of human history is over.*

When I looked up Saint Philip Neri, I learned that he was the Second Apostle of Rome, after Saint Peter. An Italian priest born in Florence in 1515, he became an Evangelist, founding the secular order the Congregation of the Oratory, with the goal of making the word of God accessible to all the people of Rome. He ministered to people who were poor or ill, sought to reform corruption in the church, and offered not just absolution but guidance. He promoted cheer, positivity, even engaged in practical jokes. "A joyful heart is more easily made perfect than a downcast one," he is quoted as having said.

And he prayed: "Let me get through today, and I shall not fear tomorrow."

Beatified in 1615 and canonized in 1622, Saint Philip is a patron saint of Rome. He is also the patron saint of humour and joy, of happiness. And he is, according to several write-ups on the Internet, the patron saint of the U.S. Army Special Forces.

Andrea continued to dig into our mother's story too. She told us that there had been a celebration planned in Kaunitz for April 1, 2020, to mark the seventy-fifth anniversary of the liberation of the seven-hundred-plus women, my mother among them. She sent a newspaper article with a photograph of some of the women from 1945. Did we recognize anyone? Our mother, perhaps?

I scoured the grainy photograph. Gucia was nowhere to be seen, but there, in the crowd, toward the left-hand side of the photo, was my great aunt, Doda Rushka, peering over her left shoulder, looking a lot more serious than the other women in the photo, with their big smiles.

Andrea sent us the text on the memorial in the meadow that we had planned to visit.

"On April 1, 1945, over seven hundred Jewish women were liberated by American soldiers. They were on the march from Lippstadt to the Bergen-Belsen concentration camp, where they were to be killed. They were brought from the Auschwitz concentration camp to Lippstadt as cheap labour workers for the arms industry," the plaque states, in German.

The text had been written and the plaque designed by ten local students who spent three years studying what had happened to these women. They happened to attend a school named for Anne Frank—who had died in Bergen-Belsen, which had been where these women were marching, where they probably would have died too.

"This memorial stone is laid to remember the suffering of these women and all victims of National Socialism. At the same time, it should warn us not to accept injustice towards people in any form, but to face it courageously."

Andrea later told me that in January 2020, when these 75th anniversary commemorations had been happening—January 27 is the day of remembrance for victims of the Nazis—Katie and Michael Flottmeier's daughter had asked them what it was all about. Her parents explained to her that her great-grandfather had camouflaged a Jew on the farm in Holsen.

"A short time later, I found the Flottmeiers," Andrea wrote to me. "It was a bit as if we had all been announced and welcomed."

Looking at these photos, reading all of this information about my parents, was a gift and a curse.

And I decided it was time to deal with my own photos. I was emotionally stronger, four years out from the separation. Birthdays no longer stung; anniversaries were manageable. And there was nowhere to go.

I was stuck at home, and my domestic to-do list was all around me, staring me in the face. Most pressing, though, was the fact that I was continuing with my writing—which felt so good and so hard—and I wanted to consult the photos I had taken in Washington and, in particular, at the Auschwitz exhibition I had toured through in New York, before the world had shut down.

In my desk drawer, I found my old iPhone; my newspaper had since issued me a new one. But once I charged it up, I had a problem. A tech disaster. Somehow the phone had been wiped.

Everything on the phone was lost. Literally thousands of photos. Photos from Jacob's eighth, ninth, tenth, eleventh birthdays. His grade five "graduation" and scene-stealing performance in that year's school musical. Our mother–son road trip through B.C. and Alberta. Visits to Canada's Wonderland and the Pacific National Exhibition. The entire life of Lucy, the cat I got for Jacob's ninth birthday in the midst of separation trauma. My sister Rachel's seventieth birthday, where the three sisters and our families had been together in Toronto, all of us toasting Rachel and having the time of our lives, sitting around her giant dining room table.

Photos from a transformative trip to Cozumel when a friend was turning fifty and invited a group of seven women to a house he had rented there for a few days. I didn't know any of them. On the first night, we went around the table, each of us introducing ourselves by explaining where we were in life. I laid it all out.

My own fiftieth birthday the previous year had been a wash, I told them. I had been unaware on that milestone birthday that my husband had left me for good. I spent the evening with him, our son and his children—my then-stepchildren—having dinner out, and it was lovely. But also so hard. Because I still had hope. This birthday was not the most devastating part of losing the life I had loved, not by a long shot, but it seemed like a relevant thing to mention as we went around the table, given the context.

I was heartbroken, I told them. My fingers still felt naked without my rings.

I also shared the practical concerns that had come with suddenly running a household on my own, in a city where I had no family and few friends at the time, and the burden I felt because of it. I told them, for instance, that I was a terrible and supremely unconfident cook; my husband had done all the cooking in the household. And when I was left holding the bag—or the pan, if you will—I was a bit lost. I was still at the point where I couldn't stand to touch raw meat.

A couple of days later, still enjoying that slice of Mexican heaven, my new friends surprised me with a do-over fiftieth birthday party luncheon. They presented me with gifts: a ring I had lingered over in a store, for my naked fingers. And a notebook filled with handwritten recipes from each of them, starting with the local woman our birthday friend had hired to cook for us that week, who had become part of our gang. Genny's Achiote Chicken. This was followed by recipe after recipe: Easiest Curry Ever! Easy Homemade Fettuccini Alfredo Sauce, Crock Pot Beef Stroganoff, Apple Cake. Apple Cake—my mother's signature dish.

I am typing this book with that ring on my finger.

The next year, when I turned fifty-one, not a milestone by any stretch, I threw a party for all the people who had helped me in some way since the separation. My little house was filled with co-workers and neighbours and chosen family and some actual family too; all these people who had helped me in a million different ways, big and small. These were the people who had helped me survive. *Mes* many *mères*.

I hadn't yet graduated from the heartbreak, but it was a hell of a summer party.

The photos from that fifty-first birthday party, when I was starting to return to myself even a little bit, had also been wiped from my phone. My progression from absolute grief to standing to really living again. The photographic documentation of all of that—gone.

I was so angry at myself. How hard would it have been to transfer those photos when I got the new phone? But I put it off and put it off and procrastinated some more—life was just so busy.

Being busy wasn't really the problem; it wasn't the real reason I couldn't deal with the phone. My last phone upload to my computer had ended with pictures from 2015. The last time I had been happily married. This is why I could not face looking at what came next. Not yet, not yet. Not yet until it was too late.

All those lost photographs—another thing I have in common with my mother, I thought. And then the return of the familiar shame.

My father had lived his entire life never seeing another photograph of his parents. I have never seen a photo of his mother or his little brother. There is no existing picture—that I know of—of my mother's little brother either, or her older brother. Even if her family photos that had been confiscated at Auschwitz had been clandestinely buried, even if I could look through that treasure trove, would I even be able to recognize the Lindzens? That toddler smiling at himself in the mirror could have been little Rachmiel, and I would have no way of knowing it.

I, on the other hand, was able to put a call out on Facebook: *Friends, if you have any pictures of us, and especially of Jacob, could you share them with me?*

The photos started arriving, creating a sort of This Is Your Life from the Cloud for the fool who had somehow neglected to store her own photos there.

Baby Jacob and me at a friend's "wine and whine" moms-and-tots get-together. One of the Salsa Babies friends, back when our boys were a few months old. Photos of post-separation rescue missions: my niece Laura, here from Toronto, organizing my linen closet for me when I couldn't stand to sift through formerly communal sheets and towels. My best friend, Marsha, here from Atlanta, taking me clothes shopping, forcing me to start wearing makeup again. Photos with two other best friends from Toronto, fellow Ryerson grads, straddling bikes on

B.C.'s Kettle Valley Rail Trail, all of us glowing with exercise in the Okanagan air. Photos from a trip to Legoland, where I had taken Jacob that first separated Christmas—a surprise on Christmas Eve, which had coincided with the first night of Chanukah that year.

I knew nobody would be able to send me the photos I had originally been after, from the New York and Washington museums. I had never shared those pictures with anyone; why would I? But as I started to write about those visits, and look back at the notes I had taken, I thought that maybe there was an upside to my no-Cloud catastrophe, at least for that trip. Maybe what stood out, maybe what I remembered, was most important.

SIXTEEN

My Intergenerational Trauma

I CARRY THE NAMES of three dead people everywhere I go and wherever I rest. They are my names.

It is traditional for Ashkenazi Jews to name a child after someone who has died. If I had been born a boy as my father had hoped, my name would have been Moshe—my Hebrew name, anyway—but my parents gave me a feminized version of the name, knowing it would be their last chance to name a child after their fathers. I am named after both of my grandfathers, Moshe Aron and Moshe Rafael, two men who were murdered in the gas chamber at Treblinka. My middle name, Estelle—Esther in Hebrew—is after the twin sister of my father's mother, Sara. I'm not sure how, where or when Esther was murdered. Esther and Sara looked so much alike it was said that only their husbands could tell them apart. I have never seen a photo of either of them.

My son is named after my father, the man who lost his entire family in those gas chambers, and survived by hiding in plain sight, secretly grieving and suppressing the trauma. Jacob Lederman became Tadek Rudnicki thanks to a Polish official and his sympathetic wife, whose names I do not know. Decades later, I created a new Jacob Lederman.

I have always loved this custom of naming after the dead, but as I immersed myself in the history of the people I had been named after, I started to wonder: Was I carrying not just the names of three murder victims, but also their burden?

Part of my return to the subject matter of the Holocaust—my decision to read, and ultimately write, about it—was my interest in learning whether this history—*their* history and mine too—had somehow affected my present life. These stories I carry around with me, whether I pay attention to them or push them deep down. Had they done something to me that had sent my husband fleeing? Or were they preventing me from somehow getting over this, let's face it, rather commonplace event?

I had the names of my ancestors, but I wanted their support from the beyond, like my friend on the stool at my kitchen counter had told me. My rational mind may have dismissed this idea as absurd, but my emotional desperation kept returning to it.

I longed to feel my grandmothers inside me, my aunt, the two boys who should have been my uncles. The third would-be uncle who had just disappeared. My Zaidies—the old men whose knees I would never be able to climb on. Moshe Rafael, who played violin with his non-Jewish neighbour but would not live to teach me to play the instrument. But it was all inside me, somewhere—the violins, the violence.

I conjured this idea during some of my worst moments. *Your ancestors are with you*, I would tell myself, picturing my friend saying this to me in the kitchen. The exercise was somehow comforting, but I never truly felt them.

What I felt was an absence. The absence of all those people from the earth, the absence of my parents from my life and from my story. The absence of my husband.

I had built the life I had craved, back when Jacob's dad and I were furnishing our home: a house that was alive. The chaos of young children, my husband cooking dinner and popping open a bottle of wine, people stopping by, the radio on, spontaneous dancing in the kitchen, shrieks and laughter and Lego scattered everywhere, bringing harmless pain to barefoot steps. I had the messy, chaotic household, buzzing with life, that had eluded me as a child.

And then I lost it. I let it slip through my miserable little fingers. And now it was Jacob and me. A quiet household once again. This was my biggest fear—to give my son a version of the heavy, not-happy upbringing I had lived through.

···

We are all shaped by who came before us, and what happened to who came before us. No matter what kind of life my parents would have lived, their experiences would have contributed to who I would become. Because of the trauma they endured, my life has been shaped by trauma—at least in part. To deny that would be folly.

But to still see myself in these terms at middle age seems, at the very least, peculiar.

In that illuminating radio interview with Krista Tippett, Rachel Yehuda observed that people in the 2G cohort—now in middle age or beyond—often describe themselves as children of Holocaust survivors. These were grown adults, still placing themselves in the world in relation to their parents, specifically their parents' experiences in the war. At a time of life when their peers, I imagine, are far more likely to self-identify as someone's parent or partner, or perhaps by their profession. Something happening in their adult life, something they have built. It seems odd for people in middle age to still define themselves in relation to their parents.

And yet a large part of me still identifies this way.

It was critical information, for sure. Was it a healthy tribute? Or was this perspective hampering my ability to move forward and have a happy life?

Because what had been going on, what was still going on, didn't seem so healthy.

An innocuous thing—still—turning into a time machine, a teleporter. A starry sky, a mobile paper shredder. A train; always, a train.

The mention of gas, especially in relation to an oven. But other things that might be less obvious: wooden clogs, striped anything—but especially pyjamas, especially vertical stripes. Anything manufactured by a company once associated, in any way, with the Nazis: a Volkswagen Jetta or a bottle of Aspirin. A Bosch appliance.

I might drive by a pastoral scene—a farmer's field with dairy cows resting. I see cows, then I think cattle cars, and I am off. I travel to the past, to what was and then wasn't.

Jacob had received a fairly realistic *Star Wars* lightsabre as a gift. It glowed red and made whooshing noises and he and I had been staging fun faux fights—me, equipped with a broom or Swiffer mop handle. Sometimes he would sneak up on me and fake slash me with the sword. We laughed a lot. But after I watched the Ivan the Terrible documentary series, the lightsabre toy transformed into a madman's bayonet for me, red with blood, maybe the blood of my aunt or grandmother. I couldn't play the game anymore.

I didn't want the tragic story I had inherited to overshadow my own story. I have my own story to tell, my own life to live. I am a parent to a child now, and this should override my identity as a former child to a former parent. It must.

I think: There has to be a way to turn this around. To play with my son like a normal mother. To look at the sky and not wonder what they saw in Auschwitz more than seventy years ago, but to just appreciate the beauty. Or to be constructive about it, wonder instead what kind of sky persecuted people are seeing right now in South Sudan, Northwest China, Syria—and what I might be able to do for them. I would like there to be a productive use for what ails me. Not just a terrible past that makes me feel powerless. There must be a reason I am here.

I recognized in the studies and in the accounts of other children of survivors so much about myself. It was, in some ways, a comfort. But also a warning.

"I do not believe that the spiritual lesson of the Holocaust is to live in mourning forever; indeed, I think the task for us literal children of survivors is to learn how to separate ourselves from the past, after fully acknowledging it, so that we can live and act in our own, sufficiently complicated present," wrote Eva Hoffman in an essay.

I'd read of 2G people who were overly sensitive, easily offended, took things too personally, perceived slights and offences where none existed. Who had a tendency to create drama—like me. Rushing to anger. Living in a state of victimhood. I really don't want to be a victim anymore, to view myself that way in the world, in the dynamic of any relationship.

The Jew as victim is familiar terrain, cultivated, with good reason, long before the Second World War. And I felt at home there, in that victim identity. Woe is me, poor me, my lackluster childhood, my husband who had done me wrong—this was a familiar place for me to dwell. I self-identified as a victim, so when circumstances turned against me—the divorce—I would rush back to that comfort zone and cling to it. I always knew I'd get here, I thought, to this misery. A victim, once again. Told you so.

...

Viktor Frankl, a Jewish-Austrian neurologist and psychiatrist, was sent to Auschwitz in 1944, when he was thirty-nine. His most important possession at the time were the notes for the book he had been working on. They were seized when he got there, causing him great anguish. There was more anguish to come. Frankl underwent brutal treatment as a prisoner and slave labourer, but he survived. His wife, who had previously been pregnant—the Nazis forced an abortion—was murdered. So were Frankl's parents and brother. After liberation, terribly depressed, Frankl wrote what would become *Man's Search for Meaning* in nine days.

Frankl had intended the book to be published anonymously, but he agreed upon the urging of others to include his name inside the first edition, on the title page only. The book, originally titled *A Psychologist Experiences the Concentration Camp* in German, was not an immediate success. Too depressing, maybe—like the initial response to Elie Wiesel's *Night*.

But when it came out in English more than a decade later, it caught on. Perhaps the world was ready to read about this. The non-German world in particular.

The book, which is a memoir and a contemplation, emphasizes that we cannot always control our circumstances. Terrible things will happen. The one thing we can control is how we respond to these events, to this suffering, however horrific—even Auschwitz-level horrific—they might be.

"... everything can be taken from a man but one thing: the last of the human freedoms—to choose one's attitude in any given set of circumstances, to choose one's own way," Frankl wrote.

I read passages like this with some mortification, knowing that I had not risen to my circumstances, my little heartbreak. I had not been proud of my behaviour as my marriage was falling apart, in particular the inability to even pretend that I was okay so that my son wouldn't suffer.

And yet here I was again, reading about Auschwitz and thinking about my stupid divorce.

In the preface to the 1992 edition of his book, Frankl wrote that he had "wanted simply to convey to the reader by way of a concrete example that life holds a potential meaning under any conditions, even the most miserable ones."

This notion that I did have some control, that I did have some agency—maybe not in the eruption of my marriage, but in how I would respond to it—was the reminder I had needed.

Edith Eger had learned this from Frankl too, and his wisdom had guided her. "Our painful experiences aren't a liability—they're a gift," she wrote. "They give us perspective and meaning, an opportunity to find our unique purpose and our strength."

Now they were both guiding me.

And not just them. I could hear my parents' voices rising up from Frankl's pages. They had been with me, like my friend had said in my kitchen that time, all along. Helping me to rise.

A central theme of Frankl's book is this philosophy from Nietzsche: "He who has a *why* to live for can bear almost any *how*."

"The question was not just survival," Frankl said in an interview. "But there had to be a why of survival." Something—or someone for whom to survive.

Ella and Gucia had been each other's whys. Each was crucial to her sister's survival.

And now Jacob, of course, was my why. But so were the birds outside and the trees. So was kayaking with my friend Josh, with curious seals popping up from the still, twilight ocean water around us. So was dancing around my living room to *Ray of Light* or bombing around in my ten-year-old Honda blasting *Beautiful Day*. Or, slightly less embarrassingly, feeling like a kid again zipping along the seawall on my bicycle. So was an excellent book, or a very cold glass of Sauvignon Blanc. So was my cat. So was I. I was also my why.

Primo Levi, weak with thirst shortly after arriving at Auschwitz, broke off an icicle to satisfy this need—only to have it snatched away from him by a cruel guard. The story is recounted in Levi's memoir *Survival in Auschwitz*. Levi, astonished, asked the guard: "Why?" The guard responded, "Here there is no why."

I was not living in Auschwitz. There were whys all around me; I was swimming in them. But I had been so immersed in my self-pity—why, oh why had this happened to me?—that I forgot to notice. It was time to come up for air. The heart is a bloom.

"The prisoner who had lost faith in the future—his future—was doomed," Frankl wrote in his beautiful book. Wait, was this like *The Secret*? Would I forever be alone and miserable if I worried that I was forever going to be alone and miserable? For the millionth time, I told myself that if I had been in my mother's tortured shoes, I never would have survived. I would have given up. And you would be reading something else right now.

My mother didn't give up, even at Auschwitz. So how dare I be contemplating giving up on the possibility of happiness now?

At liberation, Frankl himself realized that he could no longer feel happiness, even pleasure. He had to relearn it slowly, he wrote.

In my heartbreak, I too had forgotten how to feel any sort of pleasure. I could pretend, and I became quite expert at faking it, but it was always an act. Even during my best moments, I felt the weight. Laughing on a hotel balcony in the Mayan Riviera heat with Eileen, who travelled there with her daughter to meet Jacob and me for an emergency vacation the year my husband had moved out. Swimming in the ocean, minus my swimsuit, on that trip to Cozumel with brand-new friends. Discovering a kiwi bird in the New Zealand forest, and being able to hold the little thing in my hands. Even those once-in-a-lifetime moments in these exquisite places played out under a shadow, a presence that followed me wherever I went, to the ends of the earth, telling me that things were not all right, actually.

But slowly—my God, so slowly—that shadow lightened. I focused on these truly incredible experiences and my exciting job and my sweet little home and my large circle of friends and family. And most of all, on my son. Why languish on the couch when I could be playing Uno with him at our kitchen table, or baking a cake together? I can't put my finger on the exact moment it happened, but there was a point where I stopped forcing myself to do these fun things and pretending that I was okay—and actually started having fun, feeling okay. More than okay.

Even when I was by myself, on my own. I could swim in the ocean and no longer waste the submersion wishing my husband were there, no longer for a split second consider how easy it would be to just let go and disappear into the endless beauty. I was able to feel fine for a bit—and not just solely in contrast to the ever-looming sadness.

When the cloud began to retreat, it did so at a pace so slow I could not even sense it moving. Even when it was gone, or nearly gone, I understood that it would never completely disappear. Like a scar under your eyebrow to remind you of the time you were in a motorcycle accident after the war, and ended up in the hospital, where you met your husband. Scars make us who we are.

Frankl wrote that humour had helped him through—something I was somehow able to maintain. And also, curiosity. This was interesting. Shouldn't I be curious about this chapter in my life? It was unexpected, unwanted, pretty awful—but as a curious person shouldn't I at least be interested in what was happening? In the experience? That curiosity was part of the reason I had become a journalist. Maybe I could make it work for me. I had always said I wanted to experience everything at least once. Well, not everything—not rape, or the murder of a family member. Divorce hadn't been on the list either. But here I was, experiencing it. So, take notes.

With all of this reading and these conversations, I was being exposed to ideas and terminologies that were new to me but that described things I had spent my whole life experiencing.

I kept seeing the term "second generation Holocaust survivor" or variations thereof. People describing themselves as a third generation survivor, for instance. It is not a term I use. I survived nothing, beyond sad parents, quiet dinners and family gatherings devoid of grandparents. This is not so bad. My parents survived the real hell. I don't feel I deserve to use this term. I am comfortable with other people using it, but it is not for me.

At the same time, I am not comfortable blaming what had happened to my parents—and, in effect, blaming them—for my little problems. It feels self-indulgent, unfair and actually untrue. "How long can one blame the parents for the inadequacies of one's precious identity, how late demand of them that they repair the deficiencies?" wrote Eva Hoffman in *After Such Knowledge*. I felt embarrassed reading that sentence.

And this one: "It is possible, when reckoning with the deflected past, to attribute too many of one's minute miseries and neuroses to the Holocaust, thereby conferring unearned significance on problems that really are purely individual." *Guilty as charged, Eva Hoffman*, I thought.

Now I wasn't just mourning—my marriage, my way of life, my parents, my future and my past—I was feeling as if I had been unfair about it.

"If you don't get the proportions right," Hoffman wrote, "if you bring the formidable weight of the Holocaust to bear on commonplace problems of everyday life, then you may end up not so much illuminating the past as turning the searchlight on your own narcissism."

Ouch.

Maybe more than anything else, I was struck by a comment made by a science journalist I know. She remarked that in a way, because my mother survived Auschwitz and girls are born with all their eggs already formed, part of me was in the concentration camp with her, a tiny, immature egg.

The survivors themselves were helped by the act of starting new families, having children. That made me, one of those children, an agent of healing. And a healer has power. Maybe instead of thinking of myself as a victim, I needed to think of myself as someone who helped heal my parents, by giving them a purpose and sense of normalcy. And as someone who helped heal the world. I, after all, was the revenge against the Nazis. I was the thing they wanted to prevent. I was the personification of victory. I was the victor, not the victim.

There is a concept in Judaism called *tikkun olam*: to repair the world. This is often interpreted as: by helping one person, by one kind act, you help to heal the world. In a way, my birth—something I had nothing to do with—was an act of *tikkun olam*.

Like many of the 2Gs and 3Gs I was reading about, I am more sensitive to the suffering of others. That can be a burden, being constantly aware of other people's pain. But it also makes me the right kind of person to do something to help.

I liked the idea of somehow having a connection to *tikkun olam*. But I knew I had to take it further. I owe the world a lot.

I'm not sure how I fulfill that, what that looks like. But figuring it out sure is interesting.

As I try to live the rest of my little life in peace and happiness, I wonder if there is a way for people like me, the children of the people who survived an unimaginable thing, to heal. To fix ourselves. Forgiveness is important, letting go. But so is perspective. What did I really have to forgive, anyway?

I recognize how fortunate I have been, and still am. My parents, somehow, had not only survived, but survived intact enough to raise me with care and a quiet love—even if they didn't say the words out loud. It could have been so much worse, I know. They really did try. And really, they had done very well. So what if I didn't grow up with a stuffed toybox or shelves lined with children's books, or if I wasn't taken on regular stimulating outings to museums and art galleries? They did what they could. Which, in fact, was quite a lot.

That house that I recall as being quiet, dead—when I asked Pearl about her memories of it, she had a different recollection: it was a warm household, busy, with lots of visitors, she told me, and a lot of energy. The way she described it reminded me of the life I have built in my own house here in Vancouver, the house that was once home to a great love, and then a great heartbreak. There are always people here, friends and neighbours, dropping by, laughing and talking, sharing bits of their lives. Maybe I had learned this from my parents.

When I spoke with Eva Fogelman, we talked a bit about my life circumstances, and then she made a pronouncement that was, for me, transformative. About how well I seemed to be functioning in society.

"I mean just look at yourself—your father dies unexpectedly and . . . you're raising a child and you're writing a book. You must have a lot of ego strength to be doing what you're doing," she told me. "You certainly have enough trauma in your life. And you clearly didn't become a basket case."

After the few tough years I had lived through, this felt like a triumph: not a basket case.

In the afterword to *Man's Search for Meaning*, written in 2006, the year my mother dropped dead while on a trip to Miami seven days after her eighty-first birthday, the philosopher, psychiatry professor and thinker William J. Winslade wrote about Frankl's wisdom on the question of one's attitude. "A negative attitude intensifies pain and deepens disappointments; it undermines and diminishes pleasure, happiness, and satisfaction; it may even lead to depression or physical illness."

I had held off on reading Frankl's book for many years. Several people had recommended it as I spent so much time after my separation trying to claw myself back from my rock bottom. But I had resisted. I had denied myself something I knew in my bones would be helpful for me. Because I felt I somehow did not deserve Frankl's wisdom; that the reasons I needed his help were trivial. I had failed as a wife, I was failing as a parent, and I couldn't get over any of it, despite the fact that these run-of-the-mill problems could not come close to what Frankl, or my parents, had lived through.

But now this book was showing me that I could have my life back. Or a different kind of life.

In a postscript Frankl wrote in 1984—the year my father died of a massive heart attack while on a trip to Sweden four days after my eighteenth birthday—he stated, "Even the helpless victim of a hopeless situation, facing a fate he cannot change, may rise above himself, may grow beyond himself, and by so doing change himself. He may turn a personal tragedy into a triumph."

And then the sentence that has stayed with me, that I try to remember every day as I slog through whatever domestic or work-related chore, or suffer through some remnant of the heartache. "Live as if you were living for the second time and had acted as wrongly the first time as you are about to act now."

It wasn't too late. My son was still young. I still had life ahead of me. Twenty Christmases, maybe more. I was not happy with how I had been living, not just for the last five years, but for much, much longer. I could blame my ex-husband, blame my parents, blame the Holocaust, blame Hitler for screwing me up all I wanted. But that would not change a thing. What was I going to do with the time I had left? As Frankl had observed, every human being has the freedom to change at any instance. And I was free.

SEVENTEEN

The Return

WITH IN-CLASS INSTRUCTION cancelled because of the pandemic, Jacob was completing an at-home assignment, The Happiness Project. He was supposed to write a few paragraphs about something that made him happy during what was a dark time for these kids. The paragraph-writing was the point of the exercise; the happiness part, I suppose, was meant to bring something not-horrible to mind during a horrible time. He was to describe a person or thing or activity or whatever that made him happy, expanding on it enough so that it was five paragraphs long.

But there was nothing that made him happy, he protested. Nothing at all. He stomped his foot to make his point, definitely not projecting happiness. As a result of the stomping, he stubbed his toe. A shriek followed.

I couldn't help but juxtapose my son's class assignment and benign toe injury with what my mother—Jacob's grandmother—had suffered in Auschwitz, those shoes that had destroyed her feet. Or what I was suffering, reading about it, imagining my mother in those threadbare clothes, in that cold wind. The ridiculous comparison of Jacob's complaint and my mother's experience. The contrast of his grade six happiness writing assignment and the book about grief and trauma I was trying to write. The invalidity of Jacob's complaint. And then my guilt at declaring it invalid, at not being able to feel my little boy's pain. And the added guilt of knowing I had put my mother through similar *tsuris* when I was a kid, complaining about who knows what. My poor mother, the Auschwitz survivor. And then I moved on to what her suffering had done to me. And what I in turn (thanks to the suffering caused by what the Nazis had done to my parents) was doing to Jacob. The boy who could be happy about nothing. His inheritance.

I said none of this. I told him: *If nothing makes you happy, write about that. It might help.*

In the end, he wrote about our cat, Lucy. She made him very happy.

We had gotten Lucy for Jacob's ninth birthday, when he was still confused over his parents' split. He had gone from a school-loving high achiever to an anxious boy who often resisted going to school. I was sure it was because of the separation.

And the cat had worked. We liked to say we won the cat lottery. Lucy was affectionate, social, soft and sweet. Very furry. Loved to be petted and brushed. Loved to snuggle. She's almost a dog, I would tell people.

Jacob had fallen hard for Lucy, as had I. She became a landing pad for his emotions: he could tell the cat how much he loved her, call for her when he was sad or scared. She became a proxy for everything he felt after his safe, secure little world fell apart. He was powerless to change what had happened to his family or to feel better about it. That cat was a living, breathing remedy. She was the first thing he would ask about every morning, and then a conversation would ensue about where Lucy had spent the night. Sleeping on Jacob's feet, at the edge of the bed, on my chest with her butt in my face. It was our family ritual. Because this was my family now: my miracle child and my jackpot cat.

Lucy was supposed to be an indoor cat, but we had made the mistake of letting her out on a harness and leash the odd time, and lately she kept escaping. During COVID lockdown, we had been letting her wander a bit in the great outdoors; she was so eager for it and we were always around. She never went far and she always came back relatively promptly. One rule we stuck to: she was not to stay out at night. There were coyotes around. And raccoons. Also, cars.

Normally when she would enter the house at night, I would run to close the door, to ensure she was safe and home for the night. But one particular night, I was interviewing Zahava Solomon at around midnight—time zones—and it seemed unprofessional to run away from the computer in order to close the door for my cat.

So Lucy wandered in, ate something, and went back out into the night.

After the interview, I went outside to find her. I heard a rustling in one of the trees and assumed it was her. Relief; she was close by. But the rustling was not Lucy. It was a raccoon. Four raccoons, actually: three of them in that tree bridging my yard with my neighbour's, the fourth lurking right next to my front door.

I felt absolute terror. *What have you done with Lucy?* She was nowhere in sight. My fight-or-flight response motored into high gear.

The raccoons left, eventually, but Lucy did not return. I stayed up all night, searching, calling her name. Putting out her favourite food. Nothing. She had never done this.

I searched for body parts left by the gang of raccoons; nothing. That, at least, was a relief.

By 5 a.m., I had posted a lost cat ad to Craigslist. I was sick with grief and certain of the outcome: Lucy was gone. She had been eaten by raccoons or injured so badly that she was dying somewhere out of sight and I couldn't help her. She was in agony, or already dead.

And I had not closed my front door. I was too busy with my interview for my self-centred project: what had the Holocaust, this tragedy that I had not even experienced, done to me? Waah. The survivor's guilt, the catastrophizing, the dread all took hold of me, my stomach clenched with fear and my throat tight with grief. Lucy was never coming home and it was my fault.

I thought about a question I had asked Solomon at the end of our interview, about my penchant to always imagine the worst, to always imagine a tragic outcome. "Often during a happy moment, I think about the end. For instance: My son is in love with our cat; and I'll watch them and I think: 'Oh no, it's going to be awful when that cat dies,'" I told her. "Is that a typical kind of second generation neurosis?" I asked.

Solomon listened and seemed to understand. "Fearing if you're in a happy moment, that it could end in a minute. It's not long-lasting," she said. "So, you're always fearful, whatever may happen."

In those dark moments of my missing cat, I found God again. Please God, bring Lucy home and I will be a good person, I will never complain again. I bargained that night as if my life depended on it. Just as I had when my marriage was ending, when I engaged in please-Godding on a regular basis. I used to wonder how on earth people living through the Holocaust could have still believed in God, still prayed to this idea, despite the obvious divine failures all around them. But of course, they were (or had been) believers. And they were desperate—for help, for comfort, for anything. Even I, pretty much an atheist and in a situation not even close to comparably dire, almost involuntarily turned to God in my quest to save my marriage. And now to find my cat.

I wanted to take something to help me sleep for as long as the grief would live in my body, wake up only when the pain had subsided. No wait, that was how I felt when my husband disappeared. Not when the cat went missing.

But my body felt the same: my stomach, my head, my throat. The same heightened state, the same knowledge of doom in my bones.

I recognize we are talking about a cat.

Amid my Googling about what to do when a pet goes missing, I found what looked like the answer. A pet detective (cute) agency, that sends trained bloodhounds out to find your missing cat or dog. "In many cases, we are able to locate fresh scent, and have a 'live find' on the search," the website said. It all seemed so hopeful!

I had no money to spare. I was on an unpaid leave from work, trying to write this book. I was still in severe financial freefall from my divorce—in deep, shameful debt, with monthly expenses I could barely afford even when I was working, living in a house my ex owned a big chunk of and could insist on being paid out for any day. Not that he ever suggested he would do that, but it hung over my head constantly, the never-spoken-of threat.

But Lucy.

I checked out the pet detective's rates. For a silver package—an hour with a bloodhound plus high-tech live streaming cameras, thermal imaging equipment and more—it was $395. I looked at my bank balance: minus $56.04.

But Lucy.

This is what credit cards are for, I told myself. Emergencies. For a loved one. I contacted the company, had a calming conversation with the pet detective assigned to my case. She told me to go outside and spread dirty laundry around the neighbourhood for Lucy to smell. She was very encouraging. And then she sent me the contract.

With travel fees, taxes and other charges—including a night-vision camera rental that would keep an eye on my yard 24/7—the cost ballooned to $677.25. Once the contract was signed, the money was owed. Even if Lucy came back on her own, without the bloodhound or the travel fees or whatever, it was going to cost me almost $700. I thought of the dying dishwasher in my kitchen. How much would a Bosch cost?

My parents' families had bartered gold for flour, silver for sugar, who knows what for a few more days of life and something to eat to get them through it. Again, I know this imagination-leap sounds ridiculous to you, normal person, reading this. But this is where my brain went, and where it goes, without fail. When there is a stressful event, Holocaust. When there is a joyful event, Holocaust. Dead relatives, gas chambers, humiliations, horrors, survival.

I thought about my father's great love for cats, which could perhaps be traced back to the Lederman family kafehouse, the one I don't know the name of. Or maybe it had started in the courtyard of the apartment building where he lived with his family; Rachel had noticed a lot of strays there when she visited Lodz in 2016. Perhaps it originated on the farm in Holsen; was there a particular barn cat my father fell for during those terrifying years? Did it remind Tadek of life as Jacob? Of the store, and his parents, and his sister? Of the apartment house with the red stairs?

My parents supplied me with everything as a child—food (even if it was, on occasion, jellied calf's feet), a three-bedroom bungalow with a room to call my own from the time I was five, and in the basement, a piano, stereo and colour TV. And all the canned goods I could ever want. And love, in the way they knew how.

But there were very few extravagant kid-friendly surprises in my childhood. I remember so well the year at Chanukah when Pearl's family travelled to Florida—including Disney World!—and my other best friend received an electric organ with settings for marimba and other cool stuff. I got a book: *A Child's Introduction to Torah*. Another year, my parents gave me a hot air popcorn popper. "You're giving me a small appliance for Chanukah?" was my shitty teenaged response. What a bitch. No wonder my father couldn't stand me. Dinners out were rare and definitely on the family-friendly dining scale: McDonald's or a local delicatessen.

And yet when I asked Pearl, all these years later, what she remembered about my parents, she specifically brought up my father bringing us food from McDonald's, and what a sweet gesture she thought that was. And how my parents would take me on picnics all the time. It was the first time in years I had thought of those large communal picnics—which we attended on many summer weekends, their Holocaust survivor friends spread over the grass, each couple or family with their own blanket. They would spend hours there, playing cards, gossiping, reaching into coolers filled with coleslaw and sandwiches. They always took me—which, as I grew older, I began to resent, feeling like I was being dragged along to something I didn't want to do. But from their perspective, what better way for a child to spend a beautiful Sunday afternoon than in a park somewhere with a large group of friends? Just like my mother's family had done in Radom, in that beautiful park, on how many weekends, before the parks became verboten for Jews?

"Within the parameters of what they went through, they really did more than their best," Pearl said.

There was one occasion when I saw it that way, even then: my parents going out of their way to do their best, to do something very special for me. I was ten or eleven, visiting a friend, when my parents called her house and told me that I needed to come home right away. I hurried home, four blocks away; I was worried something was wrong.

When I got there, I was presented with a very large box. I opened it. Inside: a kitten.

In addition to the absolute elation of getting my own kitten, there was the joy of knowing that my parents—my father!—had manoeuvred this grand gesture for me. My father, who so rarely did anything special for me, had cooked up this giant surprise. (I suspect that someone he knew had had a cat with a litter and offered up the kittens—as opposed to him going out in pursuit of this perfect gift for his little girl, but still.)

I loved that cat with all of my heart. He was no Lucy—he wasn't mean, exactly, but very aloof, and completely uninterested in me or my love. (Sounds like some relationship foreshadowing may have been going on there.) But Frisky changed the dynamic in my house from dead-ish to alive with possibility. I would walk in the door from school and know there was a cat—if not exactly waiting for me, still there.

Frisky was an outdoor cat, and in the winter he got cold and climbed into the fan belt of my father's car for warmth. I think he did this on the regular, but we didn't become aware of it until the day my father turned the key in the ignition of the old Pontiac LeMans to warm it up, and we all heard a howl so petrifying it could have been a sound effect. Frisky, who had taken refuge in the fan belt, had been propelled from the undercarriage of the car onto our front lawn.

We rushed the cat to the vet. It seemed very touch and go. There was a lot of blood (Frisky's) and tears (mine).

Frisky, it turned out, could be saved. But it would take an expensive operation. I don't recall my parents—who were of modest means and beyond frugal—discussing whether they should go for it. Perhaps they did, out of my earshot. But somehow, I don't think so.

Frisky could be saved and Frisky would be saved, whatever the cost.

A few days later, we were able to bring him home. He was lame, hobbling, and we had to put him in a big tall box with all of his things to ensure that he did not walk too much. The boy needed to heal.

When I went to check on him a couple of hours later, the box was empty, other than the water and food bowls and the little blanket we had left in there for comfort. Frisky had escaped. Injured, fan-belt-battle-scarred, recovering from surgery, Frisky had nonetheless managed to hop the big box and hobble off somewhere more comfortable to recuperate. A survivor.

Let me emphasize, once again, the frugality of my parents. Money was not spent without difficulty in my home. Grocery store flyers were studied and sales acted upon. Family vacations were taken by car, not airplane. Nights out of town were spent at friends' homes or, in an extraordinary event, at a motel. I had not at that point taken a flight or stayed in a proper hotel, ever.

But a few months after blowing the bank on Frisky's surgery, my parents decided they were going to replace the broadloom, as they called it, in the living room and the hallway leading from our kitchen to the bedrooms. We shopped around for what felt like months—and maybe it was—going from carpet store to carpet store, looking for the right colour and the best deal.

They chose a luxurious medium-pile green. The wall-to-wall carpeting would complement the gold French Provincial chesterfield (still encased in plastic), tufted red velvet armchairs and other living room treasures—a marble and gold-leaf side table, Royal Doulton figurines, large plants and an array of Judaica.

Frisky and I hung out in the basement while the carpeting was installed that day; I remember that the house smelled like pickles. When we finally emerged upstairs, the living room looked magnificent—almost, you might say, palatial.

With that hours-old green carpeting, I felt a bit like, well, a princess. I grabbed a scratchy wool blanket from the linen closet, held the ends of it under my chin and let the rest fan out behind me, like a cape. I royal-marched into that living room with that fresh-from-today brand-new carpeting and took a few regal turns in my new palace.

On one of those turns, my cape caught on something on the ground. The sickening thunk whiplashed me back from my imagined palace into my living room. I turned to look. My blanket cape had knocked something over.

A giant houseplant.

Hunks of soil were strewn all over the installed-that-day carpeting, with a path that led from the plant to the cape and the girl wearing it.

I was in for it, I knew. And I did what any self-respecting, normal ten (eleven?) year-old kid would do. I blamed the cat.

My mother went nuts on poor Frisky, yelling at the innocent little thing while I stood by and let it happen and—I hate to report this, but it's true—she gave the cat a few slaps.

Frisky ran away. He ran and ran. For two days, I sat with the loneliness of an empty house and the heaviness of a guilty soul. He had never left for this long.

But then Frisky returned. He ate something, and went out again. All was well in the world, I thought.

But that was the last time I saw Frisky. He never came home again. My fault.

So there was a bit of pathology happening when Lucy went missing. Not just our great love for this cat and Jacob's dependence on her,

but my guilt from this previous episode. Throw in the intergenerational trauma issues with death and separation, and my added feeling
of responsibility, and I was in a tailspin.

I ordered the bloodhound. This is what credit cards are for.

Jacob woke up and trudged downstairs, asking for Lucy.

The Internet had told me during that long dark night of the soul
that being direct was best. "She didn't come home last night," I said,
my simple sentence punctuated by the even darker than usual circles
under my eyes.

He did not take it well.

As the day progressed and people in the neighbourhood found
out—through my Facebook or Twitter posts, or just passing by—a
community campaign to find Lucy was on. Jacob's friends walked up
and down the streets and laneways, calling her name. A friend up the
street designed a poster. Another dad friend a couple of blocks away
printed as many copies as the ink in his printer would allow. The kids
walked around, taping them to telephone poles.

My friend Tanis came and sat with me in my yard and made me tea.
We got pizza for all the kids. They took a lunch break in my yard and
then set out again under the warm sun.

It was Tanis who had nursed me through the worst of my marital
breakdown. I barely knew her at the time—we were mom friends—but
we happened to have a playdate scheduled on a day when things had
gotten very bad, and rather than just drop off my kid, I said, *Can I come
in?* I sat on her couch for hours and she talked me through it, and a
friendship that is more than a friendship was born.

Five summers later, she was in my catless yard calming me down,
suggesting that I needed to work on my outlook—that being certain
Lucy was dead was not helpful, or necessary. (I kept this certainty from
Jacob; I am good at feigning optimism, but I am never able to believe
my own bull.)

I am keenly aware of the value of hope, but I was always low on
it. I knew that my tendency to go to the worst place—dead Lucy—was

not helping. Tanis reminded me that this wasn't just about a cat. She wanted to talk about why I was always catastrophizing. Why could I not believe in the possibility of good?

I gestured to the pile of books sitting on the patio table next to me: *On Hitler's Mountain, Children of the Holocaust, Hitler's Willing Executioners.*

I told her about the interview I had been doing when Lucy disappeared into the clutches of the raccoons, what Zahava Solomon had said: that in many families of survivors, the children were often reminded of the many dangers of the world and warned to look out for them.

It's not a choice, I explained to Tanis. I feel it in my body. Terror and loss.

Once again, my home, my security, my joy had been taken away by invading forces. The raccoons were the Nazis. This is not a rational thought, I have to explain, because I know how ridiculous this sounds. I did not picture the critters wearing swastikas and *Sieg Heiling* with their little paws. But in my life story, where something terrible will always happen to take away the happiness in your life—unhappy husband, sudden death on a trip to Sweden or Florida, a cattle car to Auschwitz—the raccoons were just more proof, feeding into the narrative. The inevitability of loss—sudden, tragic, crushing.

Tanis gently advised that I didn't need to go there. I would be fine no matter what, and so would Jacob, but I didn't need to grieve Lucy just yet. And the way I was responding to the situation was not about what was happening now, but maybe about something that had happened to me before.

She told me she would help me work on it—later, once the Lucy crisis was over, when there was time. She didn't leave my side, this woman who had become a friend during the darkest days of my imploding marriage. She walked with me up our block and down the laneway behind the house, depositing dirty clothes—mine and Jacob's—as we had been advised to do, to help Lucy find her way home. (There were dirty socks involved, but I drew the line at underwear.)

Our other best friend, Mel, rushed over. Jacob's longtime babysitter Hannah dropped everything and came to help search. The kids were coming and going. Jacob's dad drove up and down the streets and laneways in his girlfriend's car, searching. Jacob, in this time of crisis, was distracted and even, wow, happy. A dubious second-hand report of a black cat seen sleeping under a car in the laneway was enough to convince him. "Phew, at least we know she's okay," he said. His need to believe the best was in direct contrast to my absolute certainty of the worst. Self-protection for both of us.

At some point—I was nearly delirious now with grief and lack of sleep and too much sun and too little nourishment—I looked around and recognized that something had grown out of my grief: these friend-ships—mine, Jacob's; the easy family feeling of my community, a com-munity that would come out in my time of need and help. This was not something I had had before. I'm not saying I would have traded my marriage for this, but it felt amazing to be surrounded by love and comfort in a way I hadn't as my marriage went south. People searching, texting, worrying. People who loved Lucy, but more to the point, loved Jacob and me. All these beautiful people coming to my rescue.

This was a place where I was at home, comfortable enough to air—and scatter—my dirty laundry. My now-estranged husband had brought me here. But I had made this house—this community—home. (P.S. "Estranged" is such a rotten word; we need new language around former spouses and stepchildren, please.)

I had built this. I understood what a beautiful achievement this was. I had built this community, and this community had come and rescued me, at the most difficult times. I too had been rescued. And tiny though it is, my house—like my parents' house in Pearl's memo-ries—was always filled with visitors, filled with warmth and energy.

In Eva Fogelman's essay in the book *God, Faith & Identity from the Ashes*, she advised that survivors and their descendants need a sense of belonging in order to mourn and to heal. I had it; I had built a com-munity. I belonged. And I had mourned. And now I was healing.

And then in the next moment, I thought about the Jews of 1930s Germany—or Poland—so reluctant to leave despite all the signs of doom to come. My grandparents deciding not to use those visas for Palestine. They were living their lives. They were surrounded by community, by love. What we talk about when we talk about Anne Frank.

This was home. *Everything will work out*, they must have told themselves. How bad could it get? Everything and everyone they knew and had was right there. *We'll wait it out, together.* Comfort and love, I thought, can be fatal.

Jordii, my pet detective, arrived that evening to a yard still populated (but socially distanced; it was that first COVID summer) with friends. She installed a night-vision camera on the magnolia tree at the front of our yard, the tree that had become temporary home to those rotten raccoons, rustling the leaves like they owned the place.

She would monitor the camera all night, she said, and call me if she saw Lucy. She would also call if the raccoons showed up, so that I could go outside and scare them away. Lucy would not come back if the raccoons were lurking.

She told me to pick up the dirty clothing and, equally humiliating, to leave a few items outside my home, in case Lucy needed the scent.

I hunkered down for a second night on the couch. I put the ringer on its highest volume level and laid the phone on my chest.

At 1:11 a.m., the phone rang. "Marsha?" Jordii said. *Please let it not be the raccoons.*

"Lucy is in your yard."

I opened the door, and there she was, lying on the walkway, just chilling. She let me pick her up—usually she runs away if I try to bring her inside from the great outdoors (which she would never ever experience again, I vowed). But she let me hold her and bring her into the house.

After bursting into tears on the phone, and possibly telling Jordii that I loved her, I gave Lucy some food and sat on the floor next to her, watching her eat. She was starving. Then I brought her upstairs, woke Jacob up and presented his beloved Lucy to him.

"Oh my God," he said after a confused moment, folding his little body over her and holding her close. "I thought I was dreaming."

Lucy, nonchalant, padded over to the edge of the bed and went to sleep.

On a drive to the pet store the next day to buy a collar with a bell and a retractable leash and a new harness to keep Lucy from wandering beyond our yard, Jacob and I were recounting the story to each other. I told him that when the pet detective said "Marsha, Lucy is in your yard," it was the best sentence anyone had ever said to me. He responded, not missing a beat, "Even better than 'It's a boy'?"

EIGHTEEN

Life

EXACTLY FIFTEEN YEARS TO the day after my mother died suddenly in Florida, I settled in to watch a nine-hour-plus documentary about the Holocaust. I hadn't planned it that way—it just so happened that this was when *Shoah*, which I'd placed on hold at the public library way back when, had become available. Jacob was spending the weekend at his dad's, so the timing was right. I would need two days for it; there was no way I could consume all nine hours and sixteen minutes (plus related documentaries and interviews—a total of five DVDs) in one sitting, or even one day. My pandemic weekend was set. I hit play at 6 a.m.

I had known about *Shoah*, of course—French filmmaker Claude Lanzmann's epic document of the Holocaust, made over eleven years and released in 1985. But I had never had the opportunity—or the courage—to watch it.

What I somehow had not known was its particular focus. These weren't just ("just") interviews with Holocaust survivors. The film focuses very specifically on the death process. How did the Nazis accomplish the actual killing? What happened when the trains rolled into Treblinka, and afterward? Inside those gas chambers at Auschwitz? On those trains chugging thousands of people toward their death?

Very few Jews had witnessed this part of the process and lived to speak about it. Lanzmann found some of them, including a Jewish man who had been forced to cut women's hair, just moments before they were gassed at Treblinka. Lanzmann interviewed this unlikely survivor in a Tel Aviv barber shop. He also found some Nazis and others who had been in their employ or living nearby. And he got them to talk.

I was particularly interested in what had happened at Treblinka, death site of all of my grandparents, my aunt and two uncles. A Polish witness who owned land close to the extermination camp told Lanzmann that he had a field less than a hundred metres from the site. He saw how the Jews were asphyxiated; he heard them scream. There was a small hill with a view, so he could see quite a lot. If the local Poles stopped to watch, Ukrainian guards would shoot at them, so they had to observe the horrific scene furtively.

But they could hear the screams, awful screams. I think about my aunt screaming, my grandmothers. Sara and Rachel. "It didn't bother you to work so close to the screams?" Lanzmann asked, through his translator.

"At first it was unbearable," the man said. "Then you got used to it."

In another scene, one of the Germans employed at Treblinka— taped secretly by Lanzmann and his crew—described the procedure in detail. "You're a very important eyewitness," encouraged Lanzmann, posing as an academic. He promised not to use the man's name. I felt a moment of delight at this deception.

The delight was quickly erased by the man's recollections, such as what happened when they opened the gas chamber doors after the procedure. "People fell out like potatoes," he said.

My aunt. My uncles. My grandparents. Potatoes.

"We went back and sat on our suitcases and cried like old women," the old Nazi said.

He explained that each day one hundred Jews were chosen to drag the corpses to the mass graves. In the evening, the Ukrainians drove those Jews who had worked all day into the gas chambers. Or shot them. Every day! It was in the hottest days of August. The ground, crammed with bodies, undulated like waves. "It was hell up there," he said. The smell was infernal, he explained. You could smell the gas for miles around. "We puked and wept."

And then the worst detail: there was some sort of backlog and the Jews had to wait their turn to die—for one day, two days, three days. "They foresaw what was coming. They foresaw it." Some Jewish women slashed their daughters' wrists at night, then cut their own.

Had twenty-year-old Isaac been one of those men who had to drag the corpses from the gas chambers to the graves? Had Sara slashed Devorah's wrists in the night?

Something inexplicable happened while I was watching this movie.

As a survivor walked through Chelmno, and pronounced that this is where the gas had happened, the little lamp of resilience that my friend Mel had bought me, which hadn't been working lately because the batteries had run out and I'd been too preoccupied to change them, suddenly lit up. A few metres away but in my line of sight, it lit up bright as day. The lamp, right next to the photo of my mom in the satin dress, in that happy glamour shot of my parents. And as the man in the movie with the sad, sad eyes walked down a gravel road in green, green Poland, the twinkly lights in my living room faded and died out.

I know this sounds crazy. I promise, I am not making this up. I don't believe in the supernatural. I am not a spiritual person, not that way. But there was no explanation for it, no logical explanation. Maybe I had imagined it, I told myself. Trauma can do things like that, inherited or otherwise.

I kept watching the film.

The Polish man who drove the locomotive to Treblinka—the one whose weathered face, emerging from the window of the front wagon and looking back down the length of the train, appears on the film's poster—was being interviewed by Lanzmann. Did the train conductor hear screams coming from the passengers? "Obviously," he says.

They screamed, they asked for water. It was a terrible assignment, he explained. He knew that the people behind him were human, just like him. The Germans gave him and the other workers vodka to drink. Without drinking they couldn't do it. He drank every drop he got because without the liquor he couldn't stand the stench.

"We arrived in the morning," he said. And then my light went on again. It stayed on as this man described the unloading ramp, what went on. The people were desperate for water. They offered gold and diamonds. SS men took the diamonds, but didn't bring the water.

My coffee went cold, watching. The luxury of it, pouring it down the drain. The light went off.

Still at Treblinka, now a Jewish man was speaking, one of the very few to survive that experience, because he was kept alive to work at the camp. "We have no time even to look at each other," he told Lanzmann, because they were being hit over the head "with all kinds of things." It was painful, very. "You didn't know what had happened. You had no time to think. All you heard is crying and all you heard all the time was the hollering of the people," he said.

He continued: "We got out, stepping on each other."

The light went on, again. "We saw men wearing armbands; some carried whips."

The light went on and off about a dozen times that day as I watched that documentary, learned those terrible details.

It had never happened before; I asked Jacob if he had ever seen the light just spontaneously turn on and he said no. And it never happened again.

A few weeks later, when I was sitting at my desk in the bedroom, writing all of this down, I took a break to go downstairs and refill my cup of coffee. When I came back upstairs, I heard voices. Jacob was at his dad's; it couldn't have been him. Had I turned the radio on? But, no, I realized it was my mother's voice I was hearing.

"Can't believe that it happened, huh, in a normal world," she was saying.

Somehow Doris's home movie from our trip to Poland—specifically the segment where we were visiting Treblinka—was playing on my laptop. Lucy the cat slinked away. What series of buttons had she pawed to make this happen?

Whenever I get very, very thirsty, I have a visceral flashback to a train ride I took in 1987. I was in my early twenties, backpacking around Europe with my friend Eileen. Like so many young people did at the time, we had purchased Eurail Passes and often travelled overnight to save the cost of a night in a hostel. One of these overnight trips took us from Nice to Venice. We must have had some sort of sodium-laden dinner before boarding that train, and we both ran out of water somewhere between France and Italy. I had never felt so thirsty. Never. At one point, I became so desperate, I tried to drink the tap-water in the bathroom, despite the non-potable warning signs posted over the sink. It didn't matter; by that point in the journey, nothing was coming out of the tap anymore. When we arrived in Venice, I ran to the train station café and ordered a too-expensive bottle of fizzy water.

To this day, when I get very thirsty, I am transported back to that experience. It's the weirdest thing. There have no doubt been countless other times when I have been extremely thirsty and unable to access a drink. But watching *Shoah*, it suddenly made sense that this particular experience of thirst, on a train in Europe, had had such a lasting effect. The Jews crammed into the trains at Treblinka, bartering diamonds for water. "They waited, they wept, they asked for water, they died," remembered a Polish witness.

One of the Jews who had miraculously survived Treblinka explained that they had gone twenty-four hours without water, crammed on those trains.

"We couldn't drink, we couldn't have anything taken into our mouth," he said. "It was impossible that a minute or hour before you were part of a family. You were part of a wife or a husband and now all of a sudden everything is dead."

A few days before my weekend *Shoah* marathon, the world had watched a riot at the U.S. Capitol—thugs with flagpoles and zip ties and a lot of really stupid, and dangerous, ideas.

One of those half-wits was wearing a sweatshirt that read "Camp Auschwitz" on top of an image of a skull-and-crossbones, the phrase "work brings freedom" underneath it. *Arbeit macht frei.* On the back, the word "Staff."

It's been just a few decades since the ashes of real people chugged up through chimneys purpose-built for the task—and in the realm of history that is not a long time. And there are imbeciles willing to wear a shirt like this? Who specifically selected this shirt for the occasion? Proudly wearing it to what he knew would be a highly publicized event? And there's a manufacturer willing to make this sweatshirt? And to sell it to how many other horrible people?

I was so distressed by this shirt. By this point, I had been reading and writing and bathed in all things Holocaust for more than two years—in addition to an entire lifetime of obsession. To see this was, sure, evidence that what I was doing was necessary and important. But it was hard to recognize that through the full-body feeling of defeat. Some clown was walking around in a Camp Auschwitz sweatshirt. And a whole bunch of people who were around him that day saw it. And they kept working with the guy. They accepted him into their fold. Yes, I know the people storming the Capitol might not be the best examples of upstanding citizenry. But did nobody in the crowd look at that sweatshirt and think: *Oh, is this the kind of person I'm associating with? Is this the kind of person I want on my side?*

This sweatshirt tormented me. Are we at the point in society where we can blithely joke through branded apparel about this? About the throwing of babies into gas chambers? The pulling of gold teeth from corpses? The piles of bodies? Potatoes.

This Camp Auschwitz sweatshirt coloured everything I saw in the weeks that followed. It made the viewing of *Shoah* even harder, if that's possible.

Before each gassing at Auschwitz, the film explained, the SS took stern precautions—to prevent not just escape, but panic. You couldn't bring in the next transport with bodies and blood all around, one of the witnesses in *Shoah* recounted. That would increase the panic. It was a lot of work—the deception, the preparation, the operation. In the large gas chambers, the Nazis would kill up to two thousand people at a time. It took ten to fifteen minutes, the killing.

That barber, the poor man who had been forced to cut the hair of terrified women at the Treblinka gas chamber, having to lie to them about what was going to happen next. And then what it looked like afterward.

The most horrible thing, he said, was once the doors of the gas chambers were opened, the unbearable sight: people packed together like basalt, like blocks of stone. "How they tumbled out of the gas chamber! I saw that several times. That was the toughest thing to take. You could never get used to that. It was impossible."

Once the gas was poured in, it rose from the ground upward. The lights were switched off and it was a terrible struggle in the dark. The strongest people tried to climb higher, to where there was more air, where they could breathe. Also, most people tried to push their way to the door. It was psychological: they knew where the door was so maybe they could force their way out. "It was instinctive; a death struggle. Which is why children and weak people, and the aged, always wound up at the bottom. The strongest were on top. Because in the death struggle, a father didn't realize his son lay beneath him."

Camp Auschwitz. Staff.

I was all alone with my grief and outrage. The sweatshirt sent me over the edge and I didn't know what to do with these feelings. I didn't have a person, my person, to rant to or cry with. I thought about calling up Jacob's dad to discuss it with him—I knew he would share my outrage—but no, I told myself, he's not your person anymore. You have to deal with these feelings on your own, or in some other way. I had built this huge community and I could reach out to any of them. Or I could just sit with it, and process it, on my own.

In the end, I turned off the TV before Jacob got home from school and sat with him, focusing on the miracle that he was, and all that we have, in spite of it all. I told him about what had happened in Washington, but left out many details, including the sweatshirt.

And when Jacob's dad came to pick him up for dinner that afternoon, we did talk about it. Briefly. Not me pouring my heart out to my person. But me discussing this huge event with someone who had become something else in my life. And it was okay. Or it was going to be. Okay.

As the world marked the one-year pandemic anniversary, I marked my own. It had been a year since I had doom-scrolled all night, my bags packed by the door, before calling off my trip of a lifetime to Lodz and Kaunitz and Holsen. Like everyone else, I was exhausted. But I was also feeling something else: a new calm. About myself, my future. It turns out knowledge can be power. I now know the Flottmeiers, and I know about their farm. I can picture the land. I have seen, via Whatsapp, the inside of the church where my father prayed for his life. There's a plaque on a patch of grass sixty kilometres south of there that marks the spot where my mother and my aunt and their aunt and hundreds of other women were liberated from the Nazis. The sign is there. I will see it for myself one day, when I travel there. I will sit in the grass, just like my mother did. I will try to imagine the Americans coming up the road, noticing the women in the meadow, making a U-turn, giving them bread and chocolates. And life.

And I know that my father's childhood home is there in Lodz, the building still stands, and one day, when I can, I will visit it. I will walk where my father did, where he grew up as a boy, where he made trouble for his parents and looked up to his sister, where he cared for his little brother, where he played soccer badly, where he first felt the urges that years and a continent away would lead to my birth. I will bend down and kiss the stairs, like he did.

It felt, finally, like perhaps I was moving beyond that visceral response, looking at those bulldozed bodies in the Hebrew school basement and thinking "that could be my grandmother"—which had turned into, whenever hearing about a child victim of the Holocaust, "that could have been Jacob." And, in my nightmares, it could have been me.

It is an ordeal, this way of thinking. And I know it has harmed me. But perhaps it has its positives. Maybe it is not terrible to always be on the lookout for injustice—whether it's toward me and mine or someone else and theirs. This is an important legacy to carry, even if it has messed me up, a bit. Or more than a bit.

"You have to make the best with what you have and not dwell on what you have lost," said Auschwitz survivor Nathan (Nate) Leipciger, who is Canadian, in an article about how Holocaust survivors were dealing with the COVID-19 pandemic. I read this and tried to remember always to apply it to my own life. Yes, I had lost—my husband, my stepchildren, the future I thought was mine. But look at what I have. It's a lot.

...

The day Edith Eger arrived at Auschwitz, she was forced to dance for Josef Mengele. The notorious Angel of Death had saved Eger's life— and my mother's—by pointing them in the right direction.

Mengele had pointed in the opposite direction for Edith's mother, sending her to the gas chamber. As Edith danced for this monster, not long after he murdered her mother, she discovered a piece of wisdom that she says has rescued her time and again during difficulties: Mengele, she realized, was more pitiful than she was, even if she was at that moment a concentration camp inmate. "I am free in my mind, which he can never be. He will always have to live with what he's done. He is more a prisoner than I am."

He will always have to live with what he's done.

And when she was liberated, she maintained a positive attitude. "We're free *from* the death camps, but we also must be free *to*—free to create, to make a life, to choose. And until we find our *freedom to*, we're just spinning around in the same endless darkness."

I had been liberated not from anything that could come close to being compared to Auschwitz. A divorce, big deal. But it was, for me, a difficult situation. It was over, I had survived, I would never be the same, but I could be something. My life could be something. It already was.

"To heal is to cherish the wound," Eger wrote.

There was a time when I thought I would have given anything not to feel the pain I was feeling, the wound of my heartbreak. When I was tempted to wish it all away—even the happiness before. Because if there had been no happiness, there would have been no heartbreak. If the marriage had never been, I would not be feeling this grief. But how could I wish it away? I would not have my son, my job, my life. I have a whole life that came from this marriage. The marriage was over. But my life was mine—forever changed, in some beautiful ways I would never want to give up. I cherish it all.

A key to trauma recovery is agency, Rabbi Tirzah Firestone wrote. The fact that I was sick of myself, sick of my endless woe-is-me narrative, was positive. Helpless victimization was getting me nowhere. Wanting to shed it was a positive sign.

If trauma changes us permanently, we have a choice about the outcome of the story, she wrote. "We can bemoan our fate as victims of history. Or we can recognize our pain and follow the circumstances of our lives into unforeseen directions and new meanings. We can ask: What does this terrible wound inspire me to do that I would never have thought to do otherwise?" Some call this post-traumatic growth.

Carey Newman talked to me about blood memory: the Indigenous belief that memory is in our blood, that our history is inside us, passed from generation to generation biologically.

"You are made from the blood of your parents and your ancestors, and the things that have happened to them, you carry that with you," he said during a conversation we had in the early months of the pandemic.

"We are the product of and connected to those who came before us; we're part of a continuum of life. And you cannot separate from your parents, from their experiences."

I had been thinking about this as science; Carey presented it to me like story. Who or what had turned on that lamp?

A couple of days later, while reading yet another Holocaust book pulled from the piles around my bedroom, I learned that the village Brzezinka—or Birkenau—was named for birch trees.

I immediately thought about a doctor's appointment Jacob had had with an allergist. He seemed to be having an allergic reaction to pears, which would have been a rare allergy and a little strange. When the doctor tested him, she determined that he has something called pollen food allergy syndrome. He would not be able to tolerate some fruits, including pears, not because he was allergic to the fruit itself but because he was in fact allergic to birch pollen.

When I read this meaning for Birkenau—how had I not known?— I could hear Carey in my head, explaining about blood memory. I couldn't help but wonder at this weird connection. Of course I in no way believe the name of my mother's former prison and my son's pollen allergy are scientifically related. But it was still pretty interesting to me: Jacob's inability to eat pears, and the trauma my mother had experienced among the birch trees of occupied Poland.

I do believe that what happened to my family lives on in my blood and my bones.

And Carey helped me see that there are good things about that.

"We don't only talk about the trauma, we're talking about the other things, good things," he said to me. "The good things because if we are what our ancestors were in a small way, then it connects us to other sources of knowledge, other perspectives, world views."

Carey had made me a witness, a holder of the terrible stories that came out of the residential schools. I felt honoured to be entrusted with this responsibility and to be reminded of my own. Because I was already a witness, a holder of other terrible stories. Carey had placed his sister's braids on his Witness Blanket; I had seen a braid at Auschwitz that reminded me of my mother's. Our stories, braided together, across time, distance and experience.

I have come to believe and have taken a lot of solace from the conclusion of Natan Kellermann's last paper of many on intergenerational trauma, where he wrote about resilience.

The resilience of my parents, after all, must have been extraordinary. The balls it must have taken for my father to make that deal with the guard, knock on that door of the Polish official and ask for the false papers, and then assume a new identity—*on a train into Germany*. It's almost unbelievable. And for my mother to somehow survive more than five years as a slave labourer, going from one humiliating, debilitating task to another, while undernourished and grieving and only a young teenager—when I think of her this way, she is the picture of resilience, and not just the partly broken woman who did her best to raise me well.

I like to think I have inherited some of this from my parents, not just their trauma.

Morton Weinfeld and John J. Sigal called their book *Trauma and Rebirth: Intergenerational Effects of the Holocaust*. "Our main argument is implicit in the title," these early researchers into intergenerational trauma wrote. "We are struck more by . . . the general degree to which [the survivors], and certainly their children, have overcome the traumas of the past. In this observation we present a counterpoint to most of the clinical and academic literature on Holocaust survivors, which has emphasized impairment or dysfunction."

Trauma. And rebirth.

As for my parents' intolerance of my sadness, I began to understand this too. In *The Inheritors: Moving Forward from Generational Trauma*, Gita Baack wrote that survivor mothers can be unable to tolerate a daughter's feeling of pain, anger, aggression or rebelliousness. "My mother loved me so much she couldn't bear for me to be in pain," Baack wrote. That was an eye-opener: a different way to look at my mother's inability to tolerate my sadness. It was an expression of love, not derision.

I thought about how I would do anything to protect Jacob from pain caused by outside sources. How when other kids left him out or—as weirdly started happening during COVID—teased him about being Jewish, I spun out, plotting ways to get back at these children, once I could figure out who they were. (Yes, very mature, I know.)

In any case, I can't be angry at my parents for any of this. For any of their imperfect parenting or inability to express their love or whatever. I can blame the Holocaust, not them. Hitler really did fuck me up.

He fucked up a huge chunk of the world. He fucked up the Germans too, and their descendants, the innocent people whose accents make me nervous. I felt such an affinity with Nora Krug, reading *Heimat*, her graphic memoir investigating what role, if any, her own family played in the Second World War.

Krug—who moved from Germany to the U.S.—writes about covering her mouth while she speaks, trying to hide her German accent—or keeping her answers short, even putting on a different accent. When she was younger, an aunt advised her that when travelling abroad, she should tell people that she was from the Netherlands. I felt terrible when I read this.

"I can't even stretch and hold my right arm at an angle, like the other students in the yoga class, without thinking of the Hitler salute," Krug writes.

On opposite sides of descent, we were both left with such trauma. An uncle she never met, her father's brother, died before her father was born. He died on the battlefield, a German soldier. He died on July 16, 1944—exactly forty years to the day before my father dropped dead in Sweden. Franz-Karl Krug was eighteen years old. A kid dressed up as a Nazi.

As for my abandoned project of journalism that could change the world—I recognize that art, which is what I write about, actually does have that power, to change the world. And it offers so much to us as individuals. I was seeing it all around me during a global pandemic. What was saving us? Television, music, books. The escape and illumination they offer. The spontaneous kitchen dance party the right playlist could provoke. Or the cathartic tears.

So writing about the arts was changing the world, just in a different way. It was injecting some beauty into it, or allowing people to access works that would bring beauty—and meaning—into theirs.

I have often thought about that scene in *When Harry Met Sally*, when Sally tells Harry she is going to New York to study journalism. He asks, "What if nothing ever happens to you? You just write about things that happen to other people?" She looks appalled.

What I realize, after decades of writing about other people, is that these things do also happen to you, in a way, once removed. I didn't just write about the people I have had the privilege to interview. Their stories changed me as I listened to them, thought about them and then wrote them down for other people to read. Some of this stays in your blood and your bones.

When you learn about something, it becomes part of your own story—even if just a little bit. Carey Newman's story has become part of my life. And maybe now my story will become a part of yours, even if just a little bit. You are taking on the responsibility of remembering with me. We are all witnesses.

···

Time heals all wounds, they say. From a marriage breakup? Sure.

But does time heal wounds generated by being torn from your home, your family, surviving days of thirst and filth in a packed cattle car to an unknown destination, that destination being Auschwitz? Does time heal wounds that arise from surviving a selection, learning what those chimneys were chugging out, having all of your body hair shaved, standing naked for hours in front of vicious guards in order to be chosen for something that could mean life or could mean death?

I cannot imagine how someone who has seen guards pierce babies in mid-air for a lark returns to life fully. Resilience can only go so far.

And yet. People survived, people had children, they have all contributed to the world we have now.

In Canada alone, there are children of survivors who became, for instance, the first Jewish woman to sit on the Supreme Court of Canada (Rosalie Abella), or who grew up to make Hollywood block-busters (Ivan Reitman) or to front one of the coolest rock bands ever (Geddy Lee).

And they're not all household names, of course. My brother-in-law Sam, whose parents survived labour and concentration camps including Auschwitz and Majdanek, is a hematologist who has done groundbreaking work in thrombosis and hemophilia treatment and research; he has published more than two hundred studies. It's not possible to count how many people he has helped, how many lives he has saved.

As Jacob and I hunkered down at home with our cat during the pandemic, doing puzzles and binge-watching *The Simpsons*, there were descendants of Holocaust survivors—like the president of Pfizer, for instance—working to liberate us.

...

Helen Epstein, child of survivors and early documenter of intergenera-tional trauma, talks about what her parents say when asked how they survived. They said it came down to good luck—and good friends.

Eva Fogelman told me that the friend factor was common for women in particular. The research shows that very often women depended on other women in order to survive. That many women attribute their survival to the close-knit friendships they had developed.

Mes Sept Mères—this was true for my mother, and so for me. If Joseph Morder had seven mothers, so did I—because my mother had friends to keep her alive, to give her something to live for.

After the war, they found each other again. Whether they lived a couple of blocks away, like Freda did, or far off in Paris like Hela, they did. They found each other again. And they helped each other, always. Freda talks about meeting up again with my mother in Toronto, and becoming closer and closer—speaking on the phone, visiting each other. "Friendship," she says over footage of my mother dressed up for the fancy reunion in Paris, "it's very important in our lives."

And it was true in my own life. Friends and family had flown to Vancouver to help me in my sorrow, or brought me tea from up the road, or dropped off a lasagna or tandoori chicken or a bottle of wine, or taken me skiing or kayaking or simply—not simply, actually—checked in on me, as a matter of routine, making sure I had somewhere to be on holidays and hard days—birthdays, Christmas. Mother's Day.

I knew it the day Lucy went missing—how friends and community came together to help find her, and comfort me. I will never forget going back up the block and down the laneway to pick up the dirty clothing I had scattered earlier that day. I was with Mel, the friend who had bought me that lamp, and she bent down to pick up the T-shirts and stretchy pants I had worn earlier that week, a lifetime ago, when Lucy had still been with us.

When we got to the first sock drop, I noticed that someone had found its match and placed them together. Someone had thought they were being helpful, a little gift to the person who had somehow lost their laundry—maybe on the way to the laundromat or wherever. Someone had bent down and picked up a dirty sock and walked down the sidewalk and placed it neatly with its match. I lived in a place where someone would do such a thing. During a global pandemic, no less. In my grief and terror, I felt a wave of gratitude wash over me. Anonymous neighbours would not turn me in. They were pairing up my dirty socks.

Perhaps the divorce had given me something I needed: a giant upheaval now so I could examine the upheaval before, pay attention to it. And pay attention to what I had now, what I had acquired along the way. Maybe that's what was getting me to this place of healing. A breaking together.

...

In my mother's segment in Joseph Morder's film, she tells her story of immigrating to Canada and starting her new life again. There she is, in the condo we moved to after my father died, putting on mascara and lipstick at her little makeup table. In the background on the wall is the *Mona Lisa*. My parents had been visiting Joseph's mother, Hela, in Paris when they had purchased the original reproduction.

I was watching Joseph's film during the pandemic. I hadn't seen it since before my mother died. I couldn't stand to watch it at the time— too raw.

It provided some laughs. In one scene, as the women are visiting a Holocaust memorial, one of them says to Freda, "You weren't in Auschwitz, were you?" Freda responds, indignant. "Who told you I wasn't in Auschwitz?" Another woman chimes in, as if scripted by Larry David: "What's the matter with you? She was in Auschwitz." Freda gets the last word: "I was maybe longer than you in Auschwitz—I was six months there." Then they compare their numbers, the ones tattooed on their forearms.

In another scene, my mother talks about moving to Canada with two-year-old Rachel. Then a few years later, she goes on, Doris was born. And ten years after that, her third daughter was born, Marsha, in Toronto. "We were a very happy family."

She says this over footage Joseph shot during a visit to Toronto in the 1970s. Doris and I are standing in front of our bungalow with our parents. I'm wearing a multicoloured poncho, brown bell-bottoms, my blond hair in messy pigtails. Cut to footage of me bouncing around the front lawn on a toy horse that I don't remember ever owning—I recall a childhood with very few toys—and I am smiling and twirling and, after ditching the stick-horse, bouncing around, hamming it up for this French teenager's camera.

"We were a very happy family," my mother says in the film, about us. A very happy bunch.

The house didn't look so small after all; the bushes in front of it were lush and well kept. And little girl me, I am the picture of joy. Joseph had used this sequence—used my happy childhood delight—to illustrate the hope, the possibility, the happiness after the horror. Is it possible, I wonder, that I have remembered it wrong?

...

At that Holocaust conference I attended, one of the speakers I heard was Rayna Exelbierd, a granddaughter of Holocaust survivors who had become an activist after being shocked by the anti-Semitism and Holocaust denial she witnessed when she went to college. And the sheer ignorance: more than one hundred freshmen at her university in Florida had never heard of the Holocaust.

This young woman shook me out of my well-nursed misery and reminded me that I have an obligation. Not just to combat Holocaust denial and anti-Semitism (which often go hand-in-hand) but to raise the voice my parents gave me against injustices—both catastrophic and on an individual scale. In China, Syria, the United States. At the playground, in the courts, on Canadian reserves without drinking water, on the sidewalks where Black men and women are dying at the hands of police. "Education is the path to peace," this young woman told us. She reminded us that we can't think someone else will fight for this, and encouraged us to find unity in our diversity. "Be kind and have better conversations."

Challenges, she said, are catalysts to create change.

We have a legacy and responsibility, the filmmaker Melissa Hacker, who directed *My Knees Were Jumping: Remembering the Kindertransports*, told us in that same session. But we can't act only motivated by responsibility and guilt. We will burn out; that's too dark. Hacker is a 2G, like me, but with a very different story. Her mother was one of those children saved by a Kindertransport; she was able to flee Austria in 1939.

Holocaust survivor Robbie Waisman was an honourary witness to Canada's Truth and Reconciliation Commission. When he was liberated from Buchenwald at the age of eleven, it was by a unit made up of Black U.S. soldiers. "I thought angels must be Black," he said.

At the conference, he shared the podium with Éloge Butera, a child survivor of the Rwandan genocide who converted to Judaism after moving to Canada. Butera was also an honourary witness to the TRC. The Rwandan genocide was predictable and preventable, he told us. "Genocides are never accidents. They are man-made disasters."

I listened to all of these people, knowing I needed to emerge from my self-involvement and really think about what I could do, beyond wallowing, to fulfill my obligation.

"Make sure our children get a chance to be children" was one of the things Waisman urged. At the very least, I could do that.

I was out for a walk in the neighbourhood a few years earlier with my friend Lindsey, one of the people who would evolve from mom-friend to so much more, when she asked what my approach to parenting was, what I wanted to accomplish. It was a question I had not considered. I don't know, keep my son fed, sheltered and alive?

But I gave it some thought. I want to give him a life full of adventure, I told her, an exciting life. A beautiful adventure.

If I am able to rise above my inherited issues and then my marital heartbreak to boot and give that to him, that would be an achievement. Something I could accomplish in part because my parents had raised me well.

A few years earlier, when I was writing about a science fiction series filmed in Vancouver, one with a time travelling element, I had a dream that was so vivid. My husband and I time travelled far into the future and there was Jacob, a very old man, on his deathbed. We were able to ask him about his life. And he said, "I had a good mother. She loved me very much."

I don't know how good a mother I am, but I know I love that boy with everything I have. And I don't know how good a mother mine was, or how good a father, but I know my mother loved me with everything she had and I believe my father did too. They survived so I could be born. So I could be.

When I was barely eighteen, and my father died, I had to keep it together and help my mother. I became the driver, the cheque writer, the bill payer, the snow shoveller—in addition to the greeting card copy editor. I had lost not just my father, but my childhood. Not in anywhere near as brutal a way as they had lost theirs, of course. But it was a loss. And again, a loss that was not recognized as such or treated as such—either by my mother (who was so broken herself by this shock and loss) or by me; I just thought I had to plug along. What option did I have? Get good marks, get into university, don't be a problem.

I was a problem, though. I became a problem after my father died, hooking up with an inappropriate boyfriend who distressed my mother to no end. I have felt guilty about this for years, but I think I realize now it was my way of coping.

In his speech at that Vancouver conference, Robert Krell said, "People will do wonderful things if you tell the right story."

Well, I have a story to tell. It's an ugly story, with death and torture, starvation, unimaginable loss and grief. Also shame and run-of-the-mill heartbreak. But it is a story that maybe can help others. We are all plagued by something, on the inside, inherited from those before us, and in the world, acquired through the act of living.

I would do anything to not feel this heartache, I thought at one point after my divorce. It was so all-encompassing, coating every minute, every experience, every bone in my rejected body. I couldn't stop being terrified. The doom was palpable. It was keeping me under a blanket on the couch or in my bed, keeping me from the adventure of motherhood.

And then it lifted. And I knew that I would not in fact do anything not to feel the heartache. That I was grateful for it. Because if I had not been part of that life, even for a few years, that led to the crash, I would not have this beautiful boy here with me, the one who carries my father's name, and who embodies what to my grandparents being shoved into a gas chamber would have seemed like the impossible. A great-grandchild. The continuance of our family. Survival is thick with obstacles—much greater for some, like my parents—but its very name illustrates what it has to offer: life.

It's not long. Mine is winding down. I've lived longer than my grandparents got to live. I've lived more years than I have left. I need to waste as little as possible of what's left dwelling on who has left. I loved them, they built me, they brought me here, and now I get to live a little. And it is a beautiful adventure.

I have learned that my family's legacy is something I should wear like a badge, not a burden. My second-hand memories could be a gift—and not just to me. Because this is also an ethical legacy: I must commit to doing good in the world.

I look at the stars and see Auschwitz, or at a paper shredder truck and see mobile killing squads. A lightsabre toy becomes an instrument of torture used on my own family. Well, okay. It's in me. It's always here. It is me, to an extent.

Life is a gift, and heartbreak can be too. I would not be here looking at the maple tree in full bloom, with my son being hilarious playing a videogame in the next room, if all of this awfulness had not happened. I wouldn't exist. I have had moments of terrible guilt thinking that if it hadn't been for the Holocaust, I would not have been born.

I do not wish for any of it, of course. But it happened. And because it happened, I am here. This is so fraught! No wonder I'm fucked. Because of this absolutely horrific, catastrophic thing that befell millions of people—and millions more who survived, scarred for life—I got to live. This beautiful life.

I will never understand why—why a monster would wish for the annihilation of an entire race and countless people would not only follow orders but do it gleefully. Why my dad died from a massive heart attack four days after my eighteenth birthday, when he was only sixty-four. Why my husband decided he could not live with me, or tell me why.

I may not understand. But I am here. And I have a responsibility to speak up against injustice, to raise my child and launch him into a happy life, to do whatever good I can in this world to help alleviate all of the bad. I'm not sure what that looks like, but I think writing this all down has been a start.

I am here. And I know why. Because here there is a why.

...

On the Tuesday after some force turned the twinkly lights on and off next to a photo of my parents as I learned terrible details about how people like my grandparents were murdered, about what their last moments might have been like—about what my murder would have looked like, and Jacob's—Joe Biden was sworn into office. Jacob and I watched—elated, relieved, hopeful. Biden pledged allegiance on a giant, old family Bible: a five-inch-thick heirloom, which had been in the Biden family since 1893. It looked ancient, heavy. Jacob, ever one to keep things light, made a joke. I guess there's no Lederman family Bible, he cracked.

Actually, I said, there is. And I told him about his brave grandfather, what he had done to survive the war, the false identity, the church in Holsen, the Polish Bible. My father's grave adventure—minus the terrible details. This Jacob Lederman was my why, and I had found a way to tell him this most difficult of stories. By focusing on the strength and the light—in his namesake, in me, in him.

THE RAIN GAVE WAY to sun for a single weekend at the end of a stormy October in 2021, the weekend that Jacob, now 13, would have his Bar Mitzvah. The Torah portion he spent months learning was *Chayei Sarah*—literally "Sarah's life," but in fact it is about the death of Sarah, Abraham's beloved wife. It tells the story of how her sons Isaac and Ishmael, who had been estranged, came together to bury their father.

"Because above all, family is more important than anything," Jacob explained to the congregation during his Torah summary.

"In mourning their mother's death, they realized that they could understand one another," he said in his *Dvar Torah*, his analysis. "The things that had kept them apart in the past now melted away."

I, not having had a Bat Mitzvah—something that at the time was seen as optional for girls and certainly was not customary at the Orthodox synagogue I attended growing up—also learned to read from the Torah for the occasion, stumbling through weeks of Zoom lessons with the cantor. I know that my grandparents, Moshe Rafael and Rachel Chaia, and Moshe Aron and Sara, could never have imagined such a scene from the future as they lived through hell: a woman standing at the front of a synagogue, chanting from the Torah scroll. Their granddaughter. And then, their great-grandson. He did so well.

The synagogue we attend has some beautiful rituals. During the service, I presented Jacob with a tallit: the prayer shawl that had been my father's. And I told the story about how the first Jacob Lederman had had to change his name in order to survive the war. And that his survival was a miracle. And that Jacob carries that miracle inside of him.

I wore the white and silver suit that my mother had worn to my sister Rachel's bridal luncheon forty years earlier. One of the things I had saved on a whim when we cleaned out her condo, grieving over her sudden death.

The day before the Saturday service, I presented Jacob with a watch that had been my father's. Not the gold watch that had saved his life, but a reminder of it. I had given it to Jacob's dad before our wedding; he had left it behind when he left our home. It felt so good to see it ticking again, on our son's wrist.

In another ritual at this synagogue, a Torah is taken from the ark and physically passed from generation to generation. I had seen this performed at other services. On the bimah—the platform at the front of the sanctuary—the Torah is handed from grandparent to grandparent to grandparent to grandparent, then to the parents and then the child crossing into adulthood. Each person speaks for a short while about how they hope the teachings of the Torah will be part of the life of the child, now considered a man, or woman.

I was worried about how lonely it would feel up there, just me, my ex-husband, and Jacob. No grandparents for this boy-man.

Then the rabbi spoke. "Jacob, you stand in ... a chain of Jewish tradition that goes back through the generations of your family. As your mom spoke about at the beginning of our service, it goes back all the way to your grandfather and before that. We think of all of what had to happen, all that took place, the good and the bad, to arrive at this moment."

Then it was my turn. I told those who had gathered for the service that I felt a hole because of my parents' absence. "But then I thought about everyone who's here today. All of you: my family, my chosen family, [Jacob's] friends, the people watching at home"—it was being livestreamed! Again, imagine what my grandparents would have made of this; even my parents. "And I realize that Torah is something that is read in community. It's about being together and doing something important. And all of these people, Jacob, are here for you. To support you in hard times and to celebrate the good times, like today."

I missed my parents, but I was not alone. I was surrounded by people I love, and who love me. I was standing up there with Jacob; I was standing next to his dad. We had come through the worst of it—nothing even close to the trauma my parents had come through, but still. I felt whole. And I felt joy, pure joy. Something that has become part of my life, once again.

Acknowledgements

If I acknowledged every person who has helped me with this by name, it could amount to a whole other book. Basically, if I know you, you probably helped in some way.

To my sisters, first of all: thank you. For answering my constant questions and sharing years' worth of notes and charts. For asking Mummy and Daddy the questions I never did. It breaks my heart that we didn't get to take our trip. Maybe we still can.

My whole family has been so supportive. There are too many of us to name individually—each of us, a miracle. I love you all. Special thanks to my niece Laura for constant check-ins, and for being the little sister I never had.

To Jared: for believing in this project from the beginning, and even before the beginning. To Haley: oh my God, how can I ever thank you enough? For your brain, the editing, the therapy. And the friendship. And to everyone at M&S: Terrence Abrahams, Tonia Addison, Sarah Howland, Erin Kelly, Kimberlee Kemp, Chimedum Ohaegbu, Kim Kandravy, and everyone else at PRHC. Tara Tovell, for eagle-eyed copy-editing, Erin Kern for proofreading, Sean Tai for typesetting, Terrence Abrahams for insightful reader's guide questions, and Talia Abramson for the remarkable cover design. Rachel Lindzen, on the cover of a book. Imagine.

To Martha Webb, thank you for the advice, support, encouragement, and for believing in me.

I spoke to so many people while I was writing this book; they were all so generous and helpful. Special thanks to Robert Krell, Natan Kellermann, Eva Fogelman, Zahava Solomon, Morton Weinfeld, Brent Bezo, Bernie Farber, Sheryl Kahn, Chris Friedrichs, Fern Levitt, and Eli Rubenstein. And Carey Newman, thank you. To survivors Howard Chandler, Judy Cohen, Nate Leipciger and Robbie Waisman, thank you for your strength and for sharing your stories.

To Yael Danieli, Helen Epstein, and Rachel Yehuda—thank you for your help and for the important work you are doing.

Thank you to Joseph and Robi Morder for allowing me to share your mother's words.

For help with the science that confounded me, thank you to Moshe Szyf, Martin Hirst, Jacqueline Solomon, Margaret Munro, and Laura. For French translation and excellent company, merci Gary and Elana Sures. Thanks also to Norm Ravvin, and to Claire Sicherman—for shared nightmares and weird cocktails. Thank you to Pearl and the entire Gropper family.

And a very special thank you to Andrea Tebart and the Flottmeiers.

Thank you to the researchers at the U.S. National Archives at College Park and the United States Holocaust Memorial Museum, especially Jo-Ellyn Decker. And to the Vancouver Holocaust Education Centre.

I have the best job in the world and the people I work with at *The Globe and Mail* have given me so much support. Special thanks to Judith Pereira, to my dear friends in the BC Bureau, my brilliant colleagues in the Arts section and to Stephanie Chambers. And to Simon, Mark, Gabe, and Sinc. And Lisan.

Andrew Gorham, thank you for taking a huge chance on me and changing my life. Craig Offman, you have been amazing. Thank you.

To my CBC mentor friends Kathryn, Alison and Cathy. #Regina2022

My friends mean everything to me, as you know if you have read this book. Marsha, I acknowledge everything your friendship has brought to my life. I love you more. Lezlee and Eileen, you are lifelong friends who mean the world to me. Shannon and Kevin, our bonders sustain me. Rosemary, we feel you with us. To Mel, Lindsey, Tanis, Gord, and Josh—thank you for being my chosen family here on the west coast. How would I have made it without you? To Adriana: thank you for our many conversations, including one that became central to this book. I feel my ancestors now. To Deb and John for cat-sitting and human support. And to Bob and Charles for martini drop-offs, baked goods and more. I would hate to share a wall with anyone else. And to Katherine Monk, for getting it.

I am inspired by every writer I have had the privilege of interviewing; all have helped in some way. Special thanks for support and encouragement to Kevin Patterson, Anakana Schofield, and Jen Sookfong Lee.

To Hannah for helping make Jacob the person he is. You are family.

To Jacob's dad, who helped so much as I needed time and space to write this. You are a terrific father and co-parent. And friend.

And to Jacob: thank you for putting up with everything as I tried to write this in the middle of a pandemic. You were a great sport. Now get off that screen! And yes, of course, the best sentence I have ever heard was indeed: it's a boy.

To all the survivors I grew up around—thank you.

To all the people whose names I do not know, who did not survive and have nobody to remember them, this is for you too.

Suggested Reading

Here are some books—including novels—that helped inform my thinking and writing.

The Inheritors: Moving Forward from Generational Trauma by Gita Baack

The Indescribable and the Undiscussable: Reconstructing Human Discourse after Trauma by Dan Bar-On

The Light of Days: The Untold Story of Women Resistance Fighters in Hitler's Ghettos by Judy Batalion

Generations of the Holocaust by Martin Bergmann and Milton Jucovy

Delayed Impact: The Holocaust and the Canadian Jewish Community by Franklin Bialystok

I Did Not Interview the Dead by David P. Boder

A Whisper Across Time: My Family's Story of the Holocaust Told Through Art and Poetry by Olga Campbell

International Handbook of Multigenerational Legacies of Holocaust Trauma, edited by Yael Danieli

The Choice: Embrace the Possible by Edith Eva Eger

By Chance Alone: A Remarkable True Story of Courage and Survival at Auschwitz by Max Eisen

What We Talk About When We Talk About Anne Frank by Nathan
    Englander

*Children of the Holocaust: Conversations with Sons and Daughters of
    Survivors* by Helen Epstein

Where She Came From: A Daughter's Search for Her Mother's History by
    Helen Epstein

Wounds Into Wisdom: Healing Intergenerational Jewish Trauma by
    Rabbi Tirzah Firestone

Send For Me by Lauren Fox

The Diary of a Young Girl by Anne Frank

The Survivors: A Story of War, Inheritance and Healing by Adam Frankel

Man's Search for Meaning by Viktor E. Frankl
    Copyright ©1959, 1962, 1984, 1992, 2006 by Viktor E. Frankl
    Reprinted by permission of Beacon Press, Boston

*House of Glass: The Story and Secrets of a Twentieth-Century Jewish
    Family* by Hadley Freeman

*Holocaust Survivors in Canada: Exclusion, Inclusion, Transformation,
    1947–1955* by Adara Goldberg

Hitler's Willing Executioners: Ordinary Germans and the Holocaust by
    Daniel Jonah Goldhagen

*Neighbors: The Destruction of the Jewish Community in Jedwabne,
    Poland* by Jan T. Gross

After Such Knowledge: Memory, History and the Legacy of the Holocaust
    by Eva Hoffman

GIs Remember: Liberating the Concentration Camps, published by the
    National Museum of American Jewish Military History with
    Introduction by Morton Horvitz, Guest Curator

On Hitler's Mountain: Overcoming the Legacy of a Nazi Childhood by
    Irmgard A. Hunt

*21 Things You May Not Know About the Indian Act: Helping Canadians
    Make Reconciliation with Indigenous Peoples a Reality* by Bob Joseph

Plunder: A Memoir of Family Property and Nazi Treasure by Menachem
    Kaiser

Survival and Trials of Revival: Psychodynamic Studies of Holocaust Survivors and Their Families in Israel and the Diaspora by Hillel Klein; edited by Alex Holder

Sounds from Silence: Reflections of a Child Holocaust Survivor, Psychiatrist and Teacher by Robert Krell

Heimat: A German Family Album by Nora Krug

Everyone is Present: Essays on Photography, Memory and Family by Terry Kurgan

Axis Rule in Occupied Europe by Raphael Lemkin

If Not Now, When? by Primo Levi

Survival in Auschwitz (also known as *If This Is a Man*) by Primo Levi

The Book of Radom: The Story of a Jewish Community in Poland Destroyed by the Nazis, edited and compiled by Alfred Lipson

Were We Our Brothers' Keepers? The Public Response of American Jews to the Holocaust 1938-1944 by Rabbi Haskel Lookstein

Irena's Children: A True Story of Courage by Tilar J. Mazzeo

Encyclopedia of Camps and Ghettos, 1933-1945, edited by Geoffrey P. Megargee

The Lost: A Search for Six of Six Million by Daniel Mendelsohn

Far to Go by Alison Pick

Lay My Burden Down: Suicide and the Mental Health Crisis among African-Americans by Alvin Poussaint and Amy Alexander

The Girl Who Stole Everything by Norman Ravvin

Masters of Death: The SS-Einsatzgruppen and the Invention of the Holocaust by Richard Rhodes

God, Faith and Identity from the Ashes: Reflections of Children and Grandchildren of Holocaust Survivors, edited by Menachem Z. Rosensaft

Memory Unearthed: The Lodz Ghetto Photographs of Henryk Ross

The Wandering Jews by Joseph Roth

For You Who Died I Must Live On . . . Reflections on the March of the Living, edited by Eli Rubenstein

East West Street: On the Origins of "Genocide" and "Crimes against Humanity" by Philippe Sands

Imprint: A Memoir of Trauma in the Third Generation by Claire Sicherman

Trauma and Rebirth: Intergenerational Effects of the Holocaust by John J. Sigal and Morton Weinfeld

Shosha by Isaac Bashevis Singer

Black Earth: The Holocaust as History and Warning by Timothy Snyder

The Complete Maus by Art Spiegelman

In the Midst of Civilized Europe: The Pogroms of 1918-1921 and the Onset of the Holocaust by Jeffrey Veidlinger

A Vanished World by Roman Vishniac

Boy from Buchenwald: The True Story of a Holocaust Survivor by Robbie Waisman with Susan McClelland

Memorial Candles: Children of the Holocaust by Dina Wardi

Like Everyone Else But Different: The Paradoxical Success of Canadian Jews by Morton Weinfeld

Driving to Treblinka: A Long Search for a Lost Father by Diana Wichtel

Night by Elie Wiesel

The Abandonment of the Jews by David Wyman

SUGGESTED VIEWING

Claude Lanzmann: Spectres of the Shoah, directed by Adam Benzine

The Devil Next Door, directed by Yossi Bloch and Daniel Sivan

My Knees Were Jumping: Remembering the Kindertransports, directed by Melissa Hacker

Shoah, directed by Claude Lanzmann

Each of Us Has a Name: March of the Living, directed by Fern Levitt and Arnie Zipursky

The Auctioneers: Profiting from the Holocaust, directed by Jan Lorenzen

The Painted Bird, directed by Václav Marhoul

Mes Sept Mères, directed by Joseph Morder

Night and Fog, directed by Alain Resnais
Night Will Fall, directed by Andre Singer

SUGGESTED LISTENING

Tapestry, "Tapestry@25: Life Advice from Rabbi Harold Kushner,"
    interview by Mary Hynes (CBC)
Intrigue: The Ratline by Philippe Sands (BBC)
On Being with Krista Tippett, "Rachel Yehuda: How Trauma and
    Resilience Cross Generations"

Reader's Guide Questions for *Kiss the Red Stairs*

1. Lederman often forms her thoughts and reflections as questions, many of which she does not, and cannot, have answers for based on the lack of information she has about her family's history. Did her questioning inspire reflections of your own?

2. "In Canada today, immigrants are celebrated—at least in the crowds I run with. Things weren't quite that way in the 1970s (18)." Do Lederman's notes on immigrants—in this case, specifically Jewish immigrants—align with your understanding of the world's perception of Canadian culture? Why or why not?

3. Journalist Andrea Tebart, who Lederman and her sisters hired to help research their parents, says "as far as I personally know about traumas, . . . they cannot be deleted, but 'only' overwritten by good things (87)." Compare this statement to what Lederman's friend tells her: "your ancestors are singing for you, crying out to you, they are supporting you, they are sending you strength (7)." How has intergenerational trauma impacted Lederman's life? And what are examples of the strength she has inherited from her family?

4. Through her research into children of Holocaust survivors, Lederman comes to this conclusion: "I experience the world like a survivor (121)." How does her research help Lederman understand herself, the trajectory of her life, and her son Jacob with more clarity?

5. The article "The Collision"—written from Lederman's discussions with German-Canadian artist Fred Herzog— garnered hatred and animosity from the public, much of it involving Holocaust denial. How does Lederman go on to challenge the notion that there is only "one" form of such denial?

6. What does Lederman have to say about the importance of journalism throughout history—specifically between World War II and the present day? What does Lederman also note about the "evil agendas (184)" of journalism, and the dangers of fake news?

7. "Sometimes a single conversation can change your life. Or, the way you see life (189)." Lederman has many conversations in this memoir—and, overall, carries out an important conversation with herself. Highlight examples of conversations that impacted your reading.

8. Lederman's research trip to New York and Washington, D.C., helps her shed light on her family's history; she also reflects on a different journey, one she took twenty years prior, to Poland. How did these experiences, though years apart, help her with her overall writing project?

9. We learn of the importance of the red stairs—and the kiss—that make up the title of this memoir on page 296. Discuss the importance of these stairs, and why Lederman refers to her desire to see them as a "pilgrimage."

10. "I had built this. I understood what a beautiful achievement this was. I had built this community, and this community had come and rescued me, at the most difficult times (340)." Lederman has this realization after her and her son's cat, Lucy, goes missing. What about this event led her to this realization? Why do you think it was this moment?

11. "I had found a way to tell [my son] this most difficult of stories. By focusing on the strength and the light—in his namesake, in me, in him (364)." Discuss the importance of storytelling touched upon by this statement—in particular, the telling of our family's stories, and, ultimately, our own.

© Ben Nelms

MARSHA LEDERMAN is a columnist for the *Globe and Mail*. An award-winning journalist, Marsha previously worked for CBC Radio and in commercial radio. Born and raised in Toronto, she now lives in Vancouver.

FOLLOW @MARSHALEDERMAN ON TWITTER